MW00615350

Korea in the Cross Currents

A Century of Struggle
and the Crisis of Reunification

Robert J. Myers

palgrave

KOREA IN THE CROSS CURRENTS
© Robert J. Myers, 2001

First published 2001 by
PALGRAVE
175 Fifth Avenue, New York, N.Y.10010 and
Houndmills, Basingstoke, Hampshire RG21 6XS.
Companies and representatives throughout the world

PALGRAVE is the new global publishing imprint of St. Martin 's Press LLC
Scholarly and Reference Division and Palgrave Publishers Ltd (formerly Macmillan Press Ltd).

ISBN 0–312–23815–0 hardback

Library of Congress Cataloging-in-Publication Data
Myers, Robert John, 1924-
Korea in the cross currents : a century of struggle and the crisis of reunification / by Robert J. Myers.
    p.   cm.
  Includes bibliographical references and index.
  ISBN 0–312–23815–0
  1. Korea—History—20th century.   2. Korean reunification question (1945-) I. Title.
DS916.M94   2001
951.904—dc21

                                                                00–069225

A catalogue record for this book is available
from the British Library.

Design by Letra Libre, Inc.

First edition: May, 2001
10   9   8   7   6   5   4   3   2   1

Contents

To:
Choi Chang-yoon
Soldier, Scholar, Statesman, Friend

Acknowledgments

Setting out this list of acknowledgments is first of all a flight of nostalgia. I think back to 1945 in China when I had the fortune to be assigned to the Korean EAGLE Project as a junior member of the Office of Strategic Services. That began my association with Koreans and their aspirations, an activity that I have valued all my adult life.

Over those years, I have gained knowledge of Korea and its neighbors through academic study, intelligence work, and finally academic conferences and seminars for 15 years (1980–94) as president of the Carnegie Council on Ethics and International Affairs in New York City. Since 1995, I have had the privilege of being a research fellow at the Hoover Institution at Stanford University.

During three of the years at Hoover, I have benefited from a grant from the Korea Foundation which provided funds for travel to Korea and research help at the Ilmin (One People) Institute of International Relations, located at Korea University, under the direction of Professor Han Sung-joo, who was most helpful. Choi Chang-yoon, a long-time friend and president of the Korea Foundation in 1995, was an early supporter of this work; his untimely death from cancer in 1996 was a great loss to his country, his family, and to his many friends. At the Ilmin Institute, a number of individuals were of special help, beginning with David Chun through Chun S. Moon. Another friend who was of particular assistance in 1998 was former Ambassador Park Shin-il, who arranged a number of interviews and who remains a strong supporter of the opposition Grand National Party.

Since 1995 I have interviewed many Koreans of various viewpoints and persuasions. An outstanding personality I met in April 1945 in Sian, China, who has had an exceptional career, is Kim Jun-yop, a former president of Korea University, and now chairman of the Social Science Research Institute, originally established by Daewoo. His life-long interest has been Korea-China relations. He is mentioned in this book in various places, but especially in regard to the Korean Independence Movement. It is a privilege to have been his friend over these many years.

The people I tended to rely on for advice and explanations included former ambassador to the United Nations and to the U.S., Hyun Hong-choo; former chairman of the Economic Planning Council, Kim Ki-hwan; former Minister of Information under Park Chung-hee, and retired chairman of the Daewoo Economic Research Institute, Kim Seong-jin; Sun Chu-whan, former Minister of Information and president of the Korea Foundation under Roh Tae-woo; Park Ung-suh, president of KOHAP Corporation, whose previous business career was with Samsung Petrochemicals; Gong Ryo-myung, a distinguished diplomat and former Foreign Minister, whose family traces back some 33 generations to its ancestor, Confucius, the sage of China; Hong Sung-chick, chairman of the Asian Social Science Research Institute and retired professor of sociology at Korea University; Moon Chung-in, professor of political science at Yonsei University, and Professor Mo Jongryn, also of Yonsei University; Lee Hong-koo, former professor of political science at Seoul National University, former Prime Minister and most recently ambassador to the U.S.; Kim Jun-kil, former Minister of Information at the Korean embassy in Washington, D.C.; and Han Sung-soo, Deputy Prime Minister and Minister of Finance under Kim Young-sam, now a leading member of the National Assembly.

A special mention is appropriate for former Prime Minister Yoo Chang-soon, and his wife Aija, who provided extraordinary hospitality to my wife, Elizabeth, and me over the past twenty years.

In New York City, the Korean program at Columbia University was always a source of knowledge over the years, including Gary Ledyard, Steve Linton, and Charles Armstrong; and on the economic front, F. Randall Smith, a close friend, partner of Capital Counsel, New York city, was always generous with his insights and readings about the Korean economic scene. I have profited from two luncheons with Shim Jae-hoon, Seoul bureau chief of the *Far Eastern Economic Review,* in terms of the Korean economy and a fascinating trip he took to Manchuria to view North Korea from that side of the border; and Choi Won-ki, political analyst and North Korean specialist for the *Joong-ang Ilbo* in Seoul, for his friendship and many kindnesses.

Professor Ralph Buultjens of the New School, keeper of the flame of the Toynbee Prize, has enlightened me on Toynbee's work and on Buultjen's own view of history, which includes nations continually both entering and leaving the scene, including Korea, Mexico, and India.

Over the years I have also benefited from wisdom of the resident American ambassadors in Seoul, from Richard L. (Dixie) Walker, through James R. Lilley, Donald P. Gregg, and Stephen Bosworth.

Chester L. Cooper, a member of Project EAGLE and a long-time colleague in the CIA, also deserves mention, as does Peter M. Beck, director of research/academic affairs at the Korea Economic Institute of America in Washington, D.C.

The Korean Consulate General's office of San Francisco was a dependable source of support, and in particular, Mr. Lee Kee-woo, who later transferred to New York City, provided useful periodicals and books. And so to the consul generals I owe my ongoing thanks.

At the Hoover Institution, I also have a considerable debt. First to director John Raisian for taking me in; then particularly to Thomas H. Henriksen, associate director and head of the Korean studies program, who extended his hand and time toward completing this book. One of Henriksen's assistants, Piers Turner, reviewed and improved the entire manuscript. Professor Victor D. Cha, of Georgetown University, also read the manuscript and was of great assistance in discussing the contemporary Korean scene. I owe a special thanks to Ramon H. Myers, curator of the East Asian Collection at Hoover and a scholar of Chinese history and politics, who read the first six chapters; and to Mark Peattie, a senior research fellow at Hoover and Japan specialist, for reading the chapter on Japan's colonization of Korea.

Chalmers and Sheila Johnson gave encouragement to this enterprise by publishing my view of the Korean economy in "The Slow Pace of Economic Reform in South Korea" (Japanese Policy Research Institute Report No. 51, November 1998).

During all this time I benefited from the able assistance of Dan Wilhelmi of the Hoover computer services staff, both in the ways of modern computing and from his personal knowledge of Korea; and, last, but not least, Mo Ji-hye, who volunteered to take on various translations projects which added valuable information to the book.

So for all this help I am greatly in the debt of those mentioned and the many more that were not specially mentioned. To all of you, my heartfelt thanks. And the assurance that errors of fact and interpretation are mine alone.

Robert J. Myers
Hoover Institution
Stanford University, Stanford, California, 2001

Korea at the Beginning
of the Twenty-First Century:
A Guide for the Perplexed

Focusing on the last hundred years of Korea's long history, and its par-ticular relationship with China, one is in a position both to under-stand and marvel at the events of this century on the Korean peninsula. At the same time, the complexity of the division of the country into North and South Korea—not just a perennial struggle between good and evil, although that is certainly part of the story—places the future at risk. There was one terrible war that divided the twentieth century in half and there are threats of more trouble to come. This study of the history of the past century will provide some answers and open the way to informed speculations. The June 12–14, 2000 summit meeting in Pyongyang be-tween the leaders of the two Koreas may have been, as an exuberant Kim Dae-jung declared after the meeting, the "most important event in Korean history."

The Korean peninsula underwent a continuous number of earth-shaking events in the twentieth century—although it is generally out of the earth-quake zone. Jutting off the extreme northeast edge of the Eurasian landmass, and with a combined population of nearly 70 million people, North and South Korea are situated among China, Japan, and Russia. They are also pro-foundly influenced by the United States because of the circumstances of the Korean war (1950–1953). The issues of war and peace, left over from the Ko-rean war, remain unresolved; these two separate states are the residue of the Cold War. This anomaly still poses ominous prospects for war or peace in Asia, and American national security interests.

Korea passed through two distinct stages in the twentieth century. During the first 50 years, the struggle was to reclaim its national identity and territorial integrity against the most virulent form of imperialism; and the second 50 years was an unrelenting, deadly competition between the two halves of the divided country—the future in this regard still ambiguous. This left a dangerous transition to the realities of the new century. After a hundred years of dealing with substantial challenges, the South still has found no respite. The authoritarian communist North still clings to the past, even though the logic of communist Marxist dialectic demands attention to the future. The prototypical problems of the Cold War—freedom vs. tyranny, democracy against North Korean *juche* (self sufficiency)—dominate the relationship. There are these great differences, but also similarities. One Korean friend in Seoul said to me in late 1999, "They will continue in their way. They are not stupid. After all, they are Koreans." The implication was that the South Koreans are not going to change their ways, either, wherein lies the reunification dilemma.

The current president, Kim Dae-jung, offers the new dynamics of Korea. I attended a conference in Seoul in October 1999, "Peace and Democracy for the New Millennium," sponsored by the Forum for Democratic Leaders in Asia and the Pacific. This forum had been created in 1996 by Kim Dae-jung before he became President of South Korea in 1998. It expressed his political philosophy of upholding democracy and free markets, but also favoring universal values, such as human rights, as opposed to such rivals as Lee Kuan-yu, former prime minister of Singapore, who promotes "Asian values" to excuse deviations from what has become a world standard, Western-style democracy. Attendees included newly successful leaders of East Timor, exiles from Burma, Cambodian opposition leaders, and Britons, Australians, and Norwegians who were sympathetic to the Third Way version of the brave new world. This is also a new interest of President Kim, and may appear down the road as an original contribution of Korean political philosophy.

For me, considering the security situation in Northeast Asia and the heating up of the South Korean political climate for legislative elections in April 2000, this was a remarkable venue for such a conference. South Korea was the inspiration for such a theme. The conference participants—about 45 people—joined President Kim at the Blue House (the roof tiles are blue), the presidential official residence. Like all sites of sovereign political power, the building is slightly too well polished and the staff too well groomed. The evening mainly celebrated the newly acquired freedom of East Timor.

It is in comparison with previous visits to the Blue House, under heads of the developmental South Korean state from 1961 through 1997, that the magnitude of the change in its politics since 1998 becomes starkly apparent. The election of Kim Dae-jung (also referred to as DJ) as president in December 1997 was a surprise to those of us who had been active on the Korean scene for some decades and were familiar with the outlines of Korea's history in the twentieth century. Such bold moves also raise questions as to how fast and for how long a very conservative society like South Korea can be lifted in political, economic, and national security objectives that have both a narrow and shifting consensus.

In President Kim's opening speech at the conference, he said, "Democracy, a market economy, and productive welfare form a trinity. This is what we must achieve in the twenty-first century." As a follower of the teaching of the British historian Arnold J. Toynbee and his *A Study of History,* Kim Dae-jung has a long view of the future and what happens to those who are not up to the task.

South Korea has long taken pride in its leadership in economic modernization and consolidation of its own style of democracy. So it is no surprise that Kim Dae-jung—one of the three Kims who have dominated politics in Korea for the last four decades—would in his case extend Korean democracy to include a strong human rights stand. East Timor, for example, was at the top of the conference agenda in terms of immediate interest, its independence just having been achieved. The plights of Burma and Cambodia were not neglected. The traditional interest in reunification with North Korea was integral to the gathering. In fact, my own paper dealt with the new initiative of President Kim, "the sunshine policy," as a way of dealing with the North, a subject fully analyzed in chapter 8. South Korea remains eager to lead.

The South Korean entry into modern society in the 1990s was partly by plan and partly by circumstances. In its competition on all levels with Japan, South Korea resolved to enter the Organization of Economic Cooperation and Development (OECD) and joined in December 1996. The OECD is the advanced industrial club of Europe. Japan and South Korea are its Asian members.[1] But almost as the ink dried on this great accomplishment, the economy stalled, caught up in the "Asian crisis."[2] South Korea, which had qualified for membership in this exclusive club of modernity with an income of over $10,000 per capita in 1996, had seen this fall to about $6,100 by 1998.[3] While this loss was recovered by the end of 1999, does such a drastic change of fortune, such volatility, have any meaning for Korea's economic and political future? (The economic prospects for the South's rival, the Democratic Republic of North Korea, which have been on a downward spiral since the early 1980s, appear unpromising.)

Korea is a subject that has been heavily studied since Korea moved back into history, so to speak, after the end of World War II and its escape from

Japanese colonialism. Korean scholars also resurrected the history of Korea's earliest time. According to the foundation myth, Hwanung came down to the world of man and married a she-bear who bore Tangun, the first ruler of the age of theocracy. The bear cult, the core of the Tangun legend, descends from the Paleolithic period and is still prevalent among the Amu and some tribes in Siberia. And as the twentieth century progressed from 1945, books proliferated by both Korean and foreign authors, especially on South Korea. At first these books were historical, emphasizing the uniqueness of Korea. But as the South became known as an exceptional country, renowned for its economic miracles, ideas that South Korea might well have something to offer to the world as an example for economic and political development began to take hold. Conversely, for North Korea the approbation consensus was close to universal.

By 1993, these studies on the South provoked the following comment from Hagen Koo, editor of *State and Society in Contemporary Korea,*[4] "Although the literature on Korea is growing rapidly, it is overrepresented by a genre of South Korea's economic success stories." The Asian financial crisis of 1997 severely shook this economic model. By the end of 1999 the University of Pennsylvania recommended that South Korean businesses should not try to copy U.S. corporate management, but instead stick with modified *chaebol* (family conglomerates) reform. This is what South Korea has done and will be a test of whether the 1997 financial crisis was simply a banking and financial markets issue, or if something more might have been involved. By contrast, North Korea's economy exists mostly outside the global economy.

Events in South Korea since 1997 have, in fact, broken the old paradigm (as the famines in North Korea destroyed its previous image of authoritarian success over the past several years), along with other myths of the linear rise of South Korea's modern mythic society. My observations go beyond economics to politics, foreign policy, as well as today's unification prospects. A touch of twentieth-century revisionism is in order for both the North and the South, at the same time respecting the genuine accomplishments of two societies now under strain. Perhaps neither system is universal; perhaps there are Korean values such as perseverance and dynamism that allow the North and South to deal with their difficulties, each in their own way.

The central problem now facing the Koreas is the long-standing one of reunification and their mutual obstinance in regard to some form of unification. In principle this should enhance their futures, but the devil remains in the details. Their chances for success, after almost 50 years of talks, seem minimal, despite the latest imaginative and sincere efforts of the South Korean president, Kim Dae-jung, to promote an accommodating "sunshine policy." This has had limited success, both with the North and with the South Korean electorate. Both Koreas are still caught up in the problem of successful survival at the end of a tumultuous century and what may be an even more difficult time for middle powers. Which characteristics might allow them to succeed, and those leading to failure, will be noted in the course of this study.

Both Koreas went through a series of dramatic shared experiences in the first half of the century—Korea was united then, as it had been periodically during the previous 5,000 years, in a single dynastic kingdom—but the cruelty of the Cold War sent both parts of the country in different directions, so far as to become intractable enemies.

Nonetheless, there may finally be an opportunity for a "grand reconciliation" if the long-awaited and much-postponed "reunification" occurs; or the two Koreas may continue their separate ways. But with some kind of unity, even a "confederation," this larger unit perhaps would be less buffeted by the increasingly large waves of the world economy, the "globalization" syndrome that neither, for different reasons, is really prepared to handle. Still, each has its hopes and plans for a brighter future, both societies caught up in fact by a dream of idealism, a rainbow-colored utopia, with Korea and things Korean setting the new international standard for politics, economics, and even religion.

North Korea, the Stalinist model, began to fail visibly in the 1980s, while the cracks in the South Korean structure broke into the open only in 1997, leaving both societies nostalgic and puzzled over the future. How can they singly or together restart the march of progress, an article of philosophy in the North and an article of belief in the South? Or will reunification fade, and the old North-South competition continue as of old?

Over the past few years, the media has covered the "newsworthy" events in Korea, generally along four themes: (a) famine in the North; (b) Northern infiltration of hapless agents into the South; (c) possible nuclear threats from the North; and (d) the recent economic collapse and rebound in the South, the former caused by its own blunders in both politics and economics but also as it was overwhelmed by the impersonal fast-moving world economy. South Korea's basic economic problems, however, have not yet been adequately analyzed, mainly because there is disagreement on what went wrong and what requires correction. The turmoil at the World Trade Organization (WTO) meeting in Seattle in December 1999, protesting the lack of adequate attention of trade policy to environmental and labor practices, demonstrated part of the problem. In South Korea, laborers in "Export City" were concerned that liberalized trade would result in heavy inflows of foreign goods, including U.S. agricultural products.[5]

In May of 1995 I traveled to Seoul to outline a book project for the consideration of the Korea Foundation. My involvement with Korean affairs had begun some 50 years earlier, when the Office of Strategic Services (OSS), the forerunner of the Central Intelligence Agency (CIA), took me out of a Japanese area and language school at the University of Chicago and assigned me to the OSS "EAGLE Project." This assignment was to select agent prospects from the Korean Independence Army (Kwang Bok Kun) in China. After the war, I maintained my interest in Korea during the fifties and sixties as a member of the CIA, rising to deputy division chief for Asia. This continued during my journalistic career with the *Washingtonian* magazine and *The New Republic,* and finally as president of the Carnegie Council on Ethics and International Affairs in New York City from 1980 through 1994. This position gave me an opportunity to look more deeply into the Korean scene, as well as into U.S.–Korean relations. I thought it might be a good idea in 1981 to start a discussion with Korean institutions, comparing Korean and American values, beginning with obvious differences—for example, community vs. individuals. Hence, "Values in Conflict" was the theme of our first conference in 1981 with the Asiatic Research Center of Korea University.

The head of this center was a long-time friend, Kim Jun-yop, who had been the aide-de-camp in 1945 of General Lee Bum-suk, commander of the second detachment of the Korean Independence Army at Sian, Shensi province, China. We had served together there for about four months. Professor Kim had stayed on in China after the war, attending Nanking University, where he received his Ph.D. In Korea he had a distinguished academic career at Korea University as a historian, later becoming president of that university. In 1995 he was (and remains) chairman of the Social Science Research Institute, supported by Daewoo Corporation. He was supportive of my general plans to write a book about Korea from my particular experience, from the perspective of an American interested in the world of Korea and the mutual interest of Korea and the U.S. in the new post–Cold War period. The president of the Korea Foundation, Choi Chang-yoon, was a long-time friend and associate on the conference scene and he agreed to provide a three-year grant to cover some of the travel and also research in Korea. So the project was launched in 1996, which proved by circumstance to be a particularly good time to look back over the century of events in Korea, which I had had an opportunity to witness, not for the whole century, but for the last half, the most exciting 50 years. I began this work at Stanford University, as a Hoover Institution research fellow. Korea continues to be a moving target, so some of my original interests have changed considerably in the course of the work.

The original focus was the twentieth century and the principal crises that had arisen. Although much has happened over this century, it was the years of 1997 and 1998 that proved to be of particular significance. The book might establish a marker for the starting point of the new millennium on the remaining critical unresolved issues. As President of the Carnegie Council, I had had the opportunity to travel to Korea at least twice annually, as well as to China, Japan, and Taiwan somewhat less frequently (but not to North Korea, despite unsuccessful efforts). I attended conferences and spoke frequently on Asian events.[6] The appointment at the Hoover Institution at Stanford University gave me the opportunity to pursue this work in ideal surroundings. Some of the most valuable sources for this work, however, have been interviews I have been able to conduct in Korea, particularly on economics, politics, veterans, and labor affairs. The current controversy over the "Korean development" model came to the fore in a manner not anticipated by its practitioners and promoters, although suggestions for reform during the previous decade were never far away.[7] Further, such questions as "Asian values" arose and critical views of globalization call into question South Korea's early and enthusiastic embrace of an international system that has treated it in a manner that it may not have fully anticipated. It seems almost trite to observe that both Koreas have recently lost a good deal of their autonomy in both economics and politics. This has important implications for the "middle power" concept, not only for the Koreas, but for other countries in the contemporary world as well. They are both caught up in great power struggles, although from time to time opportunities do arise for the two Koreas to advance their mutual interests, especially in the security field. Both Koreas so far have found that the cold comfort of the known, an armistice but not a peace treaty, satisfies their national interest, and the status quo has taken on a military and intellectual life of its own.

Korea attracts our attention because it is singular and unique; but it gains its significance for Americans because of its location among great powers, which augments its importance. As Don Oberdorfer writes, "Korea is at the wrong place and is not large enough."[8] This is true, and that is why the Korean peninsula sways the politics of Northeast Asia, a vital American interest. The year 2000 marks the 50th anniversary of the Korean war, which brought the U.S. and South Korea together in an unlikely security alliance that has persisted. So far, converging interests have far outweighed the inevitable stress that such relationships create.

Still, South Korea is as large as England in territory and the population of both Koreas is about 70 million (a two to one ratio for the South). A united Korea would rival Germany in population. The geography question is critical, as one can see from a glance at the map. It is dwarfed against the area of China, Russia, and Japan. (In his latest book, Bruce Cumings cleverly uses an old Korean map dated A.D. 1402, which draws Korea as the major player, as the *New Yorker* did many years later in depicting New York City as the bulk of the United States.) Its location has meant that its neighbors frequently violated its borders, most notably in the sixteenth century, when the Japanese under Hideyoshi twice invaded, ostensibly on their way to China. Two Manchu invasions in the seventeenth century were also troublesome; yet the last Korean dynasty, the Chosun or Yi, held on from 1392 to 1910 as a unified kingdom of tough, stoic inhabitants.

Is that the way Koreans really are? One has difficulty talking about Koreans or anyone else in terms of meaningful generalities. Some observers, and some Koreans themselves, describe Koreans as the "Irish of the East." In the context of a bar or restaurant scene, one presumably is talking about the enjoyment of food, drink, and song. Perhaps Irish also means people who may be irreconcilable among themselves (the 1998–99 negotiations to one side). In the period toward the beginning of the twentieth century, Koreans were described by Westerners as "lazy" and "spendthrifts." During the sixties most Asians, including the Koreans, benefited from Western journalists' discovery of Confucianism and its admirable values stemming from hierarchy—obedience, hard work, frugality, and so on—in an effort to account for Asian economic success.

Whether we like it or not, most races or ethnic groups or citizens of a particular country are often characterized, a kind of shorthand to discussion. There is no great harm in this, unless there are overtones or notions of superiority or inferiority. Anthropologists have been meticulous in their research of primitive societies to come to no such conclusions. That is my position. So with that in mind, I quote a few generalizations about Koreans through the eyes of a well-disposed American missionary, Homer B. Hulbert. While primarily interested in saving souls, he made this earthy observation in the preface of his book. He wrote of a country and a people "that have been frequently maligned and seldom appreciated. They are overshadowed by China on the one hand in respect to numbers, and by Japan on the other in respect to wit. They are neither good merchants like the one nor good fighters like the other, and yet they are by far the pleasantest people in the Far East to live amongst. Their failings are such as flow in the wake of ignorance everywhere, and the bettering of their opportunities will bring swift betterment to their condition."[9]

Hulbert was certainly right on the upside potential of the Koreans, given the opportunity for education and also to order their own affairs. Their native industry—whether Confucian or otherwise—was the key ingredient to "Miracle on the Han" of the '60s and '70s. This incredible burst of energy—under exceptional circumstances following the Korean war and the Asian economy of the day—did have miraculous results. The South Koreans were hell-bent on catching up with the world, particularly the Japanese, asserting their ability as second to none. But the possible negative effects were noted by astute Korean observers. One such article was by Professor Han Bang-jin, "Modernization and Risk in Korea Society."[10]

The reason for this article was Professor Han's reflections on the spectacular growth of the Korean economy, especially under the Park and Chun regimes. Korea's last dynasty, the Chosun (1392–1910) was marked by stagnation and intrigue in its final several decades; and the economy under the Japanese was naturally manipulated to serve Japanese interests over Korean interests (see chapter 2). Independence in 1945 and then the Korean war left industry near ground zero. It was not until the single-minded authoritarian leadership of Park Chung-hee that the framework for a modern industrial national state was established. For that reason and the historic times, the political and economic vacuum in Asia after the end of the Japanese empire, the drawn-out Vietnam war—events outside Korean control—Korea's economy inspired such adjectives as "miraculous." How else could one account for how a poverty-stricken, war-ravaged, disoriented society made its way so quickly in the shadow of Japan, China, and the Soviet Union?

These results understandably created a great sense of confidence among the South Korean people in themselves and in the unfamiliar idea of progress, that the West was correct: The trend was up, not cyclical as the Chinese claimed; the past always preferable to the future. Hard work, sacrifice, dedication, education, and anti-communism would lift up each and every Korean onto a higher and higher stage of modernization. As Senator Albert Beveridge of Indiana put it, in regard to China in the 1890s, "If Shanghai continues to progress, it may one day reach the heights of Kansas City." At the apex of the Korean economic bubble, South Korea presented itself, and was accepted in many quarters for some time without qualification, as a special new economic model suitable for emulation by other developing countries.

But to return to Professor Han and his discontent, "The mind set of Koreans is distinguished by the culture of *shimbaram*. As a social-cultural expression, *shimbaram* commonly refers to a surge of emotive energy that inspires people to work diligently toward and take ownership of a given task. This perfection of the Korean people as 'workaholics' is based on their unyielding devotion to work; once incentives and motives are identified this drive can be used as a powerful means for social change."[11] On the downside, Korean manufactured goods, such as automobiles, were dubbed "almost right," a sign that there was some way to go in quality. Today, South

Korea seems to have overcome that distinction as its cars are beginning to reach world standards.

In surveying the principal events that shaped Korea in the twentieth century, I follow the chronicle of the century—the destruction of the old Chinese imperial order and the casting of Korea into unfriendly waters; colonization by Japan in 1910; the struggle for independence in China and Washington, D.C.; the end of World War II and the reemergence of Korea into world history; the Korean war and its aftermath—the Cold War continues; the South Korean garrison state becomes the development state; politics lags behind economics in the South; the North Korean option for communism and "self-reliance"; playing China and the Soviet Union against each other; South Korea joins the international community, following the Japanese mercantile model under the slogan of "free trade"; the stage is set for economic disaster through the contradictions between the actual economic system and its professed goals; the drive for "democratic consolidation" brings unexpected results; and the struggle inside a dangerous world order.

The participation of Korea in the Chinese tributary system is our introduction to the history of northeast Asia and the politics of the day. The discussion of the Japanese colonial period tells us much about the attitude of both countries toward each other and why closer cooperation between the two is so difficult. Any signs of the possibility of better relations are usually counterbalanced by signs to the contrary.

The consideration of the independence movement has been a particular hobby of mine because of my early exposure to that activity in China in 1945. The history in part accounts for the ambiguous U.S. involvement with Korean independence leaders and accounts for critical decisions, good and bad, for future Korean-American relations. We still live in the age of "self-determination," launched by Woodrow Wilson at the conclusion of World War I (although the U.S. offered no help to Korea, which considered itself highly eligible). While this movement had a very marginal role in the course of the war against Japan, that effort provided the inspiration for today's South Koreans to visit Independence Hall, and understand their struggle against Japan. Built in 1987, now over a million South Koreans visit this site annually, filled with the intense pride of nationalism that is characteristic of the people. In the North, "independence fighters" were from a different ideology and this group also took over the leadership of their part of the country.

The Syngman Rhee period (1945–1960) was ended by student demonstrations and a brief experiment in democracy before a military coup in June 1961 ushered in the long era of the garrison state and then the economic development state.[12] There followed a stretch of military rule under

Park Chung-hee until his assassination in 1979; another general, Chun Doo-hwan (1980–87); yet another general, Roh Tae-woo (1988–92); and then a civilian regime (some say "civilian authoritarianism") under Kim Young-sam (1993–97). Finally, in December 1997, the opposition won an election, hailed mainly by academics as proof positive of the reality of South Korean democracy. Kim Dae-jung, who had suffered mightily under the ruling dictators, was elected president and was inaugurated on February 25, 1998. In his inaugural address, President Kim said: "We enjoy the proud heritage of our 5,000 year history, the spirit of our forefathers are urging us on. Just as our forefathers saved the country with indomitable will whenever they met national ordeals, let us write a great chapter in our history by overcoming today's difficulties and undertaking another chapter forward. Let us turn today's crisis into an opportunity."[13]

Based on the above summary, I will consolidate a number of issues that are especially relevant today. One is the progress of political development. I will raise a number of practical and theoretical issues that affect contemporary Korean politics. In the press of modernization, American-trained Korean scholars as well as American political scientists in particular have been eager to project South Korea to the leading edge of democracy, the "consolidation of democracy" being a current theme. I would like to establish whether this is actually taking place or whether it is at odds with the reality of a one-branch government (the executive) facing a comatose legislature and a feeble judiciary. And the long-standing political parties (often with annual name changes) need to be considered for what they actually are.

Also, I will want to analyze the present state of the South Korean economy, how the chaebol system is operating, whether it is actually being reformed, and to what extent reform is possible. The South Korean economy, propped up by grand claims for high rank in the world hierarchy, needs to be investigated. Another fascinating subject is how the desire for autonomy and freedom of action in both North and South square with today's realities. Globalization has cut like a knife into South Korea's previously protected internal market, exposing the flaws in a number of industries. The auto manufacturing sector, a "pillar of the state," would appear to be in danger of toppling over, for example, unless it can find a strong "alliance" with an international car manufacturer. Can South Korea successfully change toward the Anglo-Saxon-IMF (International Monetary Fund) model, in which it is now enmeshed, or should it cling to the Japan-German "late-industrial" model, which served it so long and so well?

South Korea's foreign policy deserves attention as an example of expansion into the world community, despite the overhanging hazard of a still-hostile North Korea. Despite the expectations by many that North Korea was on the brink of collapse, it is still very much in place and Kim Jong-il, the son of the great leader, Kim Il-sung, who died in 1994, has engineered a smooth transition of power. The limits of South Korean unilateral policy must also be considered in terms of the nuclear Agreed Framework of 1994 in an effort to end the nuclear weapons threat from the North. Four-Power talks (the two Koreas plus China and the U.S.), or six-power talks, adding Japan and Russia, are also ongoing factors in trying to work out a new order in Asia. The reasons for the delicate relations with the North, in the preference on both sides so far for the "armistice" instead of a peace treaty, need to be weighed. And what is the American interest in being tugged this way and that in the intrigues of intra-Korean politics?

Finally, I will offer observations on where the two Koreas are going and what impact that is likely to have on regional and international security and commerce. Is this a real problem, or is it simply an unburied relic of the Cold War? In the course of this work, I have interviewed dozens of South Koreans in politics, economics, and journalism to obtain their insights. I have received much assistance and cooperation; these views and information are reflected in these pages, as well as my own research, mainly at Stanford and Seoul.

Korea and the Chinese Tributary System: Will the Past Resemble the Future?

Traumatic as the Korean war was in mid-century, the Korean peninsula had had a long and bloody history of war with its neighbors. It was the fate of Korea to be located in an area surrounded, as it were, by Russia to the North, China to the West, and Japan to the South. To the East was the Pacific, and North America was 5,000 miles away. So for well over 2,000 years, Korea was dominated by the aspirations of its neighbors. The principal influence came from China, the earliest and greatest civilization in Asia. Korea was absorbed into the Chinese system of international relations, the tributary system, which was designed by the Chinese to keep their neighbors on the borders or on the periphery of their culture and power. Korea was one of the earliest and most loyal participants in this relationship, which shows in significant ways to this day.[1]

As we approach the Korean world from a perspective of some 2,000 years ago, Korea had managed through much sacrifice of blood and treasure to maintain its hold over its own peninsula. At times, under the Silla Dynasty (A.D. 668–935) and strong kings and prosperous times, it managed to extend its dominion over large areas of Manchuria as well. But by and large, the Koreans, after their long immigration from Central Asia, were content to stay on the peninsula. This offered them a degree of security and the possibility of solidifying their culture and way of life and maintaining their independence in a dangerous and hostile world.

China in the beginning was the local hegemon and the Koreans conveniently fell under the sway of the Chinese tributary system, which regulated inter-state relations along China's immense periphery. China always saw itself as the "Middle Kingdom," based first of all on geography, but above all on the internal cohesion and superiority of the Chinese (*Han*) culture. The first Emperor to succeed in unifying the contending king-doms or feudal states was Chin Shih Huang-ti, who in 221 B.C. established his dynasty. He built the Great Wall north of his capitol city of Chang An (Long Peace, now Sian). His death in 210 B.C. was the occasion for the construction of the underground burial grounds of the porcelain army that has rightly gained the ancient emperor new fame and admiration over the past two decades.

In an intellectual sense, the Chin Dynasty was marked by the efforts of the emperor and his nobles to eliminate the Confucian texts and learning, with its emphasis on virtue and accommodation, in favor of the Legalists. This was an effort to establish law rather than the ceremonies and rites of Confucianism as the pillar of government and its preeminence over inter-personal hierarchical relationships. While classical texts were indeed burned, they nonetheless survived this assault and the ascendancy of the Legalists was put to an end; the Legalist approach to government and so-ciety failed and has not recovered even today. Confucianism has undergone reform and repair, but still undergirds Chinese domestic society as well as the Chinese view of the world.

Important as this Chinese system was to Korea's external affairs, Chi-nese Confucianism also played a decisive role in the internal development of Korean society. Confucianism as an ideology and ideal of good govern-ment entered the Korean peninsula during the first three centuries A.D., gradually spreading to the south. A Confucian academy flourished in the kingdom of Koguryo; and in A.D. 682 another Confucian academy was es-tablished in Kyongju, the capital of Silla. This turned out to be preparation for the rise of the neo-Confucianism of the Chinese philosopher Chu Hsi during the Southern Sung Dynasty (1127–1279). So this Confucian her-itage exercised a powerful influence on the Koreans, both in education and in government.[2] (The importance of the Confucian philosophy in Korean life will be considered later in analyzing contemporary Korean society.)

The tributary system at first grew out of the imperial desire to deal dif-ferently with those clans and tribes that were not Han, those who were considered culturally inferior or different from the dominant group, and establish a hierarchical relationship with them. The vassal had to acknowl-edge the superior position of the Han Emperor and a system of embassies and rites was developed to handle this inferior-superior relationship. As this system developed toward fruition in the seventeenth and eighteenth centuries, it added a strong commercial and trade element that became more important than the symbolic role. Korea was an important actor in this system from the outset, around 200 B.C. during the Han Dynasty. The Koreans acquiesced in this tributary role for three reasons: (a) the power realities—if they refused to pay homage to the Chinese Emperor and his

Middle Kingdom, China might assert its power and take over militarily; (b) the Koreans admired the Chinese culture and, in the world of the day, they acknowledged Chinese superiority—as did the other members of the tributary system—and accepted an inferior hierarchical status; and (c) there were advantages to being a vassal both in terms of having good relations with China and having a claim on Chinese military support in time of need. For centuries—despite occasional clashes with China, particularly over Korean settlements in Manchuria—the system served both sides well. Yet, toward the end of the nineteenth century, the tributary system proved to be a liability for Korea and was a factor in its temporary disappearance from the international scene.

It is worthwhile to spend a bit of time explaining how the Chinese world worked in general before describing Korea's experience in it in particular, especially in the final turmoil that marked the destruction of the system altogether. Even more so now, perhaps. This is because China has reemerged in the late twentieth century as a principal world power and vestiges of its traditional worldview will once again be a factor to ponder in world politics. Since the Han Dynasty (206 B.C.–A.D. 220), according to Kenneth Scott Latourette, "the state has usually been based upon Confucian principles modified to meet the exigencies of changing conditions."[3] As an ethical mode of thought, Confucius promoted a series of virtues that governed the role of the individual in Chinese society, as well as his view of the outside world in general. Without going into his philosophy in detail, a few examples will suffice to give the sense of these ideas and how they served as a basis for the Middle Kingdom in its relations with non-Chinese cultures and alien states. The December 1999 visit to Seoul of Chinese Foreign Minister Tang Jian-xuan to discuss China's view of Pyongyang, among other things, is an example of this ancient heritage. As a special gesture, the Republic of Korea (ROK) foreign minister, Hong Young-soon, entertained his visitor for a day at a local spa.

Four principal virtues will be considered. The first is the principle of *jen,* which means "fellow-feeling," a notion of the personal and societal bond between individuals, and by extension, between groups, and even between nations. In one place Confucius says this about *jen:* "Unyielding fortitude and simple modesty approaches *jen.* " One can observe someone with these attributes: "outside the home/ treat people/ as if receiving a guest; employ the people as if performing a great sacrifice. That which one does not desire, do not do to other people. Dwelling in a feudal lord's estate, he lacks resentment. Dwelling in a great officer's estate, he lacks ill-will."[4] A person with this virtue, demonstrated by his own actions, clearly would set a good example for inter-state relations. A related virtue is *li,* which literally means the rules of propriety for ceremonies. But philosophically speaking, it has the sense of inner sincerity and virtue, an idealized way of how the Middle Kingdom wished to maintain good relations with its vassals; hopefully, after a long association with the Han society, some of the vassals would reach a level of culture that would allow them to be full-fledged members of the Middle Kingdom. This was, in fact, how the Chinese empire was consolidated inside the country; but it was difficult, despite *jen* and *li,* for non-Chinese to be admitted to the core.[5]

A third virtue, *I,* or righteousness, defined the correct conduct of the individual in all social relationships. *I* includes the meaning of appropriateness; and extended, becomes a standard for action. The Confucian in his daily activities, decides first of all which course is *I.* Discovering it, he proceeds directly along that line, regardless of material consequences.[6] This approach is similar to Kant's "moral imperative," that principles are more important than consequences: "The superior man understands about *I;* the inferior man understands about profits."[7] In political life *I* becomes particularly significant: "In holding governmental office, the superior man practices *I;* that his principles may not succeed he already knows."[8] Righteousness, then, is the only criterion for personal and political practice.

The final Confucian virtue that we will mention as the background philosophy of the tributary system is the Tao, the way or the proper way to behave and act. In the Lun Yu (the Analects), "The Master said, 'the Chun tze/ superior man/ is easy to serve and difficult to please; if one pleases him not according to the Tao, he is not pleased.'"[9] For Confucius, the Tao seems to mean an ideal way of government that has an existence of its own, just as "truth" and "beauty" have for many an independent, autonomous existence.

Uniting these ideas with the already-existing family pattern, Confucius' philosophical theory reached beyond the family to the more distant social ties. The *Hsiao Ching* (Filial Piety), a later Confucian work, provides an example of this outward extension. "The Master said, 'The Chun-tze's service to his parents is filial. Therefore, loyalty can be transferred to the ruler; service to the elder brother is brotherly; therefore, obedience can be transferred to the ruler. As the individual develops his fellow-feeling, *Jen,* it is expanded in ever-increasing radii from the family with decreasing intensity until it embraces 'all within the four seas.'"[10]

The above concepts, then, comprised the philosophical underpinning of the Chinese worldview, and how, in theory, the Han conducted its relationship with the tribes and nations along its vast periphery. The ceremonial exchange of embassies from time to time, according to the schedule maintained by the court in Beijing, satisfied the Chinese claim as the Middle Kingdom. Tribute missions by other nations acknowledged their inferiority in the Chinese hierarchical world. The Chinese often received gifts of lesser value than they gave. Over time, these tribute missions became poorly concealed trading enterprises, when China officially was not engaged in foreign trade.

And finally, this system made it unnecessary for China to station troops in these tributaries, except from time to time when power struggles and civil wars erupted, or when the dependency misbehaved in some way, such as when the Koreans expanded into Manchuria during the Silla Dynasty. In later years, Machiavelli pointed out in *The Prince* his preference for not incurring the expense of having to occupy other principalities. The Chinese tributary system created a buffer as well from the onslaughts of foreigners, and China responded to these incursions as required. During the eighteenth and nineteenth centuries, the strain on the Chinese system became severe. Western imperialism, with its superior military technology, proved to be impervious to Chinese defenses, both intellectually and militarily and through the tributary system. Power proved to be the great equalizer.

The Chinese were ignorant of the Western system of international relations and assumed that their hierarchical order, being universal and correct, was clearly superior and stronger than its neighbors. In the meantime, the West was moving in a different direction. The Treaty of Westphalia in 1648, marking the end of the religious wars in Europe, established the principle of the sovereign equality of states. State sovereignty was supposed to be inviolate. The second principle was the rule of international law, based on common consent. These agreed-upon laws were binding on the international community (although expediency and not law often determined the hard cases). Third, and perhaps the most important, was the recognition by all powers of the importance of the balance of power in their status and security in the world. Properly functioning, this balance would preserve the independence of the states within the European community and assure that no one state could emerge as the hegemon. It was with these three ideas that the Western powers began to confront the Chinese empire and its dependencies. A study of the case of Korea, one of the last and most loyal dependencies, will reveal the outcome of this unequal struggle for power in Asia.

China's long tributary relationship with Korea displays more of the power modalities of that enterprise than it does the more idealized Confucian version of just one big happy family. One Chinese writer, at a time when the West was criticized for its "unequal" treatment of China (1926), had this to say against China: "Certainly the Chinese once pursued a policy as aggressive as many of the foreign powers are pursuing now. It must be admitted that the foreign powers have been no harsher to China than China was to the surrounding tribes and kingdoms in the Han period."[11]

Wu Hung-chu and others describe the Han "chastizing" of Korea in 108 B.C. as "little more than aggression."[12] Later, during the collapse of the Mongol Dynasty (1280–1368) and the ascension of the Ming, Korea, although accepting Chinese sovereignty, played a role in northern Korea that is difficult to reconcile with Confucian principles.[13] Taking advantage of the power vacuum south of the Yalu River, Korean General Li Ch'eng-kuei advanced into this area occupied by the Sinicized Nu-chin tribes, bestowing investitures on them.[14] After Li established himself as king of the peninsula in A.D. 1392, he further extended Korean administration, even though his policy was counter to the desires of his suzerain, the Ming government. The Ming rulers intended to place the Nu-chins and all northern Korea under their jurisdiction. The Ming emperor Ch'ing-tzu (1403–1424) vigorously conducted the Nu-chin affair, obtaining the allegiance of 11 tribes in northern Korea, despite secret countermoves on the part of the Koreans. Only when it became obvious that their plans would not succeed did the Koreans petition Ch'ing-tzu for the right to govern the territory of the Nu-chins south of the Tumen river. The request was granted. China abandoned claims to territory south of the Tumen, and the Koreans give up active aspirations for northern lands.

Confucian dogma could mean several things. Action that ordinarily might be considered immoral could be justified through the ideology. When the Chinese dealt with people who did not understand the principle of *li,* they relied upon force to make their point. In fact, Confucius himself upheld "benevolent" imperialism, influencing backward people to learn about progress. The prevention of tyranny and absolutism was a legitimate function of benevolent government. After overthrowing a tyrant, if the people desired, their state could join the Chinese system without violating any ethical rules. Immoral and bad governments are also suitable prey for benevolence. There was, then, a fine but definite line of distinction between "benevolent" imperialism and plain imperialism.

This tension between the ideal and the practice, the ambivalence between theory and practice, is captured perfectly in this statement of Wang An-shih in the Sung Dynasty:

> It is quite true that the use of military force to strengthen the state is not the ideal way. A wise ruler should alternate between mild measures and strong measures. Although force should never be the only consideration, it is at present absolutely necessary for the preservation of the state. The ancient rulers held armed forces in high esteem and at the same time taught moral principles to the people. These two policies—government by force, and government by ethics—may be consistently combined.[15]

In brief, the tributary system might be compared to a large but flawed diamond; it contained imperfections but refracted resplendent light. According to Fairbank and Teng, "the tributary system was a framework within which all sorts of interests, personal and imperial, economic and social found expression."[16] Further, "there was an interplay between greed and statecraft, dynastic policy and vested interest, similar to that in any great political institution." Or, to put it another way, it was a system based on an ethical core that determined the conduct of interstate intercourse; as an ideology, the Chinese practiced international relations according to their accustomed ideals and Confucian moral principles. The projection of Chinese political and military power over the tributaries was, if not disguised, considerably moderated by adherence to the Confucian pattern: "the later Ch'ing rulers appear to have covered the tributary relationships with a sugar coating heavy enough to make it decidedly palatable."[17]

It is worthwhile recreating and reexploring the lost world of the Chinese tributary system in the context of Korea. The tributary system had a profound and disastrous effect on Korea's future at the end of the nineteenth century, which shaped Korea's fate in the twentieth century. And it is worth remembering China's own view of itself in international relations as a power is once again rising and will be on display in the twenty-first century.

Early contacts between East and West did not seriously disturb the old Chinese order. Western traders on official missions from 1655 to 1795 generally adhered to the Chinese rules, *kowtowing* (knocking the head on the floor) before having an audience with the Emperor and bringing gifts (tribute) to show respect. In the eighteenth century, however, the Chinese decreed that trade be conducted in Canton and gave a monopoly to a *cohong* (trading company) to supervise trade with the Western powers. Irritated by this system and the arrogance of the Chinese officials, the British took the lead to press China to behave like a Western nation on a basis of equality and with due regard to the Western state system based on sovereign equality, international law, and a sense of participation in the Western community.

The British reaction to China's demands was to denounce it as an uncivilized state.

China, however disposed its rulers may be to deny this fact, is one of a community of nations with common rights and obligations, and any claim to exemption from the recognized terms of national intercourse is inadequate in the interest of all other countries. To admit such a right of exemption would be to allow the arrogant superiority in power and civilization, and to pamper the hostile conceit of her people.

So long as the sovereign states of Europe will permit so obvious an in-
ference it cannot be a matter of surprise, and scarcely subject of reproach to
the Chinese, that they should be so ready to assert and so pertinacious in
acting upon it.

But even if exclusion from the territories, from all trade and intercourse
were an absolute right in the first instance, the Chinese have forfeited all
claim to its exercise—first, by voluntarily entering into relations political
and commercial in ages past with other States and people, by exchange of
embassies, by opening their ports and territories and encouraging trade; and
secondly, by aggressive wars and invasions of the territory of Europe by the
Tartar and Mongolian races who have ruled the country.

China preserves her undoubted rights of self-preservation as a political
society and an empire, but this does not involve the incidental right of in-
terdictory intercourse, because the right of decision must be shared by the
interdicted party.[18]

This passage demonstrates that Western states, like the Chinese, considered their method of international intercourse as conforming to nature
and reason, and therefore as a universal truth. The English, imbued with
the accomplishments of their own culture, which bloomed in the Age of
Enlightenment, were amazed and chagrined at the attitude of the Chinese;
action against the Chinese was rationalized on the basis of the Western
doctrine of international relations. Elijah Coleman Bridgman pointed out
that in the relations of China with Western trading nations "negotiations
becoming the character of great and independent nations, seem never to
have been undertaken."[19] The Chinese simply enroll these Western nations
as tribute bearers, who have, therefore, "frequently been treated with ne-
glect and indignity; and after all have affected little or nothing for the benefit of those who sent them, or for the world."[20] Furthermore, the Chinese
"practically deny the existence of relative rights among nations," believing
that the Emperor holds sway throughout the world.

In this assumption of all right and dominion, foreigners have acquiesced. This
acquiescence has grown out of the doctrine (very prevalent in the west), that
nations have a right to manage their own affairs in their own way, and have
no responsibilities in reference to other portions of the human family; and
that so long as one permits intercourse in a way it chooses, and refuses to interfere in any other way, or interdicts it altogether, other nations have no right
to interfere or complain. . . . The doctrine is equally opposed to the law of
God, to reason, and to common sense. Ignorance, superstition, pride, and ambition have acted jointly to strengthen, establish, and perpetuate it.[21]

Bridgman concluded that the Western powers had no alternative but to
force China to cooperate in the Western family of nations.[22] England, in-

toxicated by its own power and prestige, and proud of its commercial and colonizing success, believed it would be good for China to share in its beneficent influence. Thus we have a mirror-image conundrum of how China and England viewed the world and themselves.

Now, if the Europeans did not understand the Eastern international state system, the Chinese were even more uninformed about the West. The Koreans at this juncture were not yet directly involved in these matters but unfortunately, toward the end of the nineteenth century, they were no better prepared for this contest than their mentor, which took the following approach. The Chinese Emperor, after receiving the Macartney embassy at Jehol in 1793, issued a mandate, which read in part:

> You, o King, live beyond the confines of many seas; nevertheless, impelled by your humble desire to partake of the benefits of our civilization, you have dispatched a mission respectfully bearing your memorial. Your Envoy has crossed the seas and paid his respects at my Court on the anniversary of my birthday. To show your devotion, you have also sent offerings of your country's produce.
>
> I have perused your memorial; the earnest terms in which it is couched reveal respectful humility on your part, which is highly praiseworthy. In consideration of the fact that your Ambassador and his deputy have come a long way with your memorial and tribute, I have shown high favour and have allowed them to be introduced into my presence.
>
> Swaying the wide world, I have but one aim in view, namely, to maintain a perfect governance and to fulfill the duties of the State: strange and costly objects do not interest me. If I have commanded that the tribute offerings sent by you, O King, are to be accepted, this was solely in consideration for the spirit which prompted you to dispatch them from afar. Our dynasty's majestic virtue has penetrated unto every country under Heaven, and Kings of all nations have offered their costly tribute by land and sea. . . . It behooves you, O King, to respect my sentiments and to display even greater devotion and loyalty in future, so that, by perpetual submission to our Throne, you may secure peace and prosperity for your country hereafter. Besides making gifts (of which I enclose an inventory) to each member of your Mission, I confer upon you, O King, valuable presents in excess of the number usually bestowed on such occasions, including silks and curios—a list of which is likewise enclosed. Do you reverently receive them and take a note of my tender goodwill toward you! A special mandate.[23]

From such examples, we observe the clash of the two systems in which the outcome was not decided by superior moral philosophy but rather by foreign commercial and military technology. China reluctantly signed various treaties with the Western powers, such as the Treaty of Nanking in 1845 when the Chinese technically (but not spiritually) recognized that they were on an equal footing with the Western countries. China's leaders continued to hope that their fortunes would improve and that internal reforms, based on adopting Western technology to China's own needs while retaining its unique culture and philosophy, would turn the tide.

If the equality of states was the theoretical basis for the breakup of the Confucian state system, the Western idea of sovereignty, misunderstood by the Chinese, was the practical principle that undermined its legitimacy. For the Chinese to accept other nations as equals would have meant the recognition of equality of virtue and culture, and consequently, the destruction of the Chinese worldview. China's satellite states had for centuries clustered closely to the Chinese cultural core like iron filings to a magnet. In the absence of any counter attraction, mutual obligations and benefits whirled non-Chinese entities in an undeviating orbit. The impingement of the Western state system on the Confucian community, proclaiming the sovereign equality of states, was literally a "world-shaking" blow. The Chinese conception of the natural and social patterns having a preordained harmony in which all things had a definite and proper place was challenged by this revolutionary doctrine.[24] Forced by Western military might to accept the equality principle, the Chinese, after a series of military and diplomatic defeats, helplessly watched their tributary system disintegrate. The Liu Ch'iu islands, under pressure from the Japanese, whole-heartedly converted to the Western system, especially vis-à-vis China, and was the first tributary to be drawn from Chinese control in 1872. While the Liu Ch'iu islands in themselves were of small account, the principle involved was enormous and set the stage for the destruction of the whole system, notably for Korea. The separation of Korea from the Chinese state system highlights the principles and operations of both international orders.

With cultural contacts as well as military ones dating back to the early Han Dynasty (11 B.C.–A.D. 100), the Koreans remained in the Chinese orbit, and were generally content for centuries to stay within it. In the end, it was with great reluctance that Korea left the tributary system, which had served it well. Now a new danger appeared. Because the Western powers did not comprehend the principles of the Confucian state system, confusion arose among them over the status of Korea. This confusion played into the hands of the Japanese, who understood the situation perfectly. Western international law did not supply a definition for, or recognize, such a nebulous term as *shu pang* (dependent state). The Korean dilemma was not easily resolved; the Koreans tried to play this ambiguity to their own benefit, but this effort worked against them. "With the coming of the West, Korea attempted to maintain a double status, being simultaneously in the disintegrating East Asiatic system and in the ascendant system of the West."[25]

Korea had isolated itself from all foreign intercourse except with its suzerain. By 1846, however, the French tried to force their way into Korea, but were unsuccessful. Finally, in 1876, Japan signed a treaty of amity and commerce with Korea. In this document Korea agreed that it was as independent and sovereign as Japan, thereby, according to Western international law, disavowing Chinese overlordship. The Chinese government, anxious to avoid any more difficulties with the newest member of the foreign powers, Japan, did not press its claim as suzerain over Korea; and as in the Liu Ch'iu incident, the Chinese failed to comprehend the significance of sovereignty, thus undermining their influence upon Korea. After the Korean-Japanese treaty, the Western nations had to decide whether to recognize Korea as an independent nation, or to accept the evasive Chinese assertion of its suzerainty. In a letter from the King of Korea to the President of the United States, which accompanied the Korean-American treaty of 1882, the confusion, paradoxically, was clearly expressed. "The King of Corea acknowledges that Corea is a tributary of China, and in regard to both internal administration and foreign intercourse, it enjoys complete independence."[26]

Contradictory as this statement might seem, it describes the precise relationship of China and Korea. According to Confucian dogma, the parent, China, did not interfere in either the internal or external affairs of its shu pang except, as with a family, in times of crisis. The Western nations, however, taking a cue from the clause in the Japanese treaty and desirous of placing responsibility for signing the treaty on Korea, decided to consider Korea an independent state. In the next four years England, Germany, Italy, Russia, and France all signed treaties with Korea, all based on the Japanese model.[27]

Although the damage had already been done, Li Hung-chang, the Chinese statesman most responsible for Chinese relations with Korea, attempted to strengthen ties between the two countries. He sent the Chinese general Yuan Shih-kai to Korea to consolidate the ancient Chinese position as surrogate. This move was moderately successful, in spite of Russian and Japanese opposition. In 1882, for example, the Chinese intervened in Korea, seizing the Tai-wun-kun, the regent, and restoring the Yi Dynasty king. China then concluded a commercial agreement that openly asserted the Confucian superior-inferior relationship.[28] After this display, the Western powers began to question Korean independence, in view of the lack of Japanese protests at this intervention, and the validity of treaties with Korea that were made without the approval of the Chinese emperor. Li Hung-chang exercised control that the Westerners would recognize, although still using the traditional relationship. He also added a new element to his policy by employing Chinese commercial agents in Korea, who could function under dual roles. Japan, however, overthrew the Chinese position as a result of the Sino-Japanese war of 1894–95 and finally settled the matter for 35 years by annexing Korea in 1910. In this way, China, humiliated and reduced to a subcolony, became a member of the Western state system. Korea had many difficult times yet to endure.

Despite the injunctions of Confucius and the high-blown tones of the imperial rescripts, China's thrusts and parries with its Western tormentors revealed a leadership completely alert to interest and power as motivating factors and recourse to morality as a legitimizing principle of international relations. China tried to deal with the Western state system in a superior role as a great empire and civilization. But finally China was forced to respond as a sovereign state, as only an equal member of the Western community. For the first half of the twentieth century, China tried to become an equal to the principal Western powers. Its efforts were frustrated by the affronts of the West and undermined by internal strike, civil wars, and foreign invasion, particularly from Japan. The "unequal treaties" imposed on China by the West were among the burdens borne by Chiang Kai-shek during World War II as China strove to become one of the Big Five in the UN Security Council.

Part of the reason for the success of the communist revolution in China was precisely the perceived weakness of China on the international scene that propelled Mao Tse-tung to the fore in October 1949. China was driven internationally to regain the respect and prestige that it had lost during its long period of humiliation and entered the Korean war in 1950 in part to demonstrate that it was the revolutionary leader of Asia. China is still dissatisfied with the way the United States deals with it, somewhat short of the equal treatment China expects and insists upon. As in the United States, Chinese politics are driven by interest, power, and a certain moral view of the world. How these aspirations will be worked out, and the moral content of the reconciliation, is still unknown.

Today, even among Sinologists dedicated to promoting the uniqueness of their product, there is growing recognition that China, in its international politics, actually follows the principles of realism rather than the flowering axioms of Sun Tze in his *Art of War.* Alastair Ian Johnson, in *Cultural Realism: Strategic Culture and Grand Strategy in Chinese History,* makes the case for Chinese realism in its conduct of international relations.[29] Arthur Waldron, in his review of this book, states that "new and archivally based accounts of the Korean War have established just how involved China was, and how far from mere 'signaling' were its military objectives. There have been re-examinations of domestic policy that show power rather than ideology to have been the key factor."[30]

Johnston's book points up the distinction between Confucian theory and Chinese political practice. This is relevant, in my view, to an appreciation of the goals of current Chinese rearmament programs, based in part on the bargain sale procurement of technologically advanced Russian military equipment. To the question of what China intends to do with the new military capabilities that it is acquiring, Johnston's implicit answer is, clearly, use them. While some observers still talk about China's pride, its requirements for prestige, its desire to overcome its neighbors and so forth, Johnston reminds us that, as the *bingjia* or military writers understood, weapons are tools. His examination of China's military actions since 1949 indicates that, consistent with realist theory, China's resort to force has "been related to improved relative capabilities" while, when in a crisis, China has tended "to act in a more determined manner as it grew relatively stronger."[31]

As for contemporary ROK-China relations, they are warm and friendly, although sometimes muted by China's need to present an even-handed approach to its old ally North Korea; the war-time analogy of "as close as lips and teeth," long absent from their diplomatic vocabulary, has reappeared of late. The ROK in its geographical position has been victimized over the years by its neighbors from time to time. But it also has had the opportunity for those same reasons to play the major powers off against each other. During the Cold War, which ended elsewhere in 1989, the North kept the Chinese and Soviets at arm's length, getting separate military and economic benefits from each; while South Korea as the doughty defender of liberty profited handsomely from U.S. fears of both China and the Soviet Union.

Dr. K. W. Kim, former ROK ambassador to the UN and Washington, has commented on how fortunate the ROK is to have a "powerful friend" (the U.S.) "far away." This helps give the ROK the wiggle room it needs in pursuing its own interests, which are not necessarily identical with those of the U.S.

But the Chinese world and its worldview remain very much evident in Asia today and will continue to play a critical role on the Korean peninsula.

3

Japanese Colonialism in Korea, 1910–1945

Wrenching Korea out of the Chinese world took two wars, the first already mentioned, the Sino-Japanese War of 1895–96, and the second, the Russo-Japanese War of 1904. Korea was in a position not unlike that of a newborn calf, defenseless before the Japanese imperial wolf. Japan was the first Eastern state to understand intellectually and culturally the strength of Western industrialization and the accompanying military technology. The Japanese at first embraced these facets of the West with regret, but in the Meiji era of 1876–1920, they threw themselves into remaking their own economic structure and military establishment. While they preferred their own ways, they did not, like China, agonize over the inevitable and resist industrialization under a version of the Chinese slogan, "Chinese spirit, western science," or other diversions that got in the way of Western-style progress. One of the blessings of Japan's awareness of the West was a modern army and navy and it soon turned these to its advantage over China and then Russia, both to the disadvantage of Korea.

The Sino-Japanese War arose over the struggle for power in regard to Korea. As we have seen, China exercised an ambiguous sovereignty over Korea and thwarted Japanese interests. The war resulted in Japan annexing Formosa (Taiwan), as well as receiving trade and other concessions from China itself, and of course increasing Japan's role in Korea. China was forced to recognize the independence of Korea in 1896 at the Treaty of Shimonoseki. The U.S. Secretary of State, John Hay, tried to counter these Japanese moves against China with his "Open Door Policy," to protect American trade interests in China that were threatened by the "spheres of influence" policy of the European powers, as well as Japan. The independent status of Korea was welcomed, even though Korea was ill-prepared to deal with the increasingly dangerous politics of Northeast Asia.

With its position in Korea enhanced and its easy victory over China, Japan was now ready to deal with its other major competitor in the region, Russia. The Russo-Japanese War arose as the result of Japan's fear of Russian ambitions in that region. As Rikitaro Fujisawa, Japan's spokesman for the East Asian Co-prosperity sphere and Japanese imperialism in general, wrote quoting a colleague, Okakura, "Korea lies like a dagger ever pointed toward the very heart of Japan." On his own, he continued that "Korea in the possession of Russia, or even a weak and corrupt Korea which might fall any time an easy prey to the Russian Eagle, would place Japan's destiny in the hands of the unscrupulous 'Colossus of the North.' Japan could not accept such a fate. That the Russo-Japanese War was not only a defensive war for Japan but Japan's struggle for her very existence as an independent nation is too obvious to require either elucidation or explanation."[1] By February 1904 the Japanese were ready to strike at the Russian fleet in the ports of Port Arthur (a concession extracted from China at the tip of the Liaotung peninsula), Vladivostok, and in Korea, Chemulpo (now Inchon). Under Admiral Togo the Japanese fleet carried out a "preemptive" attack, declaring war formally only after these successful attacks had been accomplished. As Australian historian Richard Connaughton points out, this is one of the lessons of the Russo-Japanese War that the Western powers, including the United States, did not absorb.[2] The Japanese naval victory over the Russians at the Battle of Tsushima Straits in 1904 sealed the Russian defeat at sea; Korea served as a base for the Japanese to advance into both Siberia and Manchuria and humble the Russian ground forces. The U.S. achieved the settlement of this war. President Theodore Roosevelt at Portsmouth, New Hampshire, took the lead and for his efforts he received the Nobel Peace prize.

As far as the Koreans were concerned, there was a much darker side to this peace prize. This was the acquiescence, even connivance, of President Roosevelt in the Japanese establishment of a protectorate over Korea the very next year, in 1905, despite the efforts of Korean Emperor Kojong to gain U.S. support. Roosevelt's views on the situation were expressed succinctly in a letter to Secretary of State Hay: "We cannot possibly interfere for the Koreans against Japan. They could not strike one blow in their own defense." Roosevelt upheld the Taft-Katsura agreement, which in effect recognized Japanese preeminence in Korea, while Japan did the same in regard to the new American colony, the Philippines.[3]

Hulbert, a missionary in Korea at the turn of the twentieth century, was also on occasion an emissary for the Korean emperor and had unsuccessfully sought to deliver a letter from the emperor to President Roosevelt. Hulbert also wrote about these last days of the Yi Dynasty in a book, *The Passing of Korea,*[4] which has a two-part dedication. The first one is to his majesty, "The Emperor of Korea, as a token of high esteem and a pledge of unwavering allegiance, at a time when calumny has done its worst and justice has suffered an eclipse." The second dedication is to the Korean people, "who are now witnessing the passing of old Korea to give place to a new, when the spirit of the nation, quickened by the touch of fire, shall have proved that though 'sleep is the image of death,' it is not death itself."

In the preface, Hulbert goes further on his observations and lamentations.

> This book is a labour of love undertaken in the days of Korea's distress, with the purpose of interesting the reading public in a country and a people that have been frequently maligned and seldom appreciated. They are overshadowed by China on the one hand in respect to numbers, and by Japan on the other in respect to wit. They are neither good merchants like the one nor good fighters like the other, and yet they are far more like Anglo-Saxons in temperament than either, and they are by far the pleasantest people in the Far East to live amongst. Their failings are such as follow in the wake of ignorance everywhere, and the bettering of their opportunities will bring swift betterment to their condition.

The Japanese aspirations to subjugate Korea have a substantial history. Japanese pirates for centuries had raided Korean coastal shipping; and then Korea figured in the designs of Japan's powerful Shogun, Hideyoshi, who in the late sixteenth century unified Japan. His victory left him with a large army on hand with no obvious new target. Hideyoshi settled on the grand goal of conquering China; to accomplish this, he needed to advance overland through the Korean peninsula.

In 1392, the Yi family, headed by a leading Korean general, had taken over the throne from an inept despot, the last king of Koryu. This was the origin of the last Korean dynasty, the Yi or Chosun, which reigned from 1392 until 1910. The accomplishments of this dynasty over its first 200 years were substantial in economics, politics, and culture; so when the demand came from Hideyoshi to either provide passage for his army or even join in the campaign against China, the Koreans were stunned. The king tried to stall and avoid a decision, but at last he refused Hideyoshi's request. The Koreans were not prepared for the vast 1,000-ship invasion fleet and an army of over 250,000 well-equipped men, armed with firearms as well as swords and spears. The court panicked and appealed to the Ming Chinese emperor, invoking the reciprocal claims of the tributary system.

Hideyoshi assigned this campaign to subordinates who bickered among themselves; this did not prevent them from seizing the Yi capitol, Seoul, but did result in delays and dallying that allowed the Koreans to form a resistance and the Ming Chinese to send an army as well. As Japanese casualties mounted, the expectation that reinforcements would be forthcoming were dashed with the emergence of a Korean naval hero, Admiral Yi Son-sin. He developed an iron-clad "turtle" boat (something like the Confederate *Merrimac*) that all but destroyed a Japanese fleet containing 60,000 reinforcements. With this disaster, the Japanese retreated to fortified positions around Pusan, an early trading post, and finally negotiated their way back to Japan.

While the Japanese casualties were perhaps as high as 200,000, this only whetted their thirst for revenge. So in 1596 another armada of similar size invaded Korea, with much the same result. The defeated Japanese were again expelled, this time taking with them a large quantity of pickled Korean ears and noses, which were buried in a temple in Kyoto.[5] One of the unanticipated results of these two invasions was the weakening of the Ming emperor, who had twice provided assistance to the Koreans, so that when the Manchus struck early in the seventeenth century, the Ming were unprepared. The Yi Dynasty favored the Ming, but settled for an agreement with the Manchus that finally left them in peace and ready for a new flowering of the dynasty during the next two centuries. But as we have seen, the same period saw a decline in Korean military prowess, as well as an upsurge in political factionalism, which weakened the Koreans for the coming ordeals with Japan. The final stage before protectorate and annexation was the Russo-Japanese War.

An irony of both of these wars, despite their names—Sino-Japanese, Russo-Japanese—is that a good deal of the land fighting took place on Korean territory and the principal victim was Korea, which had opened itself to world commerce in 1876. All of the Western trading powers signed commercial treaties and angled for various concessions and business opportunities, such as building railroads, supplying water and electricity for Seoul, or grabbing timber concessions on the Yalu, as Russia did during the early twentieth century. But Russian influence in Korea was short-lived because of the Russo-Japanese War. Japanese interests in Korea slowly began to dominate because of both propinquity and economic fit. Japan had need for Korean surplus grain production and Korea was a good market for Japanese manufactured products.

Korea's primary introduction to international trade, therefore, centered on Japan. The rice trade was mainly conducted through the port of Inchon. This became a thriving and highly organized activity, beginning toward the end of the nineteenth century. These faint stirrings of an independent trading establishment for the Koreans were soon blended into the economic policies of the conquerors: "Traditions of ethnic continuity, close cooperation with political authorities, commerce and guild solidarity helped mold and maintain a Korean business community at Inchon. New patterns of law and contract, business-state ties, of corporations and chartered, semi-official firms in the colony brought the brokers into an interstate and intermarket colonial system." Yet even under these adverse conditions, the Korean associations were able to obtain a separate existence as Korean *chaegye* (family enterprises) as opposed to the Japanese *zaikal* (financial institutions).[6]

One issue of a theoretical nature is whether the beginnings of Korean capitalism preceded the coming of Japan and its colonial development policies. Korean historians and economists, writing from a nationalist appreciation, speak of "sprouts" of capitalism as being indigenous to the Korean economic life.[7] This claim ultimately rests on the question of definition. Max Weber, for example, in his book, *The Religions of China,* insists that there was no sign of capitalism in the entire history of the Chinese empire.[8] Economic activity in the empire was simply merchant trading and handicraft level of manufacturing. Coinage and salt were government monopolies. But in part because of the ideology of Confucius, a capitalist class did not develop, that is, capital was not accumulated and put to work to create and dominate the means of production. Money lenders and landowners in ancient China certainly created fortunes, but as Weber states, "The legal forms and societal foundations for capitalist 'enterprise' were absent in the Chinese economy."[9] Given the Korean court's dedication to the Chinese system, there is little likelihood that the Korean economy was more modern than that of China, and as Carter J. Eckert concludes, the development of modern capitalism in Korea owes its start to the Japanese colonial era.[10] The Korean "economic miracle" period, as we shall discuss later, begins with post-Korean war developments under the leadership of President Park Chung-hee.

All of this is relevant to the general difficulty of getting a capitalist mode of production and economic development going in Northeast Asia in the eighteenth and nineteenth centuries. Commercial activity in general and the making of money specifically were low on the social totem pole of Chinese Confucian culture, which rooted itself in both Korea and Japan. In contrast, the West developed the doctrine of liberalism and individualism, which legitimized the accumulation of wealth as a constructive development, opposed to the backward feudal system and as a positive way to create a better material society.

In Korea . . . capitalism developed under very different historical conditions that had nothing to do with Western liberalism, either in an economic or a political sense. No Korean counterpart to Adam Smith appeared to raise selfishness to the level of a moral principle for Korean businessmen. On the contrary, Korean businessmen were compelled to pursue their interests within a still strongly neo-Confucian society that regarded business purely for the sake of individual gain at best with suspicion and at worst as an act of moral turpitude.[11]

A 1935 interview with a Korean capitalist by a local Korean paper on the importance of making money drew this Confucian rhetorical response: "What's money [that anyone could ever consider it so important]? There's nothing more vulgar than money, nothing more filthy than money. How could [anyone] ever say that money was the most important thing in the world? I, for one, have never once thought that money was the most important [thing]. More [important] than money are humanity and also righteousness."[12]

Whether such statements are literally true is not the principal point: They are indicative of the need in the society of the time to depreciate the accumulation of capital, a situation that similarly faced the growing bourgeoisie in Japan. The merchant class in Osaka met this need during the eighteenth and nineteenth centuries by the establishment of its own Confucian-style academy, thereby raising the status of the merchant class in the eyes of the public. These kinds of efforts resulted in the necessary public attitude in Japan that it was all right to become rich, supporting a claim of Max Weber in *The Protestant Ethic and the Rise of Capitalism,* that such an ethic is a prerequisite of capitalist economic development.[13] But also note that, as in Korea, there was a considerable divergence between ethical theory and historical actuality.[14] And the requirements for full-scale capitalist development are contained in a study by Nathan Rosenberg and L. E. Birdzell, Jr., *How the West Grew Rich: The Economic Transformation of the Industrial World.*[15]

Under Japanese imperial colonialism beginning in 1910, there was a dual effect on the Koreans as a whole: The bourgeois class began to identify with Japan as the road to riches, while the population as a whole was unsympathetic to its Japanese master's goals. There was ambivalence in the way the various governor-generals ruled Korea. The aim, of course, was to maximize the value of Korea as a Japanese colony, but what was the best way to do this?[16]

According to Stewart Lone and Gavan McCormick,[17] the 45-year colonial period can be roughly divided into decades from the perspective of Japanese imperial rule: The initial colonial administration headed by army officers, who basically ruled by intimidation. This was a new experience for Japan, actually seizing another country with its own history and civilization; in the tradition of the Western powers with colonies in Asia, the Japanese followed an imperial policy based on force. From the '20s until the '30s, there was an attempt at "cultural rule," to mitigate the harshness of the military rule. This was not without reason. The common people and the Christian community especially were restless under Japanese rule. The suppression of religious freedom and the discrimination against the average Korean in terms of wage differentials (40 to 50 percent lower than Japanese counterparts), along with restrictions on press freedoms and freedom of assembly, provided a background for a nationwide uprising. The Samil (3–1) Movement, March 1, 1919, for a brief moment challenged the Japanese authority.

Beyond Japanese repression, there were external forces that helped to trigger this apparently spontaneous nationwide demonstration. First of all, there was the aftermath of World War I and the Wilsonian slogan of "making the world safe for democracy." Integral to the Wilson position was the principle of "self-determination," which guaranteed to any nation the right to insist on its own destiny. Various Korean patriotic independence-oriented groups and their leaders, including Syngman Rhee (later to become president of South Korea) lobbied in Washington, D.C., Paris, and Geneva to try to capture the attention of the victorious Western powers to the plight of Korea. Why should it not be granted its independence from Japan, a status it had just lost nine years previously? But Japan, too, was among the winning powers and no one raised a hand to the plight of the Koreans on the international stage. In Korea itself, the movement was put down severely by the Japanese military and police, with hundreds killed and thousands imprisoned.

The Japanese authorities suspected a foreign hand, beyond the Christian missionaries and the indigenous Korean church leaders who had sparked the Samil Movement. They could not believe that the Koreans on their own could have organized such an event. This was only one element of the racism that characterized the Japanese period of rule in Korea. No more uprisings of this scale occurred during the rest of the occupation; it did, however, leave its mark on the Korean people. In an interview with Yoo Chang-soon (a prime minister under the Chun Doo-hwan regime) in April 1997, he said the following: "My father participated in these Samil demonstrations in Pyongyang. A neighbor at his side was shot and killed. He vowed he would have nothing to do with the Japanese. So my brother and I both entered into private business."[18]

Another source of alien inspiration for such subversion was to the north, in the Soviet Union, where the Communist revolution was running its course through the Soviet empire and throughout Siberia. Korea shared a border with the USSR and revolutionary ideas were easily infiltrated into the South, in an effort to begin a "new worker-peasant-led struggle against imperialism and feudalism."[19] But while North Korean historians are quick to claim credit for Lenin and South Korean historians for Wilson, the impulse came from the suffering and resentment of the Korean people themselves against the Japanese, rather than from these foreign factors, whose role was only marginal. The significance of the uprising for the Japanese was that they were required to take steps to head off the dangers of a nationalist backlash by making conditions more palatable for at least some Koreans to undercut nationalist sentiments inside Korea itself. This meant that the struggle for independence from Japan basically took place outside of Korea proper. Anti-Japanese, pro-Korean independence groups were spawned in Siberia, Manchuria, and in China proper. The history and influence of these groups and their significance to post–World War II developments inside Korea will be considered in the next chapter.

The time period from 1930 to the sudden end of colonial rule in August 1945 was characterized by an increasing effort of the Japanese authority to link Korea in the most valuable way to the growing needs of the Japanese military machine. These requirements expanded as Japan first carved out Manchuria in 1931 (creating the separate state of Manchukuo and its Emperor Henry Pu I) from China. This territory abutted Korea for hundreds of miles along the Yalu River. Many Koreans had already settled there to escape Japanese rule, but some found new commercial opportunities in this new Japanese territory.

It is worthwhile at this juncture to try to recapture the mood of the times in Northeast Asia with regard to the situation in Korea. This will help explain the general cooperation (or resistance) of the population in regard to the Japanese as well as to the politics of the Korean independence movement outside of the borders. One book that allows the reader to approach this problem from the point of view of Koreans under the Japanese rule in those days is Carter J. Eckert's *Offspring of Empire*, previously cited. Here he concentrates on the way one Korean family became caught up in the Japanese colonial policy and thrived as a Korean participant in the growth of Japanese capitalism in Korea. The Koch'ang Kims, Kim Song-su and Kim Yon-su, were the founders and operators of the first Korean-owned large business enterprise, the Koch'ang spinning mills. Later, they entered other enterprises and served on a variety of Japanese corporate boards. They were probably the most successful entrepreneurs of Korean colonial society. Their descendants still play pivotal roles in Korean society.

The Eckert book tells the story of how Japan developed Korea in what later would be considered the dependency model. In its perpetual search for "food security" and vulnerable to "rice riots" when shortages showed in the markets, Japan decided to increase Korea's rice production and tie it into the Korean export market. To this end, the colonial administration conducted a land survey to standardize land measurements and to determine land titles on a systematic basis. The lack of these procedures had plagued the previous Yi government and resulted in disputes over land titles as well as serious shortfalls in tax collection.

Another lingering matter was that some Japanese saw these proposals as a way to return to a previous scheme in the dying days of the Yi Dynasty to grab land for Japanese. Hulbert describes this situation as follows:

> We have seen that no strong attempt was made by the Japanese to secure reforms of the Korean government, and for this reason, many of the best Koreans were dissatisfied with the way things were going. Therefore it was unfortunate that on the 11th of June [1905] the Japanese authorities should make the startling proposal that all uncultivated land in the peninsula, as well as other resources, should be thrown open to the Japanese . . . there can be no question that it was a grave mistake. There is no other point on which the Korean is so sensitive as upon that of his land. He is a son of the soil and agriculture is the basis for all his institutions. The mere proposal raised an instant storm of protest from one end of Korea to the other.[20]

While the Japanese did not have the power to carry out this plan prior to complete annexation, they did not lose sight of their conviction that land was not fully utilized in the Korean countryside. So it is no surprise that one program was to expand the amount of land under cultivation; despite this effort, the total land added was only 5 percent. The real increase in rice production came about because of the introduction of new and better seed stock developed at the Agricultural Technology Bureau as well as the profligate use of chemical fertilizers.[21] This made it possible to increase rice exports by eight times to Japan, albeit at the cost of lowering Korean rice consumption per capita and forcing them to rely on millet and other grains. Concentration on rice production in the agricultural sector made most Korean farmers tenants, as Japanese interests by the end of the colonial period owned some 60 percent of Korean agricultural land. Everyone was vulnerable to market fluctuations. In the depression of the mid-1930s, agricultural prices were greatly reduced and the farm community suffered from this blow to its already meager income.

There was one positive unintended aspect of this agricultural fiasco from the Korean perspective and that was the accidental element of timing. With the land overburdened with surplus labor, the Japanese invasion of Manchuria in 1931 created new economic opportunities. The logic of developing Korea, especially North Korea, as a forward industrial base for further military adventures in China was unchallenged. The Japanese proceeded to invest large sums in steel mills, hydroelectric power, and even aircraft production. The industrialization produced better jobs for Korean laborers, although the discriminatory salary levels still prevailed. New openings for Korean bourgeoisie allowed them to participate in some management and investment roles under the aegis of the Japanese colonial government.

The situation of the Korean bourgeoisie deserves more attention, and one can extrapolate from the Eckert book as well as from interviews with now elderly Koreans on how they viewed the situation in Korea as the Japanese war in Manchuria and China unfolded. There was a growing acceptance of Japanese rule by the Korean bourgeoisie as being established and without an end in sight. The prudent thing seemed to be to opt for some degree of assimilation into the Japanese capitalist society and culture. At the same time, this group did not want to abandon altogether the "cultural" route that for a time was open to them under the Japanese so that they could have both benefits—second-class Japanese status but one foot in the Korean heritage. Among the common people, there was little opportunity to expect an improvement in their condition by a kind of collaboration; instead, they clung to their Korean culture and maintained their distance from the Japanese aspects of society, which, until the "Naisen Ittai" movement (Japanese-Korean unity) were largely outside their personal orbit.

There are two fundamental differences between the Japanese occupations of Korea and the German occupation of Europe (beyond the historic timeframe). In the Japanese case, they took over the entire governmental function; there was no effort to continue the Yi Dynasty as a Vichy-like institution. Koreans did participate in minor administrative governmental positions, but the Japanese themselves ran the show. Second, there was no vicious minority racist campaign, such as the persecution and destruction of the Jews. The Japanese were exploiting all of Korea. The collaboration idea was a difference in kind. At the end, the Japanese struggled to try finally to make the Koreans into Japanese; some Koreans found this attractive or convenient and for those some still reserve judgment. But cultural imperialism on this scale is still at the root of much bitterness in Korea against the Japanese, especially in the older generation.

Hong Sung-chick, born in 1929, is one of Korea's most distinguished sociologists. He lived in a village about 60 miles south of Seoul. He vividly recalls his grandfather's scalding bitterness over the Japanese, referring to them as "devils" and as inferior "barbarians," adopting a Chinese attitude toward outsiders. In high school, Hong had a Japanese English language teacher, a young woman, who encouraged the class to study hard so that "we could go to the United States after the war and teach English in American schools."[22]

The success of individual Koreans like the Koch'ang Kims and the attitude toward their conquerors made this route, which one would now call collaboration, seem perhaps acceptable, or even inevitable. This is made apparent if we contrast their case with that of, say, the French under German occupation.[23] In Korea, it appeared that the Japanese military was successful everywhere and that there was no likely end to the Japanese empire as success followed success in the 1930s. In contrast, French citizens could see that the prospects for the Allies against Hitler's Germany were good and that the 1,000 Year Reich might be considerably shorter than that. Collaborators might have been about 20 percent of the population. Many were reluctant to collaborate under those odds. But in the Korean timeframe, for the first 25 years at least, the subjugation of Korea seemed to be a permanent thing. Therefore, when the war ended in August 1945, fully 60 percent of the capitalist class, or the chaebol, continued to engage in business and participate in political power. The collaboration investigations conducted by the National Assembly in 1948 were inconclusive and half-hearted.

According to an article by Kim Sam-wung,[24] the Special Committee for Anti-National Investigation was established by the National Assembly in 1948. Its purpose was to examine all antipatriotic acts and pro-Japanese activities. This committee received the names of 7,000 people as pro-Japanese activists and arrested 306 people, including the highly controversial Choe Nam-son. Choe was the drafter of the March 1, 1919 proclamation of independence, which made him a national hero. His stature was compromised later on, however, by his writing pro-Japanese versions of Korean history as well as urging Korean youths to join the Japanese army.

This ambitious program was blunted, however, by the actions of President Syngman Rhee as well as many government officials and military and police officers who had served the Japanese under the colonial rule. The Special Committee for Anti-National Investigation was systematically undermined by threats and demonstrations. Only a few people were actually punished by the court and all of them were freed on parole or had their sentences suspended. The Special Committee was further compromised when, in May and June 1949, two of its members were arrested on charges of cooperating with North Korea. Then, with the assassination of Kim Ku, the old Nationalist Leader and former head of the Provisional Government, the Committee became dispirited, its work was curtailed by the National Assembly, and its investigations were ended.

So the collaboration issue was simply allowed to wither away. The Kim brothers, for example, continued to thrive and Kim Yon-su himself became chairman of the conglomeration of Korean industries, which is now known as the Federation of Korean Industries, the key lobbying group for the Korean chaebol (the equivalent of the Japanese *Keidanren*) and with close connections to the Korean government. Such was part of the heritage of the Japanese colonial economic model, which opened opportunities to favored Koreans.

As one can observe from these examples, one person's collaboration was another person's idea of how to get along for perhaps a higher nationalist purpose. Bruce Cumings is one scholar who looked the problem squarely in the eye. He is sympathetic to a point but firm. The "cultural nationalists," committed to gradualism as the best way not only to get along but to maintain their Korean culture, might have succeeded if the colonial period had been extended, as most expected. "But in the last decade of colonial rule," as Cumings writes,

> the upper strata of a whole generation was turned into a collaborationist elite. Many moderate nationalists who were not forced into open collaboration still profited from the economic boom, tainting their nationalist credentials in the eyes of many Koreans. . . . This subject [collaboration] is so painful for South Koreans that most cannot or will not discuss it, and I have met a number of college young Koreans who have never been told that this happened. The history of this period is obscure for most Koreans, and it is made more so in the willful erasure and burying of facts. Many county histories, for example, will not name those Koreans who served as county managers in the period 1937–1945; there are simply blanks where their names should be.[25]

The upshot of the collaboration issue, for one thing, was that in the eyes of the exile groups, they were the only legitimate patriots who had actually resisted the Japanese. In the North, Kim Il-sung was a legitimate guerrilla leader who created a myth that all North Koreans were fiercely fighting the Japanese, a claim that was no more true in the North than in the South. Syngman Rhee spent the war in Hawaii and Washington, D.C., and Kim Ku was in Chungking. In any case, the exiles, South and North, seemed to have had the best political claim for legitimacy in the context of the end of the war.

The collaboration issue still stalks the Korean political scene over 50 years after the August 1945 liberation. As of 1997, for example, Choe Nam-son was the heretofore revered writer of the acclaimed Declaration of Independence of March 1, 1919, the document associated with the Samil uprising. Choe was a well-known poet and historian at that time. Now, after serving two and a half years in jail, he is described as a "turncoat and collaborator" with the Japanese colonial government. He was a collaborator with the Japanese in Manchukuo and wrote a Korean history from the Japanese perspective. He also urged Koreans to join the Japanese army to help in the conquest of Asia. His role in the March 1 movement, however, seemed to secure his place in Korean history; and perhaps his position would have remained intact, except that his independence document was proposed in March 1997 as a national treasure. This roused opposition from the Institute for Research in Collaborationist Activities, a leading private group devoted to research of Korean collaborators during Japanese rule. "It can never be acceptable historically. It is an act defaming the national spirit," said Director Kim Bong-woo. In the public debate two views emerged. Kang Man-kil, a professor of history at Korea University, argued that Choe's name should be removed if the statement is named as a treasure. But literary critic Lim Hun-young dissented: "As long as the statement is worthy of being a national treasure, the drafter's name should be indicated. But it is also important to make it clear that it was drafted by a Japanese collaborator."[26] The decision on the matter was finally made by the Office of Cultural Properties, concurring with Lim.

Another area that was ripe for Japanese infusion of know-how and investment was education. As Hulbert describes the situation in Korea at the turn of the century, education was a luxury for the *yangban* (aristocratic) families and was by and large Confucian. Education was an area of importance also for the largely American missionaries, and the influence of this very substantial effort is still evident in the Korean desire for English-language education as well as the existence of American-founded institutions of higher education, such as Yonsei University and Ehwa University for women. Hulbert, as one might anticipate, in looking about for what might still be done for Korea after the Japanese protectorate was established in 1905, was certain that the answer was in education. In his advisory capacity for the last King (and finally Emperor), Kojong, he realized that trying to mobilize international support for Korea, even from the United States where the missionary links were the strongest, was only a remote hope. In that matter his eyes were clear and unclouded. His expectations for the possibility of education as the deus ex machina, however, appeared to be unbounded.

> How can we, the American people, prove to the Koreans that we were not accessory to this act which was so contrary to the principles we have professed to hold? There is only one way—by helping them to the one thing that will enable them to hold together as a nation, and give them time and opportunity to prove the falsity of the libelous statements that have been so freely circulated, and which have temporarily alienated the good-will of so many of our people. That one thing is education. The Koreans have awakened to the fact that this, which should have been their first consideration many years ago, is now their last resort, and they are clamoring for education. . . . Korea can gain nothing by holding back and offering to the plans of Japan a sulky resistance. They are face to face with a definite condition,

and theories as to the morality of the forces which brought about the condition are wholly academic.[27]

Hulbert was convinced the establishment of a massive system of education throughout the country was Korea's best and only hope. He made this
appeal: "Is there any man or body of men in this country who will seize
the opportunity to found in the city of Seoul an institution of learning
which shall be the nucleus, the rallying ground, of a great national movement? It is the opinion of those most conversant with the feeling of the
Korean people that there is no other place in the world where money invested in education will bring larger, surer or more beneficent results."[28]

While the missionaries continued to do what they could to establish
schools to educate the Korean youth in both secular and religious matters,
it fell to the Japanese to carry out what education was to be done. Here
again they ran into the familiar paradox: Should they educate the Koreans
in the trades to prepare them for the industrialization of Korea primarily,
or should they concentrate on converting the Koreans to Japanese citizen-
ship in the New Greater East Asian co-prosperity sphere? The actual program moved in both directions.

It was not until 1938 that the Japanese decided on the assimilation of
Korea. The Naisen Ittai movement was to demonstrate that the Koreans
and Japanese were one and that Koreans should become Japanese citizens
and incorporate themselves into Japanese society and culture (albeit in a
somewhat inferior status). From then on, only Japanese language was
taught in Korean schools and the use of Korean language, even outside
work or schools, was prohibited. Koreans were even forced to adopt Japanese family and personal names. The path for the fast track in this kind of
society was to embrace the Japanese culture to the extent possible. Several
thousand Korean children of the bourgeoisie went on to Japanese universities in Japan to compete in a fairly even system. The discrimination came
about immediately upon graduation, when the best jobs in Korea were re-
served for Japanese and the salary differential prevailed. In Korea itself, at
the Keijo Imperial University, in 1939, there were 550 Japanese students
and 300 Koreans, with an almost exclusively Japanese faculty.[29]

So the education record of the Japanese colonizers was predictable,
working at exploitation and integration rather than working for the benefit of the Korean student and society. Nonetheless, during the war years
after 1937, some Koreans embraced publicly the Japanese war aims and
joined in the Japanese enthusiasm for anti-Westernism and promoted
Japanese war aims for Koreans. There was, as Lone and McCormack put it,
"a hatred of Japan's policies in Korea and respect for Japanese strength."[30]

One of the voids left in Korean society by the Japanese imperial rule was the underdevelopment of politics. During the last decades of the Yi Dynasty there were some stirrings of political roots in such groups as the Independence Club, which was a reformist group dedicated to improving the government. These efforts grew out of the turmoil associated with the great power rivalry in the Korean peninsula among China, the ostensible suzerain, Japan, and Russia who were vying openly for power over the peninsula. The Japanese assassination of the Korean Queen Min in 1887 to rid themselves of her meddling opposition to their plans stirred up an outbreak of Korean national awareness and the beginnings of a nationalist outlook as the King himself sought and obtained asylum in the Russian embassy both to escape and defy the Japanese. The Independence Club, which saw the emergence of American-educated Phillip Jaisohn as a leader, was opposed by not only the Dynastic officials but also by the Japanese. The Independence Club had only limited impact but offered prospects for the longer-term future of a revived Korean state.[31]

As we have seen, the Japanese did their best to integrate both the Korean economy and the population into the Japanese empire to pursue their war in Asia. For that reason, the Japanese colonists invested unprecedented sums into heavy industry in Korea, particularly North Korea, as well as built a modern transportation system of rails and roads. Western colonists in Asia did nothing comparable in their colonial possessions. The purpose of this Japanese effort was not to aid the Koreans per se, although this was one of the consequences. The sudden ending of the war, however, on August 15, 1945 with the American nuclear explosions in first Hiroshima and then Nagasaki, demonstrated how unprepared the Koreans were for real independence. They had had no opportunity to participate on the decision-making level under the Japanese and no freedom to organize political parties and organizations to prepare them for self-rule. All this meant that the scene in Korea as the Soviet forces entered the North and the Americans the South was confused. Much of the natural leadership inside Korea was tainted by collaboration; and the outside exiles from both the North and the South had difficulty establishing political legitimacy. To clarify the situation of the "exiles," or the Korean independence movement, we will review in the next chapter the broad outlines of this struggle, followed by a personal memoir of the author in his minor role in China with some of the personalities involved in Korean independence.

4

The Fight for Independence

The March 1, 1919, Korean uprising against the Japanese (the Samil, or 3–1, Movement) was the Korean symbolic declaration of independence. Because of the tight police and military security measures inside Korea, however, it was evident that the fight for freedom would have to be organized from the outside. The provisional government was established in Shanghai in 1919 in the Shanghai International Settlement, under international control. There the Koreans could operate in relative safety from the Japanese. The Provisional Government considered itself the successor government of the Yi Dynasty. For a time there were three self-proclaimed provisional governments. There was one in Seoul, Shanghai, and Siberia. After a "unity" conference, the government was established in Shanghai. It was inspired by the earlier Independent Association of Phillip Jaisohn, Syngman Rhee, and others. It would be a republic in polity and a democracy in political principle.[1] During its 27 years in Shanghai, its proposed form of government went through five changes, from presidential to cabinet systems. This made no real difference but provided some rudimentary experience in the ideas of democratic government. It was the doughty Kim Ku, instigator of various terrors and assassinations against the Japanese, who became head of the movement and won the support of Chiang Kai-shek. At the same time, in Manchuria and Siberia, other Korean groups began to organize and finally in the 1930s, with Soviet support, Kim Il-sung, later the leader of North Korea, came to the front. So, early on there were two separate movements. The Kim Ku group was filled with factions, which stood in the way of its effectiveness.[2]

After Japan declared war on China following the Marco Polo Bridge incident on July 7, 1937, the Korean Provisional Government (KPG) attached itself to the Nationalist Chinese retreat from Nanking to Chungking. From the relative safety of that redoubt Kim Ku and his principal aides set about to organize their supporters and to lobby principally with the Chinese Nationalists and the U.S. for recognition. This proved to be a remarkably difficult undertaking, and requires one fully to understand the formidable obstacles in the way because of inter-Allied politics. After all, why not recognize a group of patriotic exiles who proclaimed their intention to free Korea from the Japanese? Why not unleash the 23 million Koreans in revolt against the Japanese? While the Chungking KPG had its supporters in Washington, the Department of State was unconvinced of the merits of recognition, due to a variety of considerations that it did not necessarily share with the KPG.

The frustration among the leaders and supporters of the various Korean independence groups in the U.S., notably in Hawaii and Washington, D.C., was intense during World War II. Kim Ku and his supporters, safe in the fortress of Chungking and enjoying at least minimum material and spiritual support from the Chinese Nationalist government, had to consolidate their official position to try to support the war effort against Japan. Understandably, this produced a one-dimensional point of view, that is, the call for immediate recognition of the Provisional government by China, the U.S., and hopefully the rest of the Allied powers. Once again, the particular interests of Korea foundered against the wider interests of the wartime coalition of the Allied powers.

The Kim Ku government had been remarkably successful in its own way. While there was no polling operation at work in Korea to test the degree of public support for Kim Ku, Syngman Rhee, Phillip Jaisohn, and other leaders for independence, there was support among the interested. The Koreans in Manchuria and Siberia were activated much later, although some representatives did visit Shanghai. There was not then nor later any effort to form a political party to restore the Yi Dynasty, so complete had been its failure and humiliation in the public mind at that time.

The KPG had difficulty in getting organized, as one would expect. As mentioned before, at first there were three self-proclaimed provisional governments. One was at Seoul, the second was located at Shanghai, and the third was in Siberia, USSR. The representatives of these three "governments" held a conference and agreed to the necessity of forming one united government. There was a moment of compromise, rare among Koreans, and especially with such strong-minded delegates as Syngman Rhee on hand. The Siberian group played a key role and all agreed to locate the government in Shanghai for political and diplomatic reasons (since it was an international settlement controlled by a consortium of foreign powers). For the next 27 years Shanghai was the base for the KPG.

This government, however, was virtually powerless, filling a symbolic and necessary role as hope for an integrated Korea sometime in the future. The Japanese tried to undermine its credibility by efforts to include Korea as part of Japan in the Naisen Ittai movement, making the Korean people one body, one people with the Japanese. And furthermore, if that did not take hold, there was the vague promise by a Japanese premier, Hara Kei, that "in due course" the Koreans would be ready for and granted independence.[3]

The form of government changed five times during those 27 years, ranging from a presidential system to a cabinet arrangement, and finally to a chairman assisted by a legislature. All these were formal and sterile approaches, but of some value in becoming familiar with democratic systems. Whatever the form, the government all along insisted that it represented all of the Korean people. This was central to its claim of historical legitimacy, as the successor to the Yi Dynasty. This government was inspired by the independent association of Phillip Jaisohn, Syngman Rhee, and others; so the ideal was for a republic in polity and democracy in political principle.[4]

One perennial problem for the Provisional Government was the lack of a strong base area and a military presence. Its political activities were largely limited to dispatching delegations to international conferences to keep alive the plight of Korea in the eyes of internationalists. Beyond this, there was little that the Provisional Government players could all agree on. The government split into Conservative and Progressive wings; as a good-will gesture, the government dropped the presidential system in favor of a cabinet system, thereby providing room to placate dissidents with various cabinet appointments. With so little power, the road to foreign recognition proved exceptionally difficult.

Crucial to the hopes of the KPG was first of all the support of the Chinese. Two leaders who cultivated President Chiang Kai-shek in somewhat different ways were Kim Ku and Yi Pom-suk (also Lee Bum-suk); Kim as president of the KPG and Yi as a player in the establishment of the Kwang Bok Kun, the "Restoration army."

Kim Ku was born in North Korea in 1893. As a youth, he joined the Tonghak Movement, a peasants' rebellion. He continued his anti-Japanese agitation and was arrested by the Japanese for his involvement in the assassination attempts on the Japanese Governor General Terauchi and was sentenced to prison for 17 years. He was pardoned in 1914.

After the March 1, 1919 (Samil) uprising, he went to Shanghai and became director of Police Affairs of the Provisional Government. He continued his terrorist attacks against the Japanese. He planned an assassination on the Emperor of Japan in Tokyo on January 8, 1932, which failed. He also planned the incident in Honggu Park in Shanghai on April 19, 1932, in which Japanese general Shirakawa was killed. This earned him the support

of Chiang Kai-shek. In 1938 Kim became chairman of the KPG and transferred the KPG to Chungking in 1939.[5]

Yi Pom-suk was also a rebel against the Japanese and pursued his resistance through more traditional military means. He met an independence
leader, Yoo Wun-hyung, in 1915 and decided to leave Korea for China.
There he graduated from the Unnam military school in March 1917 and
became an instructor at the Shihhung military school. He participated in
the Cheongsanri guerrilla campaign against Japanese army units and
gained a certain amount of fame for these successes. He became chief of
staff of the Chinese army Third Corps and resigned in September 1940 to
help found the KPG's Kwang Bok Kun or Liberation Army under Kim
Ku. He was the deputy chief of staff of the Liberation Army's General
Command. The titles here were substantially larger than the number of
troops. Seventy Korean veterans of the Chinese Army were the core group
and on hand at the inauguration. The goal of this army was two-fold: (a)
to remove the Japanese political, economic, and military presence in Korea
and (b) to purge Koreans who supported the Japanese rule.

The Liberation Army, weak as it was, posed problems of control for the
Chinese government, just as the preparations of Allied intelligence services
did. Kim Ku and Yi Pom-suk argued the case for Korean control, and finally in April 1945 it was granted. By that time the number of Koreans had
increased to about 500, with about 100 in Yi's second detachment in
Hsian, and 300 in Anhui under General Kim Hak-kyu, commander of the
third detachment. The remainder were in Chungking.

With World War II approaching, supporters of Korean independence
living in the U.S. began to raise the desirability of enlisting "30 million"
Koreans (there were actually about 23 million) to the Allied cause. This
theme was carried on through the war years through the Korean lobbying
efforts in Washington, D.C., handled skillfully by Syngman Rhee in attracting Congressional support. The logical place to find some assistance
was from the new Office of Strategic Services (OSS), created by Franklin
D. Roosevelt (FDR) to coordinate intelligence inside the U.S. government. The head of this group was "Wild Bill" Donovan, a Republican and
friend of Frank Knox, Secretary of Navy, under FDR's unity cabinet.
Donovan was a Wall Street lawyer and a former colonel in the U.S. Army
in World War I. He was very close to British intelligence, which later
proved to be an obstacle for his China operations.

Inside the fledgling OSS, there were Korean enthusiasts, such as Oscar
Gale, who wished to make Korea a central location for OSS support,
oblivious to the geographical and security difficulties.[6] Further, inside
China itself, the Chinese government was jealously in charge of the Korean resistance potential, under the watchful eye of General Tai Li, who

did not want any foreign service, particularly the British but also the Americans, to work directly with the Koreas in China. China was understandably concerned about its territorial sovereignty; the British seemed more intent in regaining Hong Kong than anything else. All of these difficulties in mobilizing the Korean potential in China festered until 1945, when an American-controlled Korean operation, EAGLE, was allowed to establish a small base near Sian, Shensi province, just south of the Yellow River. The city had been the capitol of the empire of Chin Dynasty in 221–206 B.C., the unifier of China and builder of the great wall; it also later served as the capitol of the T'ang dynasty (A.D. 618–756). As one of the six Americans attached to this project, I will relate that story as an inductive account of this drama, after the vast deductive tale of high politics is concluded.

The Korean problem in terms of World War II was handled on three levels: (a) the general strategy, that is, how or whether the obvious potential of the Korean "independence movement" could be realized and become part of the Allied operations against Japan; (b) the story of the intelligence machinations, mainly involving the Americans, to establish an independent position in China, free of the control of the Chinese intelligence services; and finally, (c) the only concrete activity that came out of all this effort, the OSS operation EAGLE, which did not get underway until April 1945.

The Department of State from the beginning handled the liaison work with the Korean dissidents. Syngman Rhee (later the first South Korean president) was in charge of the lobbying effort. State was handicapped because of the difficulty of obtaining reliable information about the real situation among the Korean refugee groups in China, and particularly on what was going on in Korea itself. The war had severed official access through diplomatic, business, and missionary sources inside Korea. The most comprehensive general report was "Social and Intellectual Life of the Korean People," dated February 20, 1942, the Division of Far Eastern Affairs.[7]

State was interested in what Koreans in Korea thought about Japanese rule; control was "ubiquitous" but "pro-Japanese expression is largely false and insincere."[8] Conventional wisdom, however, said that Korean resistance to the Japanese was somewhat compromised after the Japanese occupation of Manchuria in 1931 and North China in 1937, because of better job opportunities that were provided for Koreans in Japanese-occupied territory. The State report also added that, "Conversely, whatever hopes of deliverance from Japanese rule that may have lurked in the minds of the Korean people flickered out. Again, with the Japanese occupation of great Chinese areas and cities, further opportunities for profit and adventure were opened to Koreans."[9]

Still, the analyst was cautious about the Korean attitude toward the Japanese:

> For reasons of material interest and because the hope of deliverance from Japanese bondage seemed dead, the mass of Koreans have found it to their advantage since 1931 to join the Japanese parade. Conversely, the wonted aloofness from the Government's Japanization program of the large Christian element in Korea, which is perhaps the most nationalistic, and irreconcilable, became more and more conspicuous and materially disadvantageous, and in consequence increased progressively. Thus, outwardly at lest, the Korean people in the past decade have become more and more Japanese in their outlook and sentiment.[10]

In support of this view of increasing Korean accommodation, one missionary with 20 years experience in Korea said in 1940 that the prevalent feeling of the Korean people toward the Japanese had undergone a profound change in the past three years and had become one of hero worship. In the young people especially, he said, a growing lack of sympathy with American missionaries was noticeable. Another missionary of long experience in Korea asserted that the Koreans had lost much of the antagonistic spirit they had at the time of the "Mansei [10,000 generations] movement." The views of an American businessman were similar, although he believed the Koreans now had more "pride of race" than under the days of the kingdom.[11]

So what would one have expected of the Koreans in February 1942? "The outward sympathy and cooperation with Japan of most Koreans . . . are after all only natural results of conditions and circumstances, and Koreans cannot be blamed for them."[12]

With this general background, the paper then directly addresses the question of Korean independence, which remained an issue among the Allies right through the war and, tragically, afterwards as well. Independence was a separate question from the recognition of the Provisional Government in Chungking. The U.S. and its European allies tried to keep these two points clearly separated, while the Provisional Government and its Washington lobbying arm, the Korean Commission, headed by Syngman Rhee, tended to squeeze them together.

As usual, cautious, the Department of State raised questions as to what Korean independence would mean at this juncture. Political difficulties were the first issue. "It must be borne in mind that in the 37 years of Japanese rule [counting from the protectorate in 1905], the Korean people have been emasculated politically. Long excluded from any participation in administration of control and local government, diplomacy, justice, law, police, finance, banking, education, and shipping, they would have no experience in managing a state if given their independence."[13] This kind of thinking influenced President Roosevelt's preference for trusteeship as a transition measure to independence, bitterly resisted later by President Rhee.

Military and economic prospects for an independent Korea were similarly deflated and the Chungking Provisional Government did not meet the requirements of a more ideal standard[14]:

> Following victory of the United Nations, the Provisional Government could be installed in Korea and could administer the country with the aid of an international commission pending the adoption of a national constitution and the setting up of a constitutional government. The sponsoring governments from the very beginning should make provisions for the functioning of the international commission until such time as they, and not the Koreans, might decide it to be no longer necessary. . . .[15]

> . . . In brief, the U.S. should not dampen hope of independence, premature commitments should be avoided . . . above all, the United States should avoid promising independence until it scores some substantial victories against the Japanese. It would only do the Korean cause harm, give the Japanese and their allies a good laugh, and irritate our own friends if we promised independence to one Asiatic people as we were being pushed out of our own possessions in Asia by the Japanese.[16]

During the summer and fall of 1942, there was an increasing barrage of letters to the President, the Secretary of State, and various members of Congress. These came from the Provisional Government, Syngman Rhee, church groups, and various friends of Korea; all demanded recognition of the Provisional Government, an announcement of independence, and the mobilization of Korean dissidents into the war effort. Some of the more telling exchanges, as they influenced Korea's hopes, require further discussion.

There were key conversations between the U.S. Ambassador in Chungking, Charles Gauss, and the Foreign Minister of the Provisional Government, Tjo So-yang (his spelling). Gauss considered Mr. Tjo "shifty" and "not of good quality." The Chinese officials also were skeptical of the quality of the KPG's leadership, more, I suspect, because of their traditional low opinion of Koreans, who they marginalized in Chinese society, rather than on a more objective standard. Also, one notes through all this long correspondence the efforts of the Provisional Government to convince the U.S. and British officials that the Chinese were about to recognize them, thus encouraging the U.S. to also recognize them. Such a step, they believed, would settle all of their problems. Ambassador Gauss thought Tjo's presentation was "most vague and unsatisfactory" at the February meeting, giving generalizations and inflated numbers of his followers. To sum up, he noted that Tjo's statement "gives the feeling that Mr. Tju [Tjo] is somewhat out of touch with the real situation and with the problems relating to independence and that the movement of which he is a member lacks concrete organization and precision of progress."

In fact, American embassy reporting did little to advance the Provisional Government's cause and undermined the efforts of private groups promoting a positive impression. A dispatch by John Service, then a junior diplomat, dated March 19, 1942, "Memorandum for the Ambassador" gives insight into the attitude of the Chinese Nationalist Government on the "Korean question" in a half-hour discussion with the Chinese representative, Yang Yun-chu, director of the Eastern Asiatic Department of the Ministry of Foreign Affairs. "The decision of these Chinese as to what attitude to be taken toward the Koreans is complicated by (1) lack of unity among the Koreans themselves; and (2) the difficulty in determining which, or whether any one of the groups of expatriate Koreans has any following among and can by considered as representatives of the people of Korea."[17]

The Korean group in Siberia, the National Revolutionary Party, was supposed to have two divisions of a total of 20,000 men under Soviet command. Koreans south of the Wall under the Kwang Bok Kun were the Independence group organized in five units. The one in Sian was perhaps 200 men.

Mr. Yang told Service the Chinese hoped for a union of the two groups (Siberia and Chungking) as a first step in "laying the ground for eventual recognition as part of a multi-step process." Mr. Yang spoke well of the "sincerity" of Kim Ku and his foreign minister Tjo So-wang, but wondered about their support in Korea. He was sympathetic with the aspirations for Korean independence. The impression Yang left with Service was that "the Koreans would eventually be given recognition."[18]

It is worthwhile to follow this chronicle in some detail to appreciate why the aspirations of the Koreans to play an important role in the war against Japan could not be realized. The U.S. and the Allies, including China, were always and sincerely sympathetic with the "independence" and "freedom" of Korea, citing the Atlantic Charter and the Four Freedoms and so on, but found themselves politically unable to grant "recognition" to the Provisional Government in Chungking. The failure of the U.S. especially to do this still rankles among important Koreans of my acquaintance, who cannot understand what President Truman was thinking about once he became president in April 1945 upon FDR's death. So a re-

view of the American record as it dealt with the Koreans' hopes during the
war years is instructive.

April 1942 was a particularly active month in regard to the prospects for
the KPG. A number of actors had intersected. Chinese President Chiang
Kai-shek had visited India and the Sir Stafford Cripps mission was there
trying to negotiate the postwar status of India, so that kind of issue was in
the air. A memo that the Chinese foreign minister T.V. Soong had left with
FDR after a meeting had indicated that the Chinese were thinking about
recognizing the KPG. The Soong memo was followed by a telegram from
Chungking from Chiang Kai-shek wanting the views of the U.S. Cordell
Hull and his staff replied on April 18, 1942, establishing a pattern for the
U.S. position that basically persisted, despite a variety of pressure. The U.S.
has been guided by two primary considerations:

> First, it has insisted that there not be made any appeal for support of any free
> movement in this country which would be incompatible with the unity of
> the United States and with the duties of Americans of foreign descent as cit-
> izens of the United States; and, second, this government has not desired to
> take steps which would tend to deprive the conquered populations of full
> freedom, when victory over the Axis aggressors is won, to select and set up
> governments of their own choosing.[19]

The telegram again makes the distinction between advocating independence in a broad statement like the Atlantic Charter, and "the according of recognition to any particular group of Koreans as the
Provisional Government of Korea." Hull said that the U.S. had "no immediate intention" of recognizing the KPG, in part because the KPG had
"little association with the Korean population in Korea," and the U.S. did
not wish to interfere with the right of the Korean people to choose their
own government.[20]

A follow-up cable also signed by Hull on April 29 raises the problem
of the Soviet Union, which still had not entered the war against the Japanese. He expressed concerns over Chinese recognition of the KPG. "There
remains the possibility, in case the 'Korean Provisional Government' at
Chungking is recognized by the Chinese government, that the U.S.S.R.
may support some of the Korean groups associated ideologically with the
Soviet Union." The telegram concludes:

> This whole question of Korean independence and the recognition of a Ko-
> rean government has many complications and delicate aspects. In view of
> China's geographical position and historic association with its neighbors, it
> is doubted whether this government should interpose strong objections to
> any course that the Chinese government may decide upon. It would seem

appropriate, however, for this government to lay before the Chinese government a complete exposition of its views.[21]

The Chinese were as aware as the U.S. about the possible dangers of opening up a competitive recognition match with the Soviets. Earlier in the month, the Chinese political Vice-Minister of Foreign Affairs, Yu Ping-chang, had in fact provided a full overview in a meeting with Ambassador Gauss:

> Such a move [recognition] would involve consideration of relations with Soviet Russia which one must admit are exceedingly delicate. He said that there are in Siberia about two divisions of Soviet troops—Koreans who have acquired Soviet nationality. Undoubtedly, in event of a Russo-Japanese war, the Soviets would use these Korean divisions against the Japanese and if they invade Korea, these Koreans more than likely would be used by the Russians to organize and set up some sort of Korean government. Now, if China should recognize the provisional government at Chungking, Soviet Russia might not find itself in accord. . . . [22]

In the Chinese government itself, Sun Fo, a son of the founder, Sun Yat-sen, publicly favored recognition of the KPG, as did other members of the cabinet; but bureaucrats like Mr. Fu, and the President's brother-in-law, T.V. Soong, were dubious, and concerned that this attitude might spread to the President himself. And then Mr. Fu mentioned another problem that was publicly muted: colonialism.

"At the same time concern was expressed as to the possible British reaction to Chinese gestures for the freeing of the 'oppressed people of the East' and the position as it affects not only Malaya, Burma, and India, but also the Netherlands East Indies."[23]

By May 18, a U.S. dispatch from Chungking indicated a further shift on the Chinese side, and the Division of Far Eastern Affairs circulated it on June 16. The Chinese were now more adamant about not recognizing the KPG and felt that "the Korean issue is one of primary concern to the Chinese Government, fearful that our [U.S.] well-intentioned efforts might readily lead to confusion as to solution."[24]

The battle over the independence and recognition questions was not contained strictly within the halls of the Department of State. Syngman Rhee's lobbying efforts were ubiquitous and effective. Through the Korean-American Commission he was able to reach out to the public at large as well as the powerful figures in the Congress. James A. Farley, for example, FDR's first Postmaster General and a pillar of the Democratic Party, wrote to Secretary Hull on April 21, 1942 on whether to support a public statement favorable to Korea. He received a "Dear Jim" letter from

Hull, saying that the U.S. Government had no plans to recognize a particular Korean faction, but referring him to a recent FDR radio address that stressed the Four Freedoms.[25]

Then on May 13, 1942 Senator Albert Chandler (A. B. "Happy" Chandler) wrote a letter on behalf of James H. R. Cromwell, President of the Korean-American Council, who was pressing for recognition of the KPG. Congressman Joseph Clark Baldwin also wrote to Hull on the same subject, beginning his letter with a quotation from the war hero Captain Edward V. ("Eddie") Rickenbacker: "Many of us still do not understand that we can lose this war. Not only can we lose it but we are losing it. We have been losing it every day, every week, every month since December 7th."[26]

But the figure that comes in and out of all this correspondence on the lobbying side as having particular clout was Mr. Cromwell, who lived in Washington at 2300 Foxhall Road, and was on familiar terms with high-level members of the administration. On June 15, 1942 Assistant Secretary of State Adolf A. Berle, Jr., sent along a Cromwell letter on organizing resistance to the Japanese to Colonel William A. Donovan, Director of the OSS. As part of the mantra, he was told by Donovan that there was not at present any intention of the U.S. Government to recognize the KPG. Clearly, Cromwell wanted something more. He began to agitate among his friends about the great opportunities for helping the war effort that an active campaign among the Koreans would provide. He clearly began to annoy the Department of State with his letters and ad hominum attacks. A brief was prepared for Mr. Berle to field the likely questions if Mr. Cromwell insisted on an appointment: "Several references are made in the letter to the matter of extension of practicable aid to the Koreans in order that they may 'begin their fight for freedom.' The Department has gained the impression that some members of the Korean-American Council feel that Koreans either cannot or should not participate in the war effort without first receiving lease-lend aid."[27]

On June 30 there was a meeting between Berle and Cromwell. Cromwell did not help the recognition cause by saying that the KPG in Chungking was "chiefly communist" but under the control of the Chinese Nationalist government. (This seems to have been an exaggeration of the factionalism of the Korean group in Chungking.) For Cromwell, "the only problem was whether they could get something done." Cromwell said his group was making plans for subversion of the Japanese and Berle said he would pass them on to Colonel Donovan, which he did.[28]

Cromwell on July 17, 1942 sent a thank you note to Berle, but also repeated his acute disagreement with the Chinese and U.S. refusal to recognize the KPG: "I cannot for the life of me understand why China and the United States are sitting idly by, twiddling their thumbs, when they have everything to gain and nothing to lose by the inauguration of a disciplined and systematic campaign of sabotage against the Japanese in Korea."[29]

Meanwhile, back in Chungking, the Chinese Government struggled with the practical problem of how to utilize the KPG and the "Independence Army." While the numbers were small, in some cases they were attached to regular Chinese units. The Chinese were sensitive to questions of their own sovereignty, still not free of the "unequal" treaties imposed by Western powers, particularly the British. They were suspicious that British intelligence was trying to prepare forces in Kwangtung province to take over Hong Kong again without reference to China. So they were wary of foreigners in their midst. Toward the end of 1942, the Chinese drew up some directives. "A Guide for Activities of the Korean Independence Army" spelled out how this army was to operate in Chinese territory. It was to be directly under the command of the Military Affairs Commission. The Chinese had clear control and avoided the problem they were having with the British. If these troops expanded and were to "push into" Korean territory, new discussions would be required.[30]

Faced with distrust and nonrecognition, Kim Ku seized every possible event to try to gain the attention of the distant American authorities. For example, he issued a "Manifesto on the First Anniversary of the Pacific War." He wrote that "32 years ago, Korea was annexed, that being one of the leading issues of the present war in the Pacific. . . . For the past half-century, the Koreans have continued these heroic struggles against Japan—the enemy No. 1 in the Pacific area." He laments, however, that "at the present moment our circumstances are still difficult. Though we have organized tens of thousands of armed forces, we have not yet got political recognition from the United Nations . . . what disappoints us is that the Allies are still keeping skeptical eyes on us—which gives us a feeling that the golden opportunity, which is hard to get and easy to lose might be lost at any moment."[31]

Had the Koreans been able to demonstrate proof of an active resistance inside Korea or particular exploits in China, they might have done better. The perennial plea for "lend-lease" aid was turned down in a State Department memo on March 7, 1943 on the grounds of disunity in Chungking and the priority requirements of the Chinese themselves. Syngman Rhee in another letter addressed to FDR of May 15, 1943, asked for recognition of the KPG: "I beseech you, Your Excellency, to recognize now the Provisional Government of the Republic of Korea and to give the Koreans every aid and encouragement so that they may do their share in fighting our common enemy, Japan, thereby rendering a material service to the United States."[32]

Rhee's major success, which ironically ended in failure, was to persuade the Congress and the Senate to prepare Joint Resolutions (H.J.R. 109 and S.J.R. 49). This was no small accomplishment in wartime Washington. Senator John Connally of Texas sent a letter to Hull, asking him what should be done about this and Hull repeated that the U.S. had no immediate plans to recognize any particular Korean group. So the attempt to end run State and the White House failed.[33] The success of Syngman Rhee and his American supporters had to await the conclusion of the war.

Whatever chance the schemes of Mr. Cromwell and associates had for the intelligence and sabotage operations that Cromwell believed were a neglected strategic asset was turned over to Col. Donovan and the OSS. The first problem for Donovan in trying to implement what he could of this idea was to obtain the flexibility and autonomy in China to do this. General Tai Li was jealous of his prerogatives. He resented the OSS' obvious closeness to the British services and tried to evoke the Sino-American Cooperative Agreement (SACO) at every turn. Joint Chinese-OSS operations sending teams into Japanese areas were well-established, along with the Navy coast-watcher operations and Air Force pilot rescue operations. So in March 1945, when the KPG and an OSS unit agreed to begin an operation aimed at Korea, the Chinese knew about it but did not object. And so it was under those conditions that all the meetings and conversations in Washington, D.C., at last came to fruition. It was certainly not on the scale of what had been envisioned, but it was a start. And it developed a certain significance in the postwar picture with regard to U.S. policy in Korea. The split in the Korean independence movement between the Communists and the supporters of the allies foreshadowed the future.

5

OSS and the Korean Independence Project

The previous chapter gave the context of how and why the OSS became involved with the Koreans in China.

I had been recruited into OSS in November 1944 from the University of Chicago Japanese language and area program after one full year of training. Five from our company entered OSS; the rest continued with their studies. I was sent to Washington, D.C., to the OSS headquarters in the old temporary buildings along the reflecting pool between the Washington and Lincoln memorials. I assumed I would go to China to interrogate Japanese POWs. I was taught Order of Battle (OB), the strength and disposition of enemy forces. The key element of intention somehow eluded us. Japanese OB was a frustrating subject. The Japanese language alone was a mystery code; the Japanese practice of using a simple code for the names of armies, divisions, and regiments in China was unfathomable. One division in China was called *Yuki,* or "snow," for example, and its location and armament were high on the OSS priorities.

Over the Himalayan Hump to Kunming, China, in March 1945, I was introduced to the commander for Secret Intelligence, Lt. Col. Paul Helliwell (his monthly reports to Washington, D.C., figure in many of the OSS documents quoted). Next I met Captain Clyde Sargent, the American commander of the OSS team assigned to Sian. (We were later friends in the CIA.) Sargent was an academic and out of place in the military. He was 35 years old, with thinning light red hair and buck teeth. His Chinese language was fluent, and this was his greatest strength. Fresh from the University, I was only a private first class. We had all expected commissions upon graduating, but that was not to be. Concerned about my low rank and my relations with the Koreans, Captain Sargent gave me civilian "technical representative" insignia, which allowed me to enter the officer clubs and presumably make a greater impression on the students I was soon to instruct. He explained briefly the assignment. I was to help train a group of Koreans, some of whom had escaped from the Japanese army, in intelligence collection techniques. They were also to learn radio communications. They were then to be organized into two- and three-man teams and reinfiltrated into Korea to report on the Japanese and to determine if the situation was ripe to organize guerrilla units. This was necessarily a long-range project and the plans were made with the expectation that the war against the Japanese would continue for some years.

In writing this chapter, I have relied heavily on previously secret OSS documents obtained by me from the CIA under the Freedom of Information Act. This has been supplemented by memory and some photos I retained (about l00) in the Anhui pocket. The Sian photos I turned over to the Korean Independence Hall some years ago. For a Korean perspective of these events, I refer, for example, to the writings of Kim Jun-yop, Korea's leading historian, former president of Korea University, a comrade in arms in Sian in 1945, and a cherished friend to this present day. His story is illustrative of the Korean saga.

In April 1997 I interviewed Kim Jun-yop again in his office in the Daewoo Building in Seoul. I wanted to concentrate on his World War II experience, how he had come to join the Korean independence movement. The previous year he had written in Korean language his autobiography, *My Long March,* which was also made into a movie. I wanted to know how he happened to arrive in Sian, China, in April 1945, shortly before I did. And how many Koreans were there? And so on. He said that there were 108 Koreans there; he had been asked to write a poem in their honor, which he had done; on one side of the war memorial plaque are the names of each of the 108 members of that detachment. He had escaped from the Japanese army to join the Kwang Bok Kun. How had he accomplished that, I wanted to know. So he explained.

Kim Jun-yop was born in North Korea in 1920. He had been studying in Keio University in Tokyo when he was drafted. He returned to Pyongyang to enter the army in the winter of 1945. Some 5,000 Koreans were being drafted at that time. The Japanese were ready to sacrifice more Koreans in the China war. "One difference between me and the other Korean draftees was that I had already started on a plan to escape from the army." He put together an ingenious plan. First, he bought a map and a compass in Seoul. "I could read it at night because it had a luminous dial. Also I got money from my mother, 700 Japanese yen. This was a lot of money. A middle school teacher, for example, received 30 yen per month. For 700 yen you could buy a small house."

He explained that his father was a landowner and was fairly rich. Why 700 yen? When he escaped the Japanese army, he thought he might have to walk as far as 700 li, at 100 li (about 30 miles) per day. Somehow he concluded that he needed 100 yen for each 100 li. There were other elements of his plan. "If I could not successfully escape, I kept my father's pocket knife to commit suicide. Also, I had a photo taken in my school uniform with my mother in her Korean clothes. That way I could convince the Chinese that I was a Korean."

On February 13, 1945, his unit left by train to Suchow, which was a big city. "This was the headquarters of a Japanese division. After a few days training, I was sent off to the eastern part of the Chiangsu province and was assigned to a company. The leader was a captain. Of the 40 newly arrived soldiers, five were Koreans. The Japanese lieutenant in charge of training was a fellow student from Keio University. His name was Yoichi. I told him I was ready to fight. Where are the Chinese, I asked. He replied that they were just down the railway. So freedom was only a few hours away."

Later, Kim Jun-yop said, "I visited Yoichi in his room and noted the maps on the wall showing the Chinese positions. Some were only 40 li (about 13 miles) away. Yoichi told me, 'If we like, we can go tomorrow to fight the Chinese.'" Kim was elated at the closeness of the Chinese, really only about four hours away. "When should I decide to escape? The guard changed every hour. There was a wall around our compound and then a moat. There was an East and West gate. One gate was guarded by Japanese troops; the other by the Wang Ching-wei puppet troops. Two soldiers were always on guard together."

There were other things Kim wanted to know. "How deep was the moat? Then I remembered a story from Japanese history when there was a revolt among the bakufu. One of these men wanted to know the depth of the moat around the castle to determine whether his band could cross it. I did what he did. He judged the depth by throwing stones into the moat. So during breaks I would throw stones in the moat and I concluded it was not too deep."

At this time, the Japanese army decided to go to the south to open up the railway all the way to Hanoi because normal supply routes had been cut. During these preparations, it seemed like a good opportunity to escape. "I was worried about not succeeding. I knew the pocket knife would not be enough if I were caught. So I stole a hand grenade from a senior soldier. In my whole life I have stole two times—one is the grenade. [I did not inquire what the other occasion was.] Then I wrote to my brother in Seoul. We had a simple code for three situations: Gaiwu, hoso, or panchu before the signature meant staying in camp, going toward the south seas, or I was escaping."

But when to make the attempt? "Then I had a dream from my deceased father. If you want to escape, he said, leave on 29 March (in just two weeks). This was the end of the lunar calendar. No moon. So I decided to leave at 2 o'clock in the morning. This meant I can reach the Chinese in about four hours. I couldn't sleep at all. Then I went out to the toilet, taking all my luggage and the grenade. Once I saw the changing of the guard, I quickly went up the wall. Then I made one mistake. I had not studied the condition of the soil along the moat. This was originally made of mud, but now it was dry. When I dropped from the wall, some soil fell into the moat. One Japanese soldier called out, 'Dare ga? Dare ga? [Who's there?]' I went on into the moat and he kept calling out. Then I reached the other side and crawled out and he could not see me. I started to run. I was certain I would meet the Chinese. I looked at my watch I had received from my mother. It was luminous. I ran only about 20 minutes. I took 140 steps for every 100 meters. I kept going for about 4 hours. This was the first time I had used the compass and I didn't know how reliable it was. It was still dark and I couldn't see anything."

Finally it began to become light. "I could see the farmers in the fields. There was nowhere to hide. I thought I had come to a large river. But it was the Grand Canal [used for barge traffic to Beijing]. It was 70 or 80 meters wide. I had to swim. The water was cold. I took off my clothes and tried to carry everything. But it didn't work. Some farmers saw me, and soon there were 10 Chinese soldiers on the bank with their rifles. I spoke no Chinese. I knew that Nationalist uniforms were blue and Puppet soldiers wore yellow. These uniforms were yellow."

"They all came up to me and looked at me as though I were a monkey. They took me into a hall around 7 A.M. One Chinese came in. I got a paper and brush and wrote down who I was. At first I said I was a Japanese scout in case the Puppet troops were loyal; then I took a chance and said I was a Korean and wanted to join the Chinese side. It turned out that these troops were not Puppet troops but were Nationalist guerrillas. I gave them my grenade and back pack. Then I showed them the picture of me with my mother to prove I was a Korean student. I knew I was safe. I felt freedom. Never in my life until I left the Japanese did I know the real meaning of freedom. Total freedom. For my whole life, I have loved freedom. Now I was safe and could join the Korean independence movement. I was not cold at all. But then I became cold. The Chinese brought hot water and some Chinese dumplings. I was so happy and excited. This moment was the highlight of my life." It took Kim Jun-yop from the end of March to the end of April to reach Chungking, via the Anhui pocket and then the Yangtze river. In April 1945 in Chungking he met General Lee Bum-suk, who persuaded him to join the Sian detachment as a student soldier, and he soon became Gen. Lee's aide.

The first mention of the Korean Project in the available OSS files was in the minutes of a staff meeting in Washington, D.C., on April 9, 1945. "REDBEARD (a cryptonym) cannot be considered as a separate enterprise. The Shantung Peninsula will probably be tackled by EAGLE and PHOENIX. . . . Arrival of the Koreans is eagerly awaited by Col. Helliwell. He believes they will fit in very well with the EAGLE project." This refers to a group of Korean Americans who had been recruited in the United States and finally arrived in Sian around August 1, a day or two before I left Sian for Kunming and the Anhui Pocket. This was an example of the OSS' long-range planning and support of the EAGLE operation and the high regard in which it was held in Washington. From Sargent's viewpoint, he hoped to replicate in the village of Tu Ch'i, south of Sian, the whole OSS headquarters operation, with training operations, reports, morale operations, security, and counter-intelligence staff. Captain Sargent's hopes and aspirations began to soar as the supply lines from India began to improve. Before then, the only American supplies, mainly of medicine and small arms, had been a 6 x 6 army truck driven by me from Kunming via Chengtu (Szechuan) to Sian, 1,500 miles over sketchy roads and pontoon bridges, and beset by Chinese bandits eager to steal our supplies, during the course of two weeks. This badly damaged truck and a jeep were the total EAGLE motor pool. The jeep, alas, later was to meet an ignominious fate.

A word on the cryptonym EAGLE. Most of the SI (secret intelligence) operations were named after birds. The use of the cryptonyms was for security purposes, to avoid the use of true names and locations. EAGLE was the most attractive name in the list of project birds and symbolized the hope of the project for the future of Korea, conjuring up the expectation that the eagle would be the legend of both Korea and the United States.

There was considerable optimism about EAGLE. From the OSS documents one finds this appraisal from a report covering April 20 to May 20, 1945[1]: "EAGLE project has some 40-odd agents under final training by General Lee Bum-suk, Captain Clyde Sargent, and Communications officer [actually, there were four more Americans, including myself, but Whitaker correctly focused on the chief players]. These agents are most impressive—hard-faced men, recently out of Korea, capable of speaking Japanese and proved by their loyal work in the underground; all have high school education and some are lawyers and the like. In a visit to their camp, I was impressed moreover by their discipline, soldierly manner, neatness, and zeal. General Lee Bum-suk asked that Col. Heffner (the Strategic Services Officer who had earlier visited Tu Ch'i) and OSS be thanked for the superlative way in which this project is being organized and supported."

The training of these promising Korean agents proceeded smoothly in May and June with the six Americans on the OSS staff and Korean counterparts. Gen. Lee played an active and inspirational role through his daily early-morning lecture to his troops; replete with exhortations for freedom and independence. The headquarters compound was in a walled Taoist temple, which also served as the training classroom, and as an office for Gen. Lee, his immediate staff, Captain Sargent, and the five other Americans. About once a week I drove Gen. Lee to the city of Sian, about 20 miles away, to look over Chinese jade and porcelain and to socialize with some of his friends from Manchurian days. During the jeep trips, he would often discharge his .38 revolver at offending crows in the rice paddies, claiming always that his shots were within an inch of the target. He also became increasingly interested in the mechanism of driving and took a keen interest in the manipulation of the pedals and steering wheel.

General Lee was a sturdy man of 46 who could walk up to a tree, grab the trunk, and hold himself parallel to the ground. At age 15 he met a Korean independence movement leader, You Wun-hyung, in 1915 and decided to leave Korea for China. There he graduated from the Unnam military school in March 1917 and became an instructor at the Shihhung military school. He participated in the Cheongsanri guerrilla campaign against Japanese army units and gained a certain amount of fame for these successes. He then became the vice chief of staff of the Chinese army Third Corps; he resigned in September 1940 to help found the KPG's Liberation Army under Kim Ku. He was deputy chief of staff of the Liberation Army General Command. About 70 Korean veterans of the Chinese army were the core group and on hand for the inauguration. The goal was to drive the Japanese out of Korea and then to deal with Korean collaborators. The problem of control of this group was ever present, but finally Kim Ku and Lee argued the case for Korean control and the Chinese acceded in April 1945. The number had increased another 100 in December 1940 and by 700 in 1945. Of the 600 or 700 members, there were about 100 in Sian under General Lee's Second Detachment, and another 200 in Anhui under General Kim Hak-kyu in the third detachment. The rest were in Chungking.[2] The June 1945 monthly report from Captain Sargent, the OSS EAGLE Field Commander, to Lt. Col. Paul Helliwell, is the most complete single report in the documents (pp. 90–98). He gives an overall view of the ideas and minutiae that affected Sargent's operational vision, although at other times it was soaring enough. He had his quarrels with Major Gus Krause, the Sian commander. A Nisei captain, Chikuo Ikeda, reported also in June, from the Sian headquarters, that EAGLE was now to run and be administrated separately, like all other Sian headquarters field projects; this development greatly pleased Captain Sargent, although his personal antagonism toward Major Krause remained. Captain Sargent wrote, "Activities and progress during the month have been personally satisfactory. Progress has been slower than we desire, but in view of all circumstances must be regarded as satisfactory. However, it will not be until the end of July that EAGLE will be functioning in a way to give satisfaction." He meant that by then some field teams would be ready for infiltration into occupied China and that a group of Korean Americans would be on hand to set up the kind of headquarters he had in mind, staffed properly to process intelligence information from the new Korean radio teams. Throughout June, Sargent's main concerns were bureaucratic in-fighting and administrative and construction work, all the dreary details in establishing a real training base, whose principal building was, as I have said, a decaying rat-infested Taoist temple.

Captain Sargent was preoccupied with security, the physical security of this compound. He used this legitimate concern to prevent visits to Tu Ch'i by the Sian headquarters personnel and to demonstrate to his superiors his own astuteness in security matters. There was considerable irony here. I have mentioned the regular trips to Sian with General Lee in the jeep, for example, which surely were not unnoticed by the cognoscenti. Further, here was a group of Koreans and Americans living on the edge of a peasant village of Tu Ch'i, surrounded by rice paddies and melon farms. The training compound was totally dependent on local food and drink. To think that any Chinese worth his salt did not know the nationality of the people living there was sheer illusion. Yet out of some Nixonian idea of a body guard, Sargent pressed on with security. "In addition to the regular training program, a special weapons class of 12 men was opened under the direction of the security officer in order to train a proper guard for area defense. This class completed its basic training about 30 June and a second class now is under instruction. A selected minimum of 18 men from these two classes of 24 will constitute the nucleus of the area guard as soon as training has been completed, and uniforms have arrived."

These uniforms were distinctive, not like the Chinese army, and complicated Sargent's concept. Then there was a Fourth of July party, which concluded with all of the Americans firing their weapons into the air, a la Arafat. Shortly all these rounds came down nearby, as attested by the shouts and complaints from the nearby Chinese peasants. Nonetheless, the Japanese troops were no more than 30 miles away, on the north bank of the Yellow River.

In Col. Whitaker's June monthly report to OSS Headquarters in Washington, he said that "EAGLE project is completing its final training and the first agents are ready to leave momentarily for this key area. Few projects have enjoyed better agent material or training and, though we have reason to believe that this region is harder to penetrate than Koreans believe who have been away for a year or more, much is expected from this operation." Whitaker had, however, raised a point that had not yet been resolved by Sargent and his staff: exactly how were these Korean agents going to be infiltrated into North China and then into Korea? This became more and more of a preoccupation as the training program approached conclusion toward the end of July.

Despite Sargent's concern with such matters as the physical security of the Tu Ch'i training base, larger ideas often came floating along. One recurring theme was the intrusion of MO (Morale Operations) into our little village. In the OSS records, there was also a June Monthly report from the MO section, which had a small staff in China and owed its influence and coverage to its habit of assigning an officer to every available project. This was the case for EAGLE, when Captain Evans was sent to operate with the EAGLE project. He was to provide MO instruction for this group. And what was this instruction all about? MO was the propaganda war. The overt "white" propaganda came from the BBC, for example, while the "black" phony propaganda came from MO. Their pamphlets were aimed at misleading and discouraging the enemy, that is, the Japanese, and conversely, helping keep Allied morale high with these phony accomplishments. The ceiling for the MO operation in all of China was 82 personnel. For this reason, the MO branch "has adopted the policy of attaching MO operatives to SO [special operations] and SI field teams, to a far greater extent than has been the case heretofore. This has resulted in economy of equipment and communication facilities and has greatly simplified the problem of finance and supplies."

Captain Evans arrived on June 27 and settled in easily, usually in a comfortable canvas lawn chair. He had the war pretty well analyzed. "It is clear to me that Shinto (the Japanese state religion) will collapse of its own weight." He did not bestir himself to write any "black" leaflets or the like, so confident was he of the futility of the Japanese cause. MO's assessment of its virtues possibly added to Evans' embrace of the philosophy of Lao Tze: "do nothing and all will be done." Under the heading of "Concrete Results," the MO report stated: "Generally speaking, the nature of MO operations is such that there is a considerable time lag between the initiation of such operations and the receipt of accurate information concerning the results thereof. In many instances it is impossible directly to evaluate the results of any given operation. In other cases, the results are known only after a period of weeks or even months."

The report continues: "To date . . . the only definite report has been from Team Chili. Material disseminated by this team was said to have been very favorably received by the Chinese targets and very displeasing to the Japanese." This was the world of the portly Captain Evans and his canvas chair. Captain Sargent, in his long range hopes of empire, found himself smitten by the MO bug:

> MO has a representative here studying the possibilities and potentialities of an MO program as part of the EAGLE operation. It is the undersigned's belief that an MO program from EAGLE will be distinctly valuable in the Allied offense against Japan, and will definitely aid other phases of EAGLE operations. An R & A [research and analysis] representative is now en route to EAGLE, and will be a distinct aid to EAGLE and in turn should be able to serve R & A interests in the area of EAGLE's interest [i.e., Korea]. It is hoped that X-2 [counter-intelligence] will send an intelligence research representative to EAGLE who will compile X-2 type intelligence needed by EAGLE. EAGLE also poses considerable potentialities for SO [special operations, that is, paramilitary-type raids], but it is believed that initiation of any SO training should be delayed until intelligence operations have justified themselves and are prepared to serve any SO development that Theater might request within the scope of EAGLE. At present, definite plans consist exclusively of plans for intelligence operations.

It was quite literally a step from the grand MO ideas back to the little compound where the real world existed for Sargent. Of his six people (including himself), one was an MO officer and another a field photographer recruited from the Navy. So the actual work of doing everything Sargent wanted done was the responsibility of the radio training officer, a general training officer, and me, who was to train the students in order of battle as well as to debrief them on their Japanese army experiences, which were popular and useful material in SO, Chungking. Part or even a good deal of Sargent's personnel shortage was due to his security concerns, which meant he would have no Chinese (except a doctor friend) on the premises. So in a land of cooks, we had none. High on his priorities was an American Army cook. (Sargent himself was a superb cook of regular Chinese food and assorted delicacies.)

> An American army cook is badly needed. We need a cook who can cook and assume responsibility of directing all messing activities. From 4–25 June we had an Army cook, but it was necessary to release him on 25 June [I have no recollection of why that was the case], and now our American staff each is cooking in turn, for one day at a turn, until a cook arrives. Even the general [Lee Bum-suk] takes "his day" at cooking, until we are relieved by a competent cook. As previously indicated our messing problem is due to EAGLE's policy of not employing Chinese who have concurrent affiliation with other organizations. This has prevented us from employing available

Chinese cooks. We have been told that arrival of two cooks, to be assigned to EAGLE, can be expected soon. This will relieve us of this problem.

Helliwell's report of June 1945 naturally was similar to Sargent's. The well-known phrase that EAGLE project "still remains in the training stage with approximately 60 agent personnel entering the final phase of intelligence and communications training" was also in this report. The objective was to first establish reliable courier routes through Manchuria into Korea. The recent experience of the trainees with these areas, largely from their assignment to the Japanese army, was expected to be of value in devising these plans. This indeed was true, but a closer analysis showed that leaving Sian, crossing the Japanese lines, and entering occupied China was no simple matter. What about documentation, cover stories, concealment of the radios, and all the thousands of things aficionados of tales of espionage tradecraft know by heart? There was much work to be done.

I could see that Sargent was getting concerned about the problem of successfully dispatching the agents. While the Korean trainees tended to downplay such problems, it was clear that just walking off to Manchuria was not in the cards. Shortly after the Fourth of July party, I was sitting in my mud-walled office before the typewriter thinking about some alternative ideas to help launch the agents. At that moment General Lee entered the tiny office and sat down on the one wooden chair. He was in particularly good humor and inquired about my health and so on. He was in an uncharacteristic light mood and I was immediately wary. What I had long dreaded came out in the open, "It is time that I learn how to drive the jeep. I've been watching you, and with a little instruction, I know I can do it. It is really child's play." His statement was certainly no request; he did not want my opinion as to the pros and cons of his becoming a jeep driver. (Technically, our base was under "joint command," but I was responsible only to Sargent.) It was not an order, but there was no graceful way I could avoid compliance. The jeep was parked outside along the wall. I picked out the key from my desk drawer and we were off for the instructional training. I drove maybe a half-mile to a rather good road, straight, 20 feet wide, slicing through miles of rice paddies located some eight feet below this highway. There were only a few bullock carts loaded with large stones for some construction work. The bullocks progressed at their usual solemn pace. There were no clouds in the sky. It was a perfect afternoon. So General Lee swung lightly into the driver's seat. I handed him the key and he started the engine. I explained about the gears, the clutch, and the brake. He repeated that the whole thing was child's play. We got off to a jerking start and off we went, north toward Sian, passing the bullock carts with no trouble. He was content to hold the speed to about 25 miles per hour. Since he was driving, he could not indulge in his hobby of firing at crows in the field; so on balance, I felt fairly comfortable as the passenger and not the driver. After about five miles, he braked to a stop and practiced starting and stopping, backing and so on, to get the feel of the jeep. After about a half-hour of this, he headed south back toward the compound. All was going smoothly.

Without much warning, however, disaster struck. There on the middle of the right-hand side of the road was a large rock that had fallen from the bullock cart. I suggested that he slow down, go around the rock to the left, and that would be it. He started to do just that when his foot left the brake and found the accelerator and we shot off the highway altogether. The right front of the jeep struck a tree trunk, knocking off the right front wheel; the jeep nose-dived like a shot-down airplane. I flew off to the right, while General Lee clutched the driver's wheel and stuck with the vehicle. I landed sprawling in the rice paddy, highly fertilized with "night soil." The jeep seemed to be sinking straight into the paddy. I finally rose unsteadily in the paddy, which reached my knees, and sloshed over to the jeep. General Lee still clutched the wheel and I could tell it had jammed into his stomach and ribs. I pulled him out of the jeep with all the dignity that I could muster. We stood side by side looking at the wrecked jeep. The right wheel was some distance away, cleanly sheered off; as the jeep straightened out as it sank, we could see that the gear box was shattered and various pieces of gears were still moving about. Both General Lee and I were acutely aware that this machine had come all the way from Detroit, Michigan, over the Hump, and hence to Sian. "It is not badly damaged," General Lee said. "It can easily be fixed." I nodded in diplomatic agreement.

After perhaps fifteen minutes, having heard various cries and shouts but no one coming to help us, we heard the sound of a truck, the other half of the EAGLE motor pool. The truck was jammed with eager Korean trainees, who without hesitation marched down the bank and into the rice paddy, picked up the jeep with a mighty effort, and helped Gen. Lee and myself to the truck cab. We were rushed back to the compound. Gen. Lee had some deep bruises and kept to his bed for several days. I showered and found nothing serious, unless smelling like a rice paddy for several days could be considered serious. The jeep was gone and no replacement was in sight. It was a somber moment. It was about two weeks before Gen. Lee felt well enough to talk to me about the accident, which of course was not his fault, and we began to laugh and drink *pai gahr* and life went on as usual. Except that something had to be done about getting the Korean trained espionage teams into action.

In setting the OSS operational scene in China in the summer of 1945, the EAGLE project was not the only OSS activity in the Sian area or, of course, in central and south China. Almost all of these intelligence activities were conducted in conjunction with Chinese Nationalist groups. Most were controlled by Tai Li, the Chinese intelligence chief. His agents were literally everywhere, and this was the group that Sargent feared. The Tai Li organization was none too reliable. Some thought it was penetrated by Japanese intelligence. OSS was in hot rivalry with the U.S. Navy, the SACO. A book, *A Secret War,* by Oliver Caldwell, a participant, outlined the intelligence war against Japan and also between OSS and SACO, and EAGLE was never mentioned. Lt. Col. Helliwell reported a number of low-level successes elsewhere. Intelligence operations were being expanded rapidly in East and South China; river-watcher units were established in the Changsha area to provide tactical information for the U.S. 14th Airforce. Coastal watchers provided 55 tactical shipping targets, involving over 264 vessels, to the 14th Air Force. QUAIL (another bird!) operation in French Indo-China (Vietnam, Laos, and Cambodia) had five radio teams in the field. Some coverage was obtained on the Liuchou peninsula and Hainan Island. Captain John Singlaub (later a two-star general in South Korea who opposed President Jimmy Carter's efforts to reduce U.S. troops in Korea) led a parachute jump into Hainan Island and rescued 400 POWs. In the Ninth War Zone, intelligence reports proved particularly valuable. "It is a matter of interest to note that SI officers in the area predicted this (Japanese) drive over a month before it commenced and that Ninth War Zone information was so complete during the period that the Japanese lost all elements of tactical surprise in this movement and have suffered very heavy losses."

Among all of this reporting, Helliwell included another paragraph in his June monthly report on EAGLE: "EAGLE sub-base is being established in the Tenth War Zone, and training and penetration will be carried on from that point." As it turned out, that notation applied especially to me and marked a new and dangerous phase of the Korean project for me. I'll explain how this sub-base idea came about. It was an offshoot of the rapid training progress in Sian and the slowness of decision-making on how to launch these eager and brand-new Korean teams toward Korea.

To recapitulate, as the training program in radio communications, reporting, and targeting (particularly order of battle) began to come to its conclusion in July, Captain Sargent was faced with how to dispatch these agents, ideally into Korea, which by land was a thousand miles away. It was no simple matter from Sian to infiltrate Korean teams through the Japanese perimeter. Even if that could be done, the regular administrative operations of the Nanking "Puppet Government" of Wang Ching-wei would almost surely notice their travel and arrival in local Chinese villages.

The most imaginative (or desperate) scheme was to send several teams into Korea itself, landing them on the coast. The vehicle for this bold venture would be a U.S. submarine based in then Ceylon (now Sri Lanka) at the British naval base of Tricomalee near the town of Kandy. This trip would be roughly 12,000 miles round-trip, going around Singapore and then north to Korea. Such a query was sent in early July to OSS Kunming. There was—understandably—no reply to this.

Another possibility—belatedly considered—was air drops. Captain Sargent in mid-July asked General Lee to select a dozen healthy Korean trainees who had done especially well in the courses, to prepare to go to Kunming for jump school. The elevation at Kunming was about 5,000 feet, in the foothills of the Himalayas. I was instructed by Sargent to accompany this group and then proceed to the sub-base Helliwell mentioned in the Anhui pocket. The idea was to establish a liaison between Tu Ch'i and Anhui, between the Second and Third Detachments. One of General Lee's senior officers, Major Kang, was also to go to the Pocket for the same purpose.

The Anhui Pocket in the Tenth War Zone took on larger and larger proportions in the mind of Captain Sargent as a way out of the agent-launching dilemma. All this happened in mid-June when Captain Oscar Jorgensen showed up in the EAGLE compound, fresh from the Pocket and eager to talk to Sargent. Sargent, for a change, was delighted (most visitors he looked upon as potential trouble, and he was often correct). Jorgensen was the liaison for the Pocket and was enthused about the possibility for operations being run from there. Sargent's June monthly report said this:

During the month Captain Jorgensen visited EAGLE for the purpose of discussing methods of coordinating the work done in and from the Pocket with work done in and from here. It was agreed that not only field operations should be coordinated but that also training and processing should be coordinated. It was agreed that recruiting and screening facilities in the Pocket are superior to those existing here, and that, consequently, these facilities would service both groups [as an aside, neither Sergeant nor I had seen the Pocket. There seems to be a law of intelligence operations that the less one really knows about the situation, the better and more plausible it seems]. At the same time it was recognized that the Pocket provides a better activating area for certain field operations, and that when such is the case the Pocket provides a better activating area for certain field operations, and that when such is the case the Pocket will be used as such for personnel from both areas. It also was recognized that this area probably will be better equipped at all times to conduct intelligence and communications training, and that the facilities of this area will be available to all OSS-sponsored agents. It also was recognized that this area will be more completely staffed with research analysis and reporting personnel, and that as such it should be responsible for processing of intelligence. Upon these general principles, co-ordination of all OSS-sponsored Korean operations was planned. It was planned also to establish a regular radio schedule daily with the Pocket as soon as possible in order to maintain intimate liaison. As a second step (and a first step by EAGLE) in effecting close liaison between here and the Pocket, EAGLE sent towards the end of the month a liaison team of three men, including the Second Detachment's second-in-command and two Americans of the EAGLE staff. At this writing this liaison group is still on its way.

The two Americans were actually just me and I had not yet gone with the putative Korean paratroopers because of lack of air transportation. In the first week of August, however, a C-47 was available. This was just a few days after the long-awaited Korean Americans arrived (and also Chester L. Cooper, whom I got to know briefly, as both of us were later in ser-vice in the CIA; he wrote such books as *The Lion's Last Roar*, on the Suez war, and was a critical and insightful observer of the Vietnam war). The flight from Sian to Kunming was not without incident. This was the first air trip for the Korean trainees and they naturally were nervous; and events proved them correct. We were soon victims of summer weather, with great gray clouds and fierce lightning. As night approached, the pilot discussed with me the possibility of the human cargo parachuting, not necessarily to safety. One problem was a shortage of parachutes, a total of six for the 12 Koreans and me. The Koreans felt that they could go two to a chute, but this did not totally answer the question. Finally, when the idea was being seriously considered, the sweat-drenched pilot got in contact by radio with the Kunming tower and the plane landed safely on the rain-slick runway.

No sooner had I enrolled the Koreans into the next jump school than news reached Kunming that an atomic bomb had been dropped on Au-gust 6 on Hiroshima. Everyone assumed the war would be over soon. The Chinese troops of Chinese Nationalist General Lung Yun used that occa-sion to attack American installations for loot. There was a spirited engage-ment before Gen. Lun retreated (he later went to Beijing and was a high-level member of the Communist military commission). Captain Jor-gensen was in favor of continuing with our liaison mission to the pocket. None of us had any formal military orders or travel documents, so Jor-gensen and I went to the airport and boarded a C-47 that was en route to the fabled pocket. It was an exceptional place in central China and the center of a variety of OSS-sponsored operations. According to the secret documents,

A fairly complete net has been set up, working from the Tenth War Zone "pocket" with particular emphasis being placed upon troop movements and identifications along the Yangtse River and in the Shanghai area. Information is also coming in relative to Japanese troop dispositions and fortifications in the north-south corridor, and considerable target data is being furnished the Air Force. During the month (June) radios have been moved northward and stations are operating from the Tsingtao and Yellow River areas. Other radios are presently moving north to Peiping and other key areas in North China.[3]

This was a natural area to collect Korean volunteers from the Japanese area surrounding the pocket. Indeed, this was the source of the manpower for the Third Detachment. As a base to launch Korean radio teams toward the Shantung peninsula and then on to Korea, it was far more attractive on the map than Sian. In brief, the Pocket was an excellent forward intelligence base and a haven for American pilots shot down over Central China.

Why, one may rightly ask, did the Japanese not try to shut it down? This was in part because of the general style of the Japanese military occupation of China and the peculiar military situation that was arising in Anhui province. Generally, the Japanese army occupied the major cities and towns, the railways, and major roads. The villages and the countryside were supposed to be controlled by the Chinese Puppet Forces of Wang Ching-wei, the former rival of Nationalist President Chiang Kai-shek, before he was made President of occupied China by the Japanese authorities. In Anhui province itself, there was a relatively good Chinese Nationalist army, the Sixth, under a General Li; and also, in the countryside in the river areas, the New Fourth Chinese Communist army under General Lin Piao. Under all of those circumstances, the Japanese were willing to leave alone this remote area of mountainous Anhui.

It was natural that in this area the Koreans would build a detachment, getting reinforcements from Koreans escaping the Japanese army. This Third Detachment was commanded by General Kim Hak-kyu. Jorgensen reported that there were about 100 Koreans in the detachment. At the OSS base there were about 15 Americans. When Jorgensen and I arrived on August 10, everyone was waiting to leave the Pocket as soon as the war ended. Jorgensen and I went directly to the Korean compound only to learn that Gen. Kim and the bulk of his men had obtained safe passage from the Japanese (who remained armed) and moved on to Shanghai en route, they hoped, to Korea. This information would be useful to us later. Having now arrived in the Pocket, we were disappointed that we were suddenly going to be without an assignment and with no clear idea what we should do. We were on our own. We had dinner with the few remaining Koreans. The

Korean emblem I wore on my cap resulted in the Koreans presenting me with a pair of leather riding boots, which I wore for many years. On August 15 there was a VJ (victory over Japan) celebration at the OSS base, complete with the setting off of large quantities of explosive charges. A few days later a C-47 plane arrived again, landing in the dry river bed. About half of the group boarded it and we stayed on. This was the last flight in, because it soon began to rain and the river bed air strip was unusable. As the war with Japan ended, however, a new war started, as Chiang Kai-shek had correctly predicted. The Communist New Fourth Army began attacking the railway line, tearing up the rails and cutting down the telephone lines. This turned out to be an exciting and dangerous phase of the Korean adventure.

At first we all took these developments quite well. There was probably no one in China more disappointed at the unexpected end of the war with Japan and then the new troubles with the Communists than Captain Jorgensen. The wonders of atomic weapons—and the American monopoly—were much discussed. In civilian life, Jorgensen had been a mate in the U.S. merchant marine. How he got to China is not clear. He was a good-natured man with a large yellow mustache, about 35, an avid walker, and an excellent cook. He also was an adventurer. He had no real intention of going back to Kunming and becoming part of the demobilization that was already going on there. His idea was to explore China while there was this opportunity; he had plenty of 50-dollar gold coins that had been issued to him for his mission to the Pocket, so finances were no problem. I was easy to persuade that this was the thing to do and we recruited a radio team from the SO personnel still there: Ted Opalinski, a Chinese language student from the University of Chicago, who was a cryptographer; and Clyde Gould, from New York City, a radio operator. We were assigned the call letters Peter Oboe Jake (POJ) and told to head for Shanghai. So wander from Anhui we did for the next two months, finding ourselves in ever-growing difficulties from the Communists.

Jorgensen's first idea was to travel north to Suchow. But we learned from our radio of an incident there: Captain John Birch (who had earlier served in the Anhui Pocket) had been killed by the Communists on August 20. The OSS secret account is as follows:

> Captain Birch [commanding] and three others were en route to Suchow [ll7-l0, 34–15, the map coordinates] to occupy the town, seize Jap documents and report on general conditions. At Huang-kou, a railway station 20 miles west of Suchow, the train in which the party was traveling was fired on by Communists of the l2th regiment of the 11th army district. Capt. Birch was killed and the three others were taken into custody along with 9

Central Government officials. A general commanding puppet forces at Suchow sent a force against the Communists and recaptured the body of Capt.
Birch, photographed it, and buried it in Suchow.[4]

This brief account was the background for the creation of the John
Birch Society, still very powerful in California. He was eulogized as the
"first American casualty of World War III." Jorgensen reconsidered his op-
tions. By this time there was no possibility of requesting a C-47 to come
in, for there were no secure landing fields. We somehow had to make our
way to Shanghai, which was the new American Mecca. By now, early September, the dynamics of war and politics in Central China formed an iron
triangle and our four-man team was caught in the center: armed Japanese
troops, the Communist New Fourth Army, and the Chinese Nationalist
Sixth Army. None of these forces was particularly interested in four Americans. Somehow we needed to interest somebody. We slowly made our way
down the river to the east, seeking safety. Our Chinese liaison team did
what they could, but the war raged increasingly louder. Every day we
heard and saw the thump of mortar rounds, the low growl of the heavy
machine guns, and the sporadic rifle fire. It continued day and night, as the
Communists and Nationalists began to fight out their civil war. By now,
both the river and the railway were blocked by the Communist New
Fourth Army. The mission of the Chinese Sixth Army was to march north
to Suchow, as part of the grand strategy of the Nationalists to defeat the
Communists north of the Yangtse. This strategy left the local Japanese reg-
imental commander as our best bet; our exit route could become his exit
route also, if he wanted to save his troops from the civil war.

The fighting became more intense. All day long there was the familiar
firing of weapons; from time to time Communist prisoners in their padded
blue uniforms, hands tied behind their backs, hatless, hopeless, frightened,
were pressed by their Nationalist guards to walk along the edges of the rice
paddies, where at any moment they would be machine-gunned into the
paddies; their black hair sticking out of the paddies looked like a fall harvest of frozen cabbage. One could also imagine similar scenes not far away,
on the other side of the river, where Nationalist prisoners were being
given similar treatment in the opening rounds of this fateful civil war.

Soon it was mid-October and still we waited, sleeping on the ground
or on occasion in the door of a hut, removed for safety from damage. We
could no longer use the river because of the fighting. Our hopes were on
the railway. Finally, one morning, our Chinese aide arrived and said the
Japanese had decided to help. Two boxcars of troops, about a company, or
125 men, were being dispatched to open the broken railway, and we were
invited to accompany them. The four of us rather gingerly got into the

boxcar with the Japanese troops. There was no effort on either side to frat-
ernize. The irony of fighting the Japanese in August and needing their assistance in October was heavy on all of us. One of the first lessons of
international politics (which I had already been taught by General Lee
Bum-suk) was revealed: Countries have permanent interests, but not necessarily permanent allies. In our case, all we wanted to do was leave Anhui
province.

The Chinese Communists, upon seeing the armed Japanese troops,
quickly left the railway for the nearby hills. They did not want to battle the
Japanese; the Nationalists were their target. The four of us walked through
the break in the railway tracks for maybe a mile, when a motorized handcar miraculously appeared. The handcar took us all the way to Nanking,
where we stayed at the home of Wang Ching-wei, the puppet president of
China. He had earlier fled to Tokyo, where he fell into the hands of the Allies and was executed as a war criminal.

From Nanking we went on to Shanghai. For us the war was over. I returned to the U.S. via the Hump and India and resumed my studies at the
University of Chicago. In 1948 I noticed in the newspaper that Syngman
Rhee had selected Lee Bum-suk as his prime minister, the first prime minister in modern Korean history. I immediately sent him a letter of con-
gratulation, and he replied with thanks and invited me to visit him in
Seoul. It was not possible to do so on the GI Bill of Rights, but I nonetheless hoped to do so someday. Although I was in Korea briefly in 1952 during the Korean war on intelligence matters, I did not see Gen. Lee again
until the fall of 1964. Then I was the deputy chief of the CIA's Far East Division. I went to his modest home in Seoul. It was already cold and dark.
He greeted me warmly, and offered me a large snifter of brandy and a Ja-
maican cigar. He had gained weight (as had I), but still had the well-
groomed mustache, the scar on his forehead, and a twinkle in his eye
behind the tortoise-shell glasses. We reminisced for about two hours, exchanged best wishes, and then I left. That part of the Korean EAGLE was
gone forever.

There is just one final incident that needs to be included in the conclusion of the OSS-Korea story in China. The last scene had a devastating
effect on the future of the KPG as a political actor in postwar South Korea,
as well as on the leadership of the future CIA. The account from the Korean side goes like this: "The Liberation army's leaders, such as Kim Ku, Yi
Pom-suk and others had an operational talk with OSS Commander Major
General William H. Donovan and OSS chief in China Paul Helliwell in
the p.m., August 7, 1945. They agreed to mount a secret operation to
Japan. A special branch unit was founded and Yi Pom-suk was named the
commander of this unit. But it failed to operate because of the Japanese

surrender on August 15." This was part of the story; the first part is the un-successful Lt. Col. Bird mission to Keijo (Seoul) to get the Japanese to sur-render, recounted by Kim Jun-yop, who went on the mission. The second part is the story recounted in Professor Yu's book on the OSS in China.[5] In the crush of the dying days of the war, Donovan was in China to try to step up OSS operations in both Manchuria and Korea, so he did not hes-itate to meet Kim Ku and his staff, who were visiting EAGLE project in Sian at that time. In addition to the operation discussion, Kim asked Dono-van for his support for U.S. recognition of the KPG. This resulted in an open cable from Kim Ku to Truman on that subject. Kim was unaware of the American politics in Washington. Truman had little use for the Re-publican Donovan. His cool reply to Donovan read: "I would appreciate your instructing your agents to the impropriety of their acting as a chan-nel of self-styled governments which are not recognized by the Govern-ment of the United States."[6] Twenty-five days later, Truman dissolved the OSS. So Donovan was out of the intelligence business and the postwar planning began on what to do about intelligence. Kim Ku arrived in Seoul a month after his rival, Syngman Rhee.

From the top to the bottom, one can see that the military efforts in-volving the KPG were unsuccessful. And the Korean forces integrated in the Soviet army did occupy North Korea, while the U.S. belatedly occu-pied the South. Syngman Rhee as head of the Korean Commission in Washington, D.C., was the big winner. After worrying about the perils of installing a government that the Korean people might not want, Rhee was chosen by the U.S. Department of State as the Korean leader and flown to Tokyo. Then he arrived in Seoul on Gen. MacArthur's plane. Kim Ku and the KPG arrived in Seoul a month later, as private citizens. While Lee Bum-suk was appointed prime minister, Rhee never fully trusted him and his influence declined during the long years (1948–1960) of the Rhee administration.

Yet one should not discount the value of this long struggle for inde-pendence by the Korean people. This movement gave the Koreans a sense of pride in themselves as making a contribution to their own salvation. Today, when one visits the Independence Hall in South Korea south of Seoul, one can see the sense of pride that the annual one million visitors have in this period of history. Also located there is the Institute of Korean Independence Movement Studies, whose staff members are diligently compiling all the facts and stories about this difficult period of Japanese occupation, leading to today's equally engaging efforts for economic and political success in a difficult environment.

6

The Cold War Erupts in Korea

"War is the father of all things," said Heracleitus, a sixth-century B.C. philosopher. This aphorism proved to be painfully evident in the twentieth century in Korea, which, in part by accident and in part by design, became the first fiery crucible of the Cold War. The drama of the international struggle for post–World War II power was played out to the full on the impoverished Korean peninsula, the crossroads of the superpower competition that most expected to occur in Europe. Instead, it erupted in full force, to the surprise and chagrin of the United States. The latter was caught off guard strategically, tactically, and psychologically. China and the Soviet Union, as we shall see, were in the position of the sorcerer's apprentice. Korea was once again the victim of great-power rivalry.

While World War II was not fought with the goal or expectation of ending war forever or "making the world safe for democracy," there was no real anticipation that a major war would occur again soon. It was hoped that the Soviet Union would lose its stripes, but if not, competitive rivalry was expected to be contained within the normal restraints of diplomacy backed by sufficient military power. And if nothing else, there was the comfort of Professor Quincy Wright's two-volume *The Study of War*,[1] which, among other things, assured us that the period of time between wars of major consequence was increasing. Clearly, with the improvement of military technology and the element of nationalistic fervor that had transformed the devastating potential of war, each war brought more destruction and a longer time was required for preparation for the next round.

There was also the possibility that the new United Nations organization, aware of the deficiencies of the old League of Nations, would function as its sponsor hoped at the preparatory meeting in San Francisco in

April 1945, and that through the hard work of the United States, the Soviet Union would enter the "family of nations" and behave in the manner of a regular nation, participating in the world community, where global responsibilities would temper national interests. This was the philosophy of Yalta in February 1945, when the Allies made concessions to the USSR over Eastern Europe with this expectation in mind. Potsdam in July of the same year demonstrated more resolve and determination on the part of the Americans, but it was over 50 years before these well-intentioned errors were corrected.

Contrary to Korean political mythology, the question of Korean independence was not a primary purpose of World War II nor an immediate goal of the Allies. At the Cairo four-power conference in 1943, the Korean question was not dealt with conclusively. It was simply agreed (with Chiang Kai-shek, the Chinese Nationalist supreme leader, present) that Korea would be granted independence "in due course" (as the Japanese had already promised), thereby righting the wrong inflicted on Korea by Japanese imperialism in 1910, when Japan annexed Korea.

At the Yalta conference in February 1945, shortly before FDR's death in April, the Big Three—the U.S., the Soviet Union, and Britain—dealt with the postwar Korean settlement in a most general way. Korea would be handled by a four-power trusteeship—the U.S., China, the USSR, and Britain—which would prepare the way for an independent Korean government. The specifics of this idea were not spelled out then or at Potsdam in July 1945. This was in large part because of President Truman's caution and belief, bolstered by Secretary of the Army Henry Stimson, that such matters would be delayed pending information on whether the atomic bomb tests, scheduled for July 1945, were successful. Successful tests were anticipated as a major bargaining weapon, although their direct and specific use in dealing with the Korean problem was not evident. The big American concern was to assure Soviet support for the U.S. China policy, that is, Soviet support for the Nationalist leader, Chiang Kai-shek, in establishing his authority over China. For a time, Stalin went through the motions of supporting Chiang; but Chiang's desires far exceeded his military reach and the Communist forces seized more and more territory, for example, Manchuria. Soviet cooperation in China soon became a forlorn hope, but nonetheless, this was the short-term American vision of postwar Asia.[2]

With the success of the atomic bombing of Japan on August 5 and 7, the end of the war was imminent; the American military team (including future Secretary of State Dean Rusk) drafted General Order Number 1 on August 10–11, which was approved by President Truman and issued by General MacArthur on August 15, dividing Korea at the 38th parallel for the purpose of accepting Japanese surrender. Four-power occupation faded into the reality of the Soviets in the North and the Americans in the South. Any possibility of nationwide elections being held steadily deteriorated as relations between the Soviet Union and the West worsened. By the time UN elections were held in September 1948, they occurred only below the 38th parallel. The Soviet-sponsored regime of Kim Il-sung in the North would have no part of free elections. The gauntlet was clearly down. Both sides clamored for reunification, but on their own terms, which increasingly were expressed by threats of force. The situation in Korea could be described as low simmer; the degree of heat was controlled for the time being by the presence of occupying forces, Soviet and American, in the two parts of divided Korea. The antagonism between the two regimes has prompted some to claim that the Korean war was simply a civil conflict.[3]

Returning to the scene in the U.S., by the fall of 1948 the citizens were faced for the first time since 1932 by a presidential election without FDR. The traditional inward focus of the American public was apparent in the closeness of the presidential race between Harry S. Truman, the successor to FDR, and the Republican candidate, Thomas E. Dewey. In foreign affairs, both sides favored the reduction of military expenditures and the streamlining of the American armed forces, already substantially decimated by the enthusiasm for demobilization that shaped the new American dream at home.

President Truman won the election by the narrowest of margins; on defense, the task was to allocate available limited resources to the best effect. This meant, as it did in World War II, that the reconstruction of Europe was the priority against the menace of the Soviet Union. The Iron Curtain, as Winston Churchill dramatically put it, was coming down in Europe.

It is against this background that we need to examine the Far Eastern situation in general and the Korean situation in particular. In Japan, the American forces under MacArthur, as well as token Allied units, formed the Supreme Command, blocking out Soviet desires to send troops to aid in the occupation. Japan was seen by some as an anti-Communist lynch pin, from the American policy perspective. In July 1945, James Forrestal, the Secretary of the Navy, had raised the question of how thoroughly the U.S. should defeat Japan, considering the uncertain future in Northeast Asia.[4] The situation in China was increasingly worsening from an American perspective, as Mao Tse-tung and his associates went from victory to victory, driving Chiang Kai-shek farther and farther to the South. The mission of former army chief of staff George C. Marshall to China concluded that without far-reaching reforms of the Nationalist government, the U.S. could not successfully intervene in China. This was the subject of a partisan Republican cry for the heads of those who "lost China," and a White Paper response in 1949 from the Truman administration, placing the blame on the Nationalists and not the Truman administration. American leaders and elites wanted to hunker down and define new priorities.[5]

In this context and from this grand viewpoint, it is no surprise that the Truman administration, in terms of its defense allocations, had to make choices both in terms of strategy and the accompanying resources of men and material. Part of this was disclosed in January 1950 in a now-famous speech at the National Press Club in Washington, D.C., by Secretary of State Dean Acheson:

> The US defensive perimeter essential to military security in the Pacific runs along the Aleutians to Japan and then goes to the Ryukyus. . . . The defensive perimeter [then] runs from the Ryukyus to the Philippine Islands.
>
> So far as the military security of other areas in the Pacific is concerned, it must be clear that no person can guarantee these areas against military attack. But it must also be clear that such a guarantee is hardly sensible or necessary within the realm of practical relationship.
>
> Should attack occur . . . the initial reliance must be on the people attacked to resist it and then upon the commitments of the entire civilized world under the Charter of the United Nations which so far has not proved a weak reed to lean on by any people who are determined to protect their independence against outside aggression.[6]

While retrospectively this Acheson speech was considered by his critics as a betrayal of both Korea and Taiwan, it was all of a piece with well-published American statements since National Security Council study 8 (April 2, 1948), limiting the U.S. commitment to defend Korea.[7]

This is an extraordinary report, seen from today's perspective, extraordinary because of its paternalism and its awareness of the strategic importance of the Korean peninsula, making the Acheson statement a year later almost incomprehensible, except that the study specifically warns not to allow events in Korea to lead to war.

The study begins by complaining about the "political immaturity" of the Korean people making it particularly difficult to establish a democratic sovereign government: "The tendency of Korean political elements to polarize into extremes of right and left and to pursue their ends through the use of violence acts as a serious deterrent to the achievement of political stability on a democratic basis in Korea."[8] The study points out that the traditional source of raw materials (North Korea) had been cut off, and, as things stood, the South was dependent on the importation of raw materials for industry as well as food. This was blamed on the refusal of the Soviet Union to deal "in good faith" to resolve the Korean problem. This intransigence "has made inescapable the conclusion that the predominant aim of Soviet policy in Korea is to achieve eventual domination of the entire country. Clearly indicative of this aim is the action of the Soviet occupation authorities . . . in fostering the establishment in north Korea of a satellite regime claiming authority over the entire country and backed by the arms of a Soviet-trained and equipped army."[9]

There was a detailed appreciation of what such a development might mean to the security situation in North East Asia: "The extension of the Soviet control over all of Korea would enhance the political and strategic position of the Soviet Union with respect to both China and Japan, and adversely affect the position of the U.S. in those areas and throughout the Far East."[10] This posed a quandary on the anticipated withdrawal of U.S. troops after the UN-supervised elections that fall. Unless the U.S. left the South Koreans well enough armed to handle anything but "an act of aggression," such a withdrawal might be interpreted as a "betrayal by the U.S. of its friends and allies in the Far East and might well lead to a fundamental realignment of forces in favor the Soviet Union throughout that part of the world."[11]

This bleak outlook led to a series of five recommendations: (1) expand the training and equipage of South Korean troops; (2) provide sufficient funds to prevent the economic collapse of Korea; (3) after the formation of the new South Korean government in September 1949, "every effort should be made to create conditions for the withdrawal of occupation forces by 31 December 1948"; (4) set up a diplomatic mission after withdrawal of the occupation forces to recommend what economic and military aid measures should be considered; (5) "the U.S. should not become so irrevocably involved in the Korean situation that any action taken by any faction in Korea or by any other power in Korea could be considered a *casus belli* for the United States." It is fair to say that the U.S. was pursuing a policy in Korea principally of hope, that against the dire predictions of Soviet intentions, the U.S. could somehow withdraw its forces, yet hold the Soviets and their puppets at bay; not appear weak and appeasement-oriented, but under no conditions become involved in a war in such an uncongenial spot.

The developments on the other side, so to speak, which made this formulation hopeless, were the ongoing Communist revolution in China and the implications for the Communist movement in Asia, especially in North Korea. The battle over Korea had actually begun during World War II, with the Communists in Yenan and the Soviets supporting Korean groups, the North China Korean Volunteer Army and the Northeast Anti-Japanese United Army (in which Kim Il-sung served as a division commander); the Kuomintang government in Chungking supported (but did not recognize) the Korean Provisional Government in China.[12] This set in motion two contending forces, a drama that was later performed on the Korean peninsula in June 1950.

While Mao Tse-tung was preoccupied with completing his victory over Chiang Kai-shek in 1949 (the People's Republic of China was not officially declared until October 1, 1949), he nonetheless paid attention to the overtures for support of the invasion of South Korea proposed by Kim Il-sung. Until Soviet and Chinese official archives became open and reported, the time frame of all these events leading to the Soviet and Chinese planning, support, and entry into the Korean war were largely the subject of speculation and some educated (and then not-so-educated) guesses. These ranged from the belief that Mao himself was surprised by the June 25 invasion, to the view held by I. F. Stone and Professor Bruce Cumings that the actual invasion may have been launched by the South and that the North simply responded to this attack. Fortunately, with the partial opening of the Chinese and Soviet archives and the provision of selected documents on the subject, a much clearer picture is now available. Two of the authorities in this matter, Kathryn Weatherbee and Chen Jian, have provided Russian and Chinese archival material that I accept at face value. New evidence supports new interpretations. Unless there is a deception going on here on a grand scale that would be difficult to create and then to sustain, the archival material offers reliable insight into these matters. Clear-cut as this is, namely that North Korea, with the support of the Soviet Union and China, initiated the Korean war, it is necessary to deal with this one point in greater length. Some still claim, despite this new evidence, that (a) the culprit is unknown and (b) it does not matter anyway. It is this latter point, the ethical issue of intervention and responsibility, that warrants devoting extra time to this question.

The first attempt by an American to place the blame for the Korean war elsewhere than North Korea was by I. F. Stone in his book, *The Secret History of the Korean War*.[13] As an iconoclast and muckraker from a liberal-left tradition, Stone was susceptible to circumstantial evidence, which we will mention later in connection with the speculations of Bruce Cumings, who is a Korea specialist in academic life; two of his books are on *The Origins of the Korean War*.[14] The problem is not with his scholarship, but with his premise that the villain is not known. The first volume was published in 1980. The second volume, published in 1990 with the subtitle, "The Roaring of the Cataract, 1947–50," provides the details for his conspiracy thesis, condensed but essentially unchanged in his most recent book, *Korea's Place in the Sun*.[15]

Cumings advances three hypotheses on how the Korean war began[16]:

Who started the Korean War? This question cannot be answered. Instead, the reader is asked to consider three mosaics, each explaining how the war might have "started." All three are conspiracy theories including the established American, South Korean position: that the Soviets and North Koreans stealthily prepared a heinous, unprovoked invasion. The first mosaic is this "official story," and especially the documentary evidence behind it. Mosaic three is the North Korean account, which precisely reverses the first position: the South launched a surprise unprovoked invasion all along the parallel. The most absorbing perhaps, is Mosaic Two: the South provoked the war. Then there is a set of intelligence mosaics of report and counter report, which meander in and out and raise the question, who knew what, when?[17]

The size and complexity of Cumings' book is highly dependent on maintaining the fiction of ambiguity on who started the war. In chapter 16, Cumings provides a highly speculative hypothesis on Mosaic Two, that the Taiwan problem and South Korea might have been linked in a domestic U.S. political maneuver to reverse U.S.–China policy, that is, to refuse to intervene on Taiwan's behalf against a Chinese Communist attack. To appreciate this, one must go back in time to the post–World War II political atmospherics. This was the era of vast disorder in Asia in the wake of the collapse of the Japanese empire, the rise of anti-colonialism as well as of Communist China. Both Taiwan and Korea had been excluded from the U.S. defense perimeter by Dean Acheson in his January 1950 speech, as already mentioned. There was then (as now) a powerful Taiwan lobby. The immediate issue then was military aid to Chiang following the Nationalist defeat on the mainland. Assistant Secretary of State Dean Rusk (now Truman's man for drafting a peace treaty with Japan) and Louis Johnson, the Secretary of Defense, visited MacArthur in Tokyo at about the same time, in June 1950. This amounts to possible evidence of a deep conspiracy to attack North Korea, in Cumings' mind. John Foster Dulles visited Seoul and spoke to the National Assembly about the vice of Communism; Johnson was keen on reversing U.S. China policy and had an ally in MacArthur. (In an interview after the Korean war, Acheson said in regard to the impact of the Dulles visit in June 1950, "Foster up in a bunker with a homburg on—it was a very amusing picture."[18])

Cumings reads into these coincidental visits a plot to start a war in Korea to save Chiang and then possibly reopen the mainland war with China to achieve a "roll back" of Communism, a favorite Dulles theme (honored in the breach in the case of Hungary). Cumings wishes to make Taiwan a significant actor at this juncture of history. For the Nationalists, the desire may have been there but the body was weak. Having arrived in Taipei in May 1950 as a CIA officer to dispatch intelligence agents into mainland China, I observed at first hand the demoralized and ill-equipped troops of Chiang Kai-shek. The expectation was that Chinese Communist junk fleets assembled across the 90-mile wide strait along the Fukien coast would soon attack. President Truman said the U.S. would not intervene. There was not much public American clamor to reverse this decision, after the debacle on the mainland and the retreat from Shanghai to Taiwan. No one expected that the Nationalists could hold back the anticipated attack. There was interest from many high Chinese officials about where they might go, principally to the U.S. or the Philippines. In any case, Chiang had no plans to invade Korea a la Hideyoshi in 1592 en route to Beijing.

I had my own one-time code pads for communicating with Yokosuka, Japan, the Seventh Fleet base, which provided the CIA station with cover. The CIA group was called the Field Research Unit, Far East Command (FRU/FEC). It was the lineal descendent of External Survey Detachment 44 (ESD 44), which had been established in the fall of 1945 in Shanghai (after the closing of the OSS by President Truman), under the aegis of the U.S. Seventh Fleet, then commanded by Admiral Charles Cooke. (In Washington, D.C., the Central Intelligence Group was soon established to allow such organizations as ESD 44 to continue China operations until the CIA was established in 1947.) Once the Korean war was on, South Korean Prime Minister Lee Bum-suk became South Korea's ambassador to Taipei. But no Nationalist troops as such were ever sent to Korea to resume the Chinese civil war. The Taiwanese/American role was largely restricted to small-scale guerrilla raids along the Fukien-Chekiang coast. This was attempted by Western Enterprises, a CIA front.[19]

The offensive capability of Chinese Nationalist troops remained nil. In March 1951, Lt. Col. Richard Stilwell (later a four-star general in the 1970s in command of UN and U.S. forces in South Korea) came to Taiwan for a meeting with President Chiang. Madame Chiang was on hand to interpret. Stilwell's mission on behalf of the CIA's OPC (Office of Policy Coordination, the covert action wing) was to persuade Chiang to send a force to Hainan island to seize it as a diversion. It had fallen to the Chinese Communists in April 1950 without any real resistance, further reducing the credibility of the Nationalists as a fighting force. This island was then occupied by the Chinese Communists. Located southwest of Hong Kong and east of Hanoi, it was about 500 nautical miles from Taipei. As the discussion began, Madame Chiang handed me a note, "Is he serious?"

So much for the Chinese Nationalist military and the Korean war. Did Syngman Rhee provoke the war? Certainly Rhee and his followers, following the 1948 elections, proposed to march on the North, and there were often scrimmages along the 38th parallel initiated by both sides. So far so good for Cumings' argument. But in the end, it was the North under Kim Il-sung's leadership, with the connivance of the Soviet Union to provide tanks and the Chinese to return Korean veteran troops from the Chinese People's Liberation Army, that made feasible the invasion across the 38th parallel. The South Koreans, if they had been provided with U.S. tanks and artillery, may have done the same thing. But this is counterfactual.

Cumings' approach to scholarship, he writes, is that "the scholar's only concern must be with truth as he sees it, pursuing the truth wherever it takes him."[20] As of 2000 and his book *Korea's Place in the Sun* of 1997, he apparently has not yet looked into the materials released from the Soviet archives. For example, in a research note published in the fall of 1994 issue of the *Journal of Northeast Asia Studies*,[21] the riddle, if it ever existed, is resolved. In 1993 the Russians declassified a number of documents on Russian involvement in the Korean war and made this information available to scholars. Then, in the summer of 1994, President Yeltsin presented the visiting South Korean Foreign Minister, Han Sung-joo, with a file of sensitive documents related to the war. One such document, classified "Top Secret," dated August 9, 1966, with copies to Breznev, Kosygin, et al., reads as follows:

"On the Korea War 1950–53, and the Armistice Negotiations"

I. Background to and Preparations for the First Stage of the War.

> After separate elections in 1948 in South Korea and the formation of the puppet government of Syngman Rhee, on the one hand, and the formation of the DPRK, on the other, relations between the North and the South of the country were sharply aggravated. The Seoul Regime, as well as the DPRK, declared its claim to be the authority of all of Korea. The situation at the 38th parallel became even more tense in 1948 after the withdrawal of Soviet and American troops from Korea.
>
> During this period, Kim Il-sung and other Korean leaders were firmly determined to unify the country by military means, without devoting the necessary attention to studying the possibility that existed at the time for peaceful reunification through the broad development of the democratic movement in South Korea.
>
> In the DPRK, a people's army was created that in manpower and equipment significantly surpassed the armed forces of South Korea. By January 1, 1950, the total number of DPRK troops was 110,000; new divisions were hastily being formed.
>
> Calculating that the United States would not enter a war over South Korea, Kim Il-sung persistently pressed for agreement from Stalin and Mao Zedong to reunify the country by military means (telegrams #3–51, 233, 1950:
>
> Stalin at first treated the persistent appeals of Kim Il-sung with reserve, noting that "such a large affair in relation to South Korea . . . needs much preparation," but he did not object in principle. Stalin gave the final consent

to support the plan of the Koreans at the time of Kim Il-sung's visit to Moscow in March–April 1950. Following this, in May, Kim Il-sung visited Beijing and secured the support of Mao.

The Korean government envisioned realizing its goals in three stages.

1. concentration of troops near the 38th parallel
2. issuing an appeal to the South for peaceful unification
3. initiating military activity after the South's rejection of the proposal for peaceful unification.

At the time the document indicates, there are more details on the war and the long peace negotiations. The paragraphs quoted are sufficient to make the case of what precipitated the war and where the responsibility lies. (One can make a distinction between what "caused" the war and what "started" the war. Factors causing the war were vast and complex, but not so with the actual "start" of the war.) The only defenses against the archival evidence would be a proven claim that these documents are fabricated or deception material. No such claims have arisen. For now, this settles this part of the question of who started the Korean war.

In *Korea's Place in the Sun,* Cumings gives a shorter version of his argument on guilt for the Korean war.

> Whatever happened on or before June 25, it was immediately clear that this war was a matter of "Koreans invading Korea;" it was not aggression across generally accepted international lines. Nor was this the point at which civil conflict began. The question pregnant with ideological dynamite, 'Who started the Korean War?' is the wrong question. It is not a civil war question; it only holds the viscera in its grasp for the generations immediately afflicted by fratricidal conflict. Americans do not care any more that the South fired first on Fort Sumter; they still do care about slavery and secession. No one wants to know who started the Vietnam War. Someday Koreans in North and South will reconcile as Americans eventually did, with the wisdom that civil wars have no single authors. It took American about a century to do; it is therefore not surprising that Korean reconciliation is still pending after fifty years.[22]

It is important historically to have the record straight; we need to identify the aggressor to help in the final closure of this offense. A number of Asian countries, including Korea, are keen on identifying wrong-doing and equally demanding of national apologies. Japan's offenses against Asian countries in World War II readily come to mind. Fixing war guilt is part of the healing process. This will factor into the final resolution of the unification issue between North and South Korea.

The South Koreans, after a couple of decades of revisionist literature on the Korean war, as well as the now-defunct "dependence" theory, are picking up the guilt issue. A critical view of Cumings' two volumes on the origins of the Korean war says "his two volume study of the Korean war does not pass, I am afraid, either the scientific or artistic test, despite his time-consuming and painstaking research into official documents, memories and interviews. In my opinion, this disappointing outcome is his own making in which he clings to the erroneous concepts, assumptions and theories even when the evidence has indicated to the contrary."[23] Nowadays, Cumings does speak of a "northern invasion," but downplays this in the context of the then-ongoing civil war as he sees it. After this digression, I return to the historic international conflict.

I have mentioned the highlights of the American strategic appreciation of the world in quoting National Security Council studies. The counterpoints to these pronouncements, particularly in Asia, were the statements issued by Mao Tse-tung and not Kim Il-sung. On June 30, 1949, Mao proclaimed his famous "leaning to one side" policy: "Externally, unite in a common struggle with those nations of the world which treat us as equal and unite with the peoples of all countries. That is, ally ourselves with the Soviet Union, with the People's Democratic countries, and with the proletariat and the broad masses of the people in all the other countries, and form an international united front. . . . We must lean to one side."[24]

This view was contrary to the advice of a newly arrived former Chinese Nationalist general, who recommended that "the new China, while existing with the Soviet Union, should seek accommodation with the United States and other Western countries." He believed that such a policy could be in the interests of the Chinese nation. Mao disagreed, arguing that the attempt to pursue the doctrine of the mean "in international politics would be dangerous to the cause of the Chinese Communist revolution because it could weaken the inner dynamics of the Chinese revolution and blur the distinction between revolution and counter revolution."[25] Mao's choice changed Korean history.

In regard to Korea, Mao and the People's Liberation Army (PLA) command had earlier agreed to some minor measures, like sending the 184th and 166th divisions of the PLA to Korea, along with their equipment, as earlier requested. These troops were mainly ethnic Koreans who had caused some disciplinary problems in central China because they wished to return home. Then on January 21, 1950, General Nieh Rong-zhen, acting general staff chief of the PLA, agreed to send some 16,000 Korean PLA troops with their equipment in the spring of 1950.[26] This did not appear to be a systematic plan on the part of the Chinese to prepare for an invasion of the South, although it might well have been part of Kim Il-sung's plans. In April 1950 Kim stopped in Beijing on his way back from Moscow and told Mao of the general plan to invade the South, as agreed with Stalin, but did not specify a date.[27]

The actual outbreak of the war on June 25 was marked by Mao's denunciation of Truman's decision to protect Taiwan; Mao's statements about Korea were not provocative. He settled for the moment for "moral support" of the North's campaign, hopeful that Kim Il-sung's prediction of a six-weeks war would prove correct. The Truman statement about Taiwan on June 27 brought joy to Taiwan. There was an immediate lift to the real estate market and to those Chinese who were resigned to "leaping into the sea." Now, however, they began to put their energy into commerce and talk of the future. The vast collection of Chinese junks that the Communist forces had assembled across the Taiwan strait was soon dispersed, against the American promise of the protection of the Seventh Fleet. Mao's involvement in Korea certainly cost him Taiwan, and another unintended consequence of the Korean war has become a fact of history.

Against this hope of an early and easy Kim victory, however, the Chinese Communists became agitated. They were surprised that the U.S. was able to send troops so quickly from Japan, particularly against the previous U.S. claim that Korea was not in its defense perimeter. They decided to organize their own contingency plan. On July 2, just one week after the invasion, Chou En-lai traveled to Pyongyang and met with Soviet representative Roshchin. Chou advised that if the Americans crossed the 38th parallel, the Chinese would send troops into North Korea as "volunteers" to oppose the Americans and their allies, without formally declaring war. He asked Roshchin for assurances of Soviet air support for Chinese forces in North Korea. On July 5 Stalin responded that it was appropriate for the Chinese to assemble troops for use in the war and if the enemy crossed the 38th parallel, he would provide air support. Specifically, Stalin was willing to send an air force division to China, composed of 124 Z fighters.[28]

Briefly, the Kim Il-sung attack was pushed back by General MacArthur's masterful landing at Inchon, the port to the west of Seoul, and by late September the UN began an ill-fated advance across the 38th parallel toward the Yalu River, which demarcates the border between Korea and Manchuria, the "Northeast" region of China. The British, although staunch and faithful allies of the U.S., were becoming chary of their involvement in Korea. Sir John Slessor, Chief of the Air Staff, wrote a letter to the Chiefs' committee just prior to the Inchon landing. "What is the object of the exercise? I think the Americans would agree with us that we have really no strategic interest in Korea whatsoever."[29]

The Inchon landing and the drive North sent the Chinese military security apparatus into a frenzy. On October 2, as an "urgent" matter, Mao assembled the Standing Committee of the Party Politburo and emphasized the seriousness of the situation. "The question now is not whether we should send troops to Korea or not, but how fast we can do this. One day's difference will be critical to the whole situation. Today we will discuss two urgent questions—when should our troops enter Korea and who should be the commander." The outcome was to enter Korea around October 15 and to make Peng Tehuai field commander.[30]

In the meantime, at the SCAP (Supreme Commander of Allied Powers) headquarters in Tokyo, Gen. MacArthur and his intelligence chief, Major General Charles Willougby, were convinced (or, more correctly, convinced themselves) that the Chinese would not enter the war. There were many indications to the contrary, including a statement by Chou Enlai on September 30, 1950. It is important to understand his position in terms of the international picture, especially the growing ties between the USSR and China. "The People's Republic of China resolutely stands on the side of the world camp of peace and democracy headed by the Soviet Union and has, moreover, established the closest fraternal relations with the Soviet Union. During Chairman Mao's visit to the Soviet Union, China and the USSR concluded a Sino-Soviet treaty of friendship, alliance and mutual assistance which has enormous significance for world history."[31]

After recounting the success of China in liberating its own territory, Chou had this to say:

> The Chinese people absolutely can not tolerate foreign aggression, nor can they stand idly aside while their own neighbors are outrageously invaded by imperialists. Whoever attempts to exclude the nearly 500 million Chinese people from the United Nations and whoever tries to blot out and violate the interests of this fourth of humankind and vainly thinks about an arbitrary solution to any Eastern issue of direct concern to China will certainly bloody their skulls.[32]

As a personal aside, I was from May 1950 through September 1952 the CIA liaison with the Chinese Nationalist primary intelligence service, the Pao Mi Chu (PMC, the "Bureau for the Protection of Secrets"). This was the linear descendant of the famous or infamous organization, BIS (Bureau of Information and Statistics), of General Tai Li. The BIS handled the lion's share of intelligence liaison with U.S. military forces, except the OSS, which was in the coalition but tried to maintain a free hand. The deputy chief of the PMC, Gen. Pan Chi-wu, was the Tai Li commander of the "Happy Valley" intelligence base near Chungking during World War II. The current PMC chief was Mao Jen-feng, who enjoyed the support of Madame Chiang Kai-shek. Beginning in July, after the Korean war broke out, the PMC began reporting on the northward movement of Chinese army units on the mainland. The PMC was still in contact by radio with many of these army units, who had turned over to the Communist side after being defeated on the battlefield or simply surrendered to the superior force facing them. These units were still run by their old commanders and were in fact the illusionary basis for Nationalist hopes that with the war in Korea, these troops might again be able to opt for the Nationalist side. In any case, our small group in Taipei forwarded these reports to the CIA China operations headquarters in Yokosuka, from which they were passed on to MacArthur's headquarters. There was no claim that these troops would proceed from Manchuria into Korea, but this was the obvious implication. MacArthur and his staff had no use for this information; William Duggan, the CIA chief in Yokosuka, was told not to send this information anymore, on pain of being sent back to the U.S. But still the reports from the PMC arrived and they were still forwarded to SCAP.

In defense of SCAP, one can of course say that these reports were from an interested source, that is, the Chinese Nationalists. The wider the war, the more hopes they had for their "back to the mainland" aspirations. The PMC was careful not to speculate on the final destination of these former Nationalist troops, but it seemed clear to those of us handling the material. These troops definitely were not willingly in the Communist camp. One can in fact speculate that the "human wave" tactics the Communists used for a time in North Korea on their drive south were based on these troops of doubtful loyalty, whom the Communists wanted to dispose of in a productive way. Of the Chinese prisoners taken and finally repatriated in 1953, most of the 20,000 troops opted for Taiwan.

While this minor drama was being played out, the U.S. Joint Chiefs and the U.S.' principal allies, especially the British, worried about the northern campaign and the possibility of Chinese and Soviet intervention. This would vastly escalate the war that they were all trying to contain within its current parameters. An alarmed President Truman flew out to Wake Island to obtain at first hand MacArthur's vision and version of the war. The relevant Truman-MacArthur conversation was as follows:

Gen. MacArthur: I believe that formal resistance will end throughout North and South Korea by Thanksgiving. There is little resistance left in South Korea—only about 15,000 men—and those we do not destroy, the winter will.

In North Korea, unfortunately, they are pursuing a forlorn hope. They have about 100,000 men who were trained as replacements. They are poorly trained, led and equipped. But they are only fighting to save face. Orientals prefer to die rather than to lose face.

It is my hope to be able to withdraw the Eighth Army to Japan by Christmas. That will leave the X Corps . . . I hope the United Nations will hold elections [presumably in all of Korea] by the first of the year.

The President: What are the chances for Chinese or Soviet intervention?

Gen. MacArthur: Very little. Had they interfered in the first or second months it would have been decisive. We are no longer fearful of their intervention. We no longer stand hat in hand. The Chinese have 300,000 men in Manchuria. Of these probably not more than 100/125,000 are distributed along the Yalu river. Only 50/60,000 could be gotten across the Yalu River. They have no Air Force. Now that we have bases for our Air Force in Korea, if the Chinese tried to get down to Pyongyang there would be the greatest slaughter.

With the Russians it is a little different. They have an Air Force in Siberia and a fairly good one. . . . The Russians have no ground troops available for North Korea. They would have difficulty in putting troops into the field. It would take six weeks to get a division across and six weeks brings the winter. The only other combination would be Russian air support of Chinese ground troops.[33]

MacArthur's speculation on this final point was exactly what Mao and Stalin had in mind. Following Mao's decisions on when to intervene and who was to command, Chou En-lai flew to Moscow to be certain all was as agreed. He was in for a shock. "Contrary to previous agreement, Stalin now did not want to send an airforce, but only equipment for 20 divisions. So Chou cabled Beijing on 10 October, asking whether to reconsider."[34] Mao had delayed sending his troops to cross the Yalu and convened another meeting of the Politburo on October 13. He then cabled to Chou in Moscow:

I have consulted with comrades in the Politburo. The consensus is that it is still advantageous to send our troops to Korea, at the critical stage of the war, we can concentrate on fighting the [South Korean] puppet army, for we may cope with the puppet army with certainty. We can establish bases in the vast mountainous areas to the line between Wonson and Pyongyang. This will encourage the Korean people. If we are able to eliminate several puppet divisions in this stage, the Korean situation would take a turn in our favor. The above positive policy will be very advantageous to China, to Korea, to the East, and even the whole world. If we do not send off our troops and allow the enemy to reach the Yalu River, the enemy will be swollen with arrogance. This will result in a variety of disadvantages to us, especially to the Northeast [Manchuria] area. The whole Northeast Border Defense Army will be tied down there, and electric power in south Manchuria will be controlled [by the enemy]. In short, we think that we should enter the war; we have to enter the war. To enter the war will be very rewarding; not to enter the war will be extremely harmful.

On October 19 the PLA crossed the Yalu River.[35] As noted, the major decisions after the first week of war were all made by non-Koreans. The way the war developed with massive foreign intervention made it difficult for the Korean commanders, South and North, to make their own strategic plans.[36]

The entry of China into the Korean war with the growing support of the Soviet Union escalated the conflict into higher American strategic stakes, in exactly the region that complicated U.S. defense plans on a global scale. Washington was determined to contain the war within the Korean peninsula; this was considered a Soviet feint, with the main blow to come next in Europe. This was why MacArthur's calls to enlarge the war by bombing Manchuria and the China coast were rejected by the Joint Chiefs and in April 1951 led to MacArthur's dismissal by President Truman. By this time General Mathew Ridgeway had not only blunted the Chinese offensive but, for the most part, had also pushed the Chinese back over the 38th parallel in a fierce and bloody campaign.

There remained the problem of the war spreading. Soviet pilots were involved in missions over North Korea and this was well-known to the UN command. This was not played up, however, in order to keep the lid on. China for its part stuck to the "volunteer" fig leaf. All of these measures were part of the Orwellian term "limited war," that is, the political and military goals of this kind of war were incomplete and "victory," as MacArthur argued, was no longer the objective. This kind of war, repeated in Vietnam and to a considerable degree in the Gulf War of 1991, ushered in new uses of military power that did not sit well with the military or the citizenry. So, as with the Korean conflict, inconclusive warfare suited the Cold War strategy of the twentieth century.

The UN Command's success in the winter and spring of 1951 provided the opportunity for General Ridgeway to issue "peace feelers" to the "Communist command." Actual negotiations began in June 1951, about a year after the invasion, which had seen during that interval the ebb and flow of battle with Pyongyang overrun by the United Nations Command (UNC), and the brief Chinese taking of Seoul before the retreat again to the North. Fighting continued during the negotiations; about half of American casualties, for example, occurred between the opening of negotiations and the final armistice at Panmunjom on July 27, 1953.[37]

Mao Tse-tung seemed eager to conclude negotiations quickly, but Stalin's position was ambivalent, although ostensibly for a settlement.[38] The Chinese negotiators were clearly the "superior" and the North Koreans the "inferior." This was sound Confucian doctrine and a continuation, in effect, of the old Chinese tributary system, with Mao addressing Kim Il-sung affectionately as "hsiao" (small) Kim, in the older brother-younger brother tradition.[39] The Indian government, mistrusted by the Truman administration, played a role through the UN in New York City as well as through its embassies in Beijing and Moscow. Chester Bowles, the U.S. ambassador to Delhi, after talking with Nehru and other Indian officials, concluded that China had everything to gain from a settlement, but that the Soviet Union "had everything to gain" through more fighting, since the war clearly drained the strength of both China and the U.S. to the advantage of the USSR.[40] The talks got nowhere over almost two years, until Stalin died on March 4, 1953.

Another factor that may well have entered into Communist willingness to conclude the war was the election of Dwight D. Eisenhower in November 1952. He was in favor of negotiating a truce; but he was well aware of technological advances in nuclear weapons, making possible the use of nuclear artillery and small bombs. This would give his administration new confidence, if provoked by Communist intransigence; the use of tactical nuclear weapons in Korea and China was feasible.

On May 19, 1953, the Joint Chiefs recommended direct air and naval operations against China, especially Manchuria, including the use of nuclear weapons.[41] On May 20 the Security Council endorsed this position. While Max Hastings says it is not possible to be certain whether this new attitude toward the use of nuclear weapons was only a bluff, the self-assurance of the administration may have convinced the Communists that a truce was preferable to a nuclear phase of the war.

By July 1953 a truce and cease-fire—not a peace—was agreed to by the two sides. While the Americans considered a coup to replace Rhee, in the end a mutual security treaty between the U.S. and the Republic of Korea was concluded. The armistice agreement was signed by the UNC, China, and North Korea, but not South Korea, a problem that still plagues a final settlement.

One other cause for the drawn-out character of the peace negotiations was the issue of the prisoners-of-war. This is another good example of how issues that did not particularly concern the South Koreans stood in the way of South Korea's interests. Mao had assumed that the issue of POWs was already resolved in the terms of the 1947 Geneva Conventions, which provided for their expeditious return. President Harry Truman, however, had other thoughts, based on the way POWs were repatriated at the conclusion of World War II in Europe. The Western powers allowed hundreds of thousands of their German prisoners, including large numbers of Russian and Eastern European troops who had fought on the German side, to be repatriated to the USSR, where they faced an uncertain fate.[42] In light of that experience, Truman insisted on "voluntary repatriation" so that those involved could make a choice. When the Eisenhower administration took power in January 1953, John Foster Dulles held to the Truman position, but with an additional twist in mind: If repatriation were voluntary, then Communist countries would think twice about invading other countries and risking capture of their troops, who would not return. In the case at hand, there were about 20,000 Chinese prisoners, of which only 5,100 chose "voluntary expatriation." This infuriated the Chinese Communists, who considered it an international humiliation, and accused the Taiwan Nationalists of luring the POWs to their side.

There was indeed something to this argument. The Chiang Kai-shek government had provided the assistance of interpreters for the POWs as well as spiritual comfort through the sending of Buddhist monks, all of whom worked on behalf of the Chinese intelligence services. Having been responsible on the CIA side for making these arrangements with the PMC, I can vouch for these facts. Whether these agents played an important part in persuading the majority of Chinese troops to proceed to Taiwan is another matter. If we remember that these troops were in the first instance Chinese Nationalist troops newly minted as PLA, then this may be easier to understand. After their experience in the PLA, the Chinese solders may well have concluded that life on Taiwan would be better.

From the perspective of the South Korean government, one can understand Syngman Rhee's outbursts. As many as three million Koreans of a total population of about 25 million on both sides perished and additional millions were dislocated. Military casualties were: U.S. 33,629 dead/105,785 wounded; South Korean 415,000 dead/429,000 wounded; the Commonwealth 1,263 dead/4,817 wounded; other Allies 1,800 dead/7,000 wounded. The U.S. estimated that 1.5 million Chinese and North Korean soldiers had died.[43] And after all of this sacrifice, the division along the 38th parallel still remained. In fact, the division was much deeper and more rigid than it had been, so conquest appeared still to be the only solution. "Peaceful" reunification was not even on the horizon.

Yet the lure of instant reunification was still the sharpest arrow in the quivers of both Rhee and Kim Il-sung. For Rhee, it was virtually his only motivation. He was not intellectually caught up in "economic development" or the other political and economic goals that may have crossed his limited horizon. During the seven remaining years of his regime, he became increasingly out of touch with the future of Korea as many of his citizens saw it, and his illusions were finally shattered by the student disorders in April 1960 that shook the foundations of his regime.[44] There was no longer any place for him in the country he had helped to create through his own dedication and leadership, with the support of the U.S. A new and different society was emerging in the South.

In the North, an equally disappointed Kim Il-sung took a somewhat different course right after the war. He embarked on a program of reconstruction and political consolidation that, for a time, as seven-year-plan succeeded seven-year-plan, seemed to be succeeding. The contrast between progress in the North and ongoing poverty in the South was not lost on anyone. This was behind the civil unrest in the South and the first shoots of democracy, while in the North, under the slogan of *juche* (self-sufficiency), two different Koreas were taking shape. They were significant because to many, they symbolized the intensifying Cold War.

Some argue that retrospectively the positive value of the Korean war was that it sowed the seeds for the Sino-Soviet split a decade later. Stalin's failure to provide timely air support for the Chinese in October 1950 was one item. This distrust may have led to the U.S.–Chinese rapprochement in the 1970s. But in itself, the war was a bitter disappointment to both North and South in terms of their mutual passion for reunification. The war settled nothing. Both sides began to think about how best to prepare for the next round.

7

The Bumblebee Economy

Acording to specialists in aerodynamics, the bumblebee is not supposed to be able to fly. The wings are too small and the body is too large, for example. Yet the bumblebee does fly, perhaps not in the most gracious, straightforward manner, but fly it does. That has been the case as well for the South Korean economy. The truly heroic efforts of President Park Chung-hee started the authoritarian developmental state in 1961, and it worked. In the view of some, South Korea literally pulled itself up by its bootstraps (albeit with an exceptionally fortuitous set of circumstances, detailed later). The Korean developmental model, not well understood either by the Koreans or their would-be copiers, rang up the cash registers and annual GNP gains consistently in the 8–9 percent range.[1] This remarkably quick V-shaped recovery of the Korean economy from the 1997 financial crisis is testimony to the durability of a nation of dedicated workers.

There were Cassandras, who received the usual punishments meted out to the poor devils who are prematurely correct about impending perils.[2] The South Koreans themselves were not without their own skeptics. The doubts raised were not about the empirical success of the system (new manufacturing plants, a leading trading state), but whether the methods employed (loans, not equity; market share, not profit), would finally run a cropper. *Sansa* (*Thought*), Korea's most sophisticated intellectual magazine, published two pertinent articles in its spring 1997 issue. Choi Woo-sock, president of Samsung Economic Institute, wrote "Why the Korean Economy is in Crisis," and Chung Un-chan, professor of economics at Seoul National University, produced "The Present State of the Korean Economy." Both articles expected a coming economic depression. Government reports remained positive.

The reasoning of the critics was similar and correct. Choi cited problems in Korea's major industries—semiconductors, shipbuilding, steel, automobile, and petrochemical. They were going downhill and bringing with them low growth, high unemployment, and social instability. He felt the Korean economy needed a dose of the American system for a systematic restructuring, increasing research and development investment, easing of regulation, and a new emphasis on creativity and new ideas. He wanted to strengthen the information network, political stability, and "elevate work ethics and the elite's moral values."[3]

Professor Chung criticized monopolistic supply markets, the closed financial sector, inefficient government, and unfair economic practices, all of which resulted in conflict and not harmony. "In the past, the Korean economic system was run by competitive limitations, and the government's artificial resource distribution policy. The government gave favors and resources to the conglomerates." This resulted in distorted resource allocation, worsened corruption, and created huge bad debts. This made it possible for these large companies to prey on the medium and small companies. In the 1960s and 1970s it was easy to get advanced technology from developed countries and economic growth could be achieved by a favorable economic environment, low wages, and government policy. But now, Professor Chung concluded, all this is difficult to achieve. Technology is hard to come by; wages are higher, yet skilled workers are in short supply; real estate prices are too high; and the international environment is complicated. He was also for structural improvement and economic reform.[4]

A more fundamental critique of the South Korean economy over the last three decades also needs to be weighed. Some revisionists claim that the "Miracle" should be attributed to America. The combination of American financial input into Korea for the Vietnam war, easy and cheap technology exchange as part of the security package, and easy loans was really the basis for Korean economic success.[5]

The Hanbo steel scandal was out on the street by the spring of 1997; but sophisticated observers concluded that this was unique, that the whole chaebol system was not at risk. While the Korean domestic financial debt situation was ripe and vulnerable, it required the external market to set off a series of events that finally crash-landed in Seoul. The economic boom in Southeast Asia was due to vast quantities of foreign bank loans, far more than the internal markets of Thailand, Malaysia, and Indonesia could absorb. So part of the funds were invested unwisely, creating over-capacity in manufacturing and real estate projects, for example. Then there was the inevitable due date of repayment of the loans—money was generally borrowed at short-term rates for long-term projects, and "hot money" flowed back and forth to take advantage of discrepancies in interest rates. Malaysia darkly accused financier George Soros and his associates of being the primary cause of its misery. Japanese yen was a popular currency to borrow and relend at much higher rates. In any case, the whole jerry-built system came crashing down in Thailand in July 1997. The Thai finance minister reportedly wondered how foreigners had acquired so much *bhat* (Thai currency), not realizing the futures trade required no bhat at all. (Thailand, with a GNP of around $200 billion, half of General Electric's gross, was a minor player in the drama.) All the Southeast Asian currencies were instant inflation victims and the International Monetary Fund (IMF) was called in as the financial instrument of last resort. Designed at Bretton Woods in 1944 to oversee and control international currencies in the new postwar world order, the role of the IMF had dramatically changed since that time. It was the only open short-term window around, the World Bank blissfully doling out long-term low interest loans in the name of economic development for the backward states. How to prevent a similar future crisis was much on the mind of the "international financial community."[6]

By November in South Korea, the won began to inflate, rising from the 880 level to about a thousand, on the way, briefly in January to 2000 to the dollar. Creditors naturally wanted their money back in a hurry. They were no longer willing to lend money to the Korean banks, even though they were backed by the government at just over U.S. Treasury rates, and automatically roll them over as good business. Japanese and American banks were technically exposed to billions of dollars worth of debt, but smug and secure in the certainty that the U.S.-backed and -controlled IMF would come to the rescue in the last resort. And so that scenario soon played itself out.

For Korea, the economic moment of truth arrived in early December, 1997, when then-President Kim Young-sam claimed to have learned for the first time of the seriousness of the liquidity crisis. South Korea could not pay its short-term foreign debts. He and his advisors decided that the IMF offered the best immediate solution and quickly arranged, through their long-time good connections, a $58.8 billion bailout. This came as a shock to the South Korean public and was an immediate source of embarrassment to many successful Koreans, who felt this borrowing represented a blot on the honor of the nation. It was rich fare for the man-in-the-street kind of interview, perfect material for today's journalists intent on encapsulating great issues through a one-paragraph lead with John Q. Public.[7] The bailout, however, held off the creditor banks and shored up Korea's sovereign credit. This was about two weeks before the elections for President on December 18 and all three candidates were pressed into agreeing to this step, however reluctantly. At first career opposition leader Kim Dae-jung insisted that if elected, he would renegotiate the terms of the agreement; but he soon thought better of that approach. The responsibility for not receiving the loan was something no candidate wanted to accept.[8]

The question of who was responsible for this state of affairs, plunging the Korean economy into both despair and depression, remained an issue into 1999, when hearings in the National Assembly were still being proposed. Others, like John A. Mathews, for example, in JPRI Working Paper No. 46 ("Fashioning a New Korean Model Out of the Crisis," May 1998), were positive and upbeat about the South Korean economic situation. The country was in the process, he believed, of turning the old economic model in for a bright new one, better and sleeker, attuned to the realities of economic competition in the twenty-first century. The problem, as he saw it, "was the redemption of $30.6 billion in debts out of a total external debt for domestic financial institutions of $103.2 billion, that encapsulates the core of the Korean crisis."[9]

Earlier, economists like Larry Lau of the Stanford Economics Department and Harry Rowen, director of the Asia Pacific Research Center, and investors like Harry Seggerman, president of the International Investment Advisers, were convinced that the tightening of credit and the reduction of debt would lead to enough restructuring to begin industrial growth again. They were correct. The Korean economy began to show recovery by the end of 1988. Others, like myself, thought the recovery would take longer and that more restructuring of the chaebol would be required; and that while that went on, recovery would be slow.[10] Reform of the chaebol has decimated the top 20, and the number two chaebol, Daewoo, has been allowed to slip into receivership and bankruptcy. Daewoo's problems were the business story of 1999. The bankruptcy of Daewoo Motors was somehow delayed until November, 2000. The "too big to fail" slogan was no longer operative. Nonetheless, a review of some of the difficulties is worthwhile in documenting the scope of "DJnomics" under tough conditions.

The reason for the buildup of this debt (in an economy of then $400–500 billion GNP) was in large part due to the liberalization of the credit market beginning around 1990, when businesses could begin to borrow money abroad without government approval but with the tacit assumption of government guarantees. Alice Amsden and others have pointed out that this amounted to a premature relaxation of government control on borrowing. It contributed to the over-extension of credit to major South Korean businesses and accelerated the South Korean system of substituting loans for equity to finance business expansion.[11] Because of the Japanese colonial experience, the Korean fear of a financial "recolonization" was real. Korean nationalism had reached a level at which any foreign control was unacceptable. I once asked a leading member of the securities industry in the early 1980s when the Korean stock market would be open to foreigners. He replied with a smile, "Only after we Koreans have made all the money possible." Korea as a place to do international business always ranks near the bottom. In April 1999, Korea's international competitive ranking dropped to thirty-sixth (from 35) of the 47 ranked countries, behind Malaysia (27), the Philippines (32), and Thailand (34). Categories rated include price controls, GDP growth, shareholders' rights, protectionism, new information technology, corporate responsibility, and college education.[12] A reversal of this position is one of the aims of the current "New Korea" program. The current campaign for reversing this super-nationalistic attitude, however, is beginning to show signs of success. Foreign direct investment for long-term growth is essential, as opposed to short-term speculation in the stock market.

Suspicions of the true financial condition of the chaebol deepened over the resolution of the Hanbo steel case. The bribery of former president Roh Tae-woo was aired. And about $2 billion of the $5 billion Hanbo investment could not be accounted for. In the end, the Hanbo chairman and his son were convicted of taking a mere $400 million of company funds. These are the conditions that made shareholders in Korean stocks wonder when the dividends would arrive.[13]

The collapse of Kia auto in July of 1997, then the tenth largest conglomerate, added to the growing debt pool and also signified the tightening of the saturated world auto market. But both of these major indicators, Hanbo and Kia, were largely ignored or considered exceptions. And as John Mathews pointed out, "Korea has faced huge crises before and emerged stronger from the experience."[14] Chalmers Johnson opened a wider discussion of the Korean/Asian problem that, in my opinion, can help us understand what is going on in South Korea. In "Economic Crisis in East Asia, the Clash of Capitalism,"[15] Johnson goes beyond the liquidity crunch explanation to wonder whether the general world industrial over-capacity and the end of the Cold War in East Asia are also factors in what happened to the Asian economies.

This is getting closer to the complexities that face Asian and South Korean policy-makers as they begin repairing the bumblebee economy. The first reaction of the new Kim Dae-jung administration in its dedication to the twin principles of democracy and free markets was to arrest the former deputy prime minister and minister of finance, Kang Kyong-shik, and the senior Blue House economic adviser, Kim In-ho, for failing to see the coming clouds and put up the umbrella in good time. The two were released after a few months, but the example cast a pall over the kind of democracy the "New Korea" was going to have. The best that can be said about these arrests is that it is important to find out what went wrong. The facts of over-extension of credit and foreign and domestic investment excesses answer the immediate problem; but the structural reform issues, while noted, have been faced only obliquely.[16] The handling of both chaebol reform and failure are key indicators of full recovery and the shape of the future.

Having been caught up in the Asian financial turmoil, South Korea lost a lot of its Southeast Asia market, as well as its market share in the U.S. and China. Where are the new markets to allow for not only South Korea but Asia in general to develop in order to expand exports? Chalmers Johnson has been onto the question for some time and has written that what was needed for continuing prosperity in Asia was another major market, which he hoped would be Japan. "One problem has always been Japan's comparison of East Asian Economics to a V-formation of flying geese with Japan always as head goose. . . . No one ever asked where these geese were flying. Up to now, they have been flying to Los Angeles, but in the post–Cold War era, the United States can no longer play its traditional role. A new primary market for Asian manufactured goods must be found."[17] The search for such a market continues, and no one is more anxious to find this new El Dorado than the Koreans. The U.S. is staggering along with an ever-expanding trade deficit in the $200–300 billion range. Eventually, such deficits will kill off American jobs and lead to a sharp decline in the value of the American currency.

The inclusion of South Korea in the chain reaction of financial events sent a mighty shock wave throughout Asia. Aside from Japan and China, which, because of their size and in the case of China, a currency that could not be externally traded, South Korea had a strong economy and its success story had created both envy and emulation. Popular journalism went into a frenzy of reporting how disastrous this fallout was; no story, usually based on anecdotes, about the South Korean economy seemed too outrageous or indicative of the shape of the future. The Jindo fur company, which had become a sprawling weak chaebol, was highlighted in the *Wall Street Journal* in a piece from Seoul by Namju Cho, "Jindo Group Provides Apt Case Study for Korea Inc." The president and founder, Kim Young-jin, had been forced to put up both his house and Jindo shares to obtain an emergency loan.[18] Stories of the bankruptcy of auto manufacturer suppliers also were singled out as the multitude of bankruptcies began to expand the ranks of the unemployed.

By October 1998 the gross domestic product was expected to contract by 6.7 percent during the third quarter and by 6.5 percent for the year, according to the Korea Development Institute.[19] The Hyundai Institute took a look at the per capita income with these estimates: "The nation's per capita income, which had declined to the $9,500 level last year from

$10,548 in 1996, is projected to drop further this year to about $7,000." Recovery to the $10,000 level was anticipated by 2003. Korea's per capita GDP was $5,883 in 1990, $6,745 in 1991, $6,988 in 1992, $7,484 in 1993, $8,467 in 1994, and $10,037 in 1995.[20] The over–$10,000 level was reached again in 1999 and South Korean trade with Asia generally recovered. And Korean trade with the U.S. rose from 2.7 percent to 2.9 percent of the U.S. domestic market, thus adding billions of dollars to South Korean exports.

In view of all these manifest economic difficulties, President Kim Daejung offered a 1997 "economic press conference" to deal with the public concern about the condition of the economy and what to anticipate. The first question from the reporters was, "What warrants your optimism about the prospects for the economy?" Here he cited the restructuring and refinancing of banks as an indication that loans, based on credit worthiness, would soon be operating, leading toward recovery. The IMF program, still being criticized, was actually not so much different than his own, that is, more exports, lower interest rates, fewer imports, and so on, to improve the economy. "It is supportive of our plan to expand the fiscal deficit and money supply. It is demanding that we lower interest rates. The IMF is hoping our economy will recover."[21] He did not convince everyone. The *Chosun Ilbo,* South Korea's largest newspaper, criticized the business and government reforms, for example, as "bogus." Many observers, in fact, saw the reforms as having little substance. This perception continued, for good reason. "Restructuring" actually consisted of having the weaker firms go under and their employees becoming unemployed. Nonetheless, DJ's analysis and action in lowering unemployment through works (like the Inchon International Airport) was a good short-term measure, although, at some juncture, the public deficits would have to be faced.

After the IMF loans, there were many optimists—Korean, American, and at the IMF—who were confident that the Korean economy would bounce right back. And bounce it did, although obviously the deeper problems could not all be addressed in that short a time. This would only have been possible if the cause was simply overextended bank loans; but the crisis was much deeper than that. Faulty analysis resulted in faulty expectations. To understand the full panorama of difficulties the Koreans faced especially, one needs to see how the whole alleged "miracle on the Han" happened, and what the ingredients were that made South Korea's success possible. Establishing South Korea as an export platform in the 1960s required a serendipitous coming together of a number of factors: (1) a global demand for low-priced, high-quality goods that allowed Korea to follow behind Japan in supplying them; (2) a determined leader, President Park Chung-hee, who saw trade at ever-higher levels of technology as the key to Korean wealth and national security; (3) a desire on the part of the U.S. to see Korea succeed—despite its reluctance to have Korea enter into steel and high-tech—as part of its own security alliance against China and the Soviet Union. (The U.S. market access and technology transfer were exchanged for national security.) And (4) the Vietnam war spurred Korean economic growth. A final, more recent reason for Korean economic growth was the country's high expectations due to its participation in globalization.

Today, however, none of original four conditions prevails. China has moved into the niche Korea once held and will continue to move up the technological ladder. China trade will continue to expand in the region and in the world; Korea cannot compete in overall export effectiveness. The Korean leadership today is determined but still undecided about which direction to take in economic policy and is divided on other important issues. President Kim's bold announcement on the fiftieth anniversary of the founding of the South Korean government on August 15, 1998 that "nation building will restart" failed to note whether his then-Prime Minister, Kim Jong-pil, or the labor unions, for example, were on board. There is today considerable ambiguity about how far the U.S. will go to promote economic competitors in Asia. It may well be, as Chalmers Johnson has predicted, that the U.S. trade-off between trade and security in both Japan and Korea may have ended. And a limited war in Asia as an economic stimulus does not seem likely.

Finally, globalization, once considered a potential boost, is instead taking its toll. In 1993, during the early days of Kim Young-sam's administration, it was embraced as a sign of modernity and trade opportunities without carefully weighing the negative possibilities.[22] Thus, Korea joined the Organization of Economic Cooperation and Development (OECD) in December 1996. In retrospect, this seems to have been much too soon and some warning voices (one of them P.M. Kim Jong-pil's) were raised at the time. Once South Korea's domestic market was exposed to the full range of international competition as a result of the World Trade Organization (WTO) and OECD agreements, it immediately went into a trade deficit. The IMF has dramatically corrected that.

The first item, Chinese competition, deserves more attention. In a February 1999 report by the Export-Import Bank of Korea, it was stated that because of high wages and low productivity in South Korea, Korean manufacturers were lagging behind their Chinese counterparts, and that this trend appeared to be widening. Freer trade with China will benefit Korea in the short term, but in the long term it is likely to be disadvantageous to the Korean balance of payments. Fears of Chinese devaluation of the yuan to boost exports had so far not materialized. The strengthening of the Korean won to about 1,200 to the U.S. dollar was considered unfavorable. An OECD report listed China's international trading market share at 1.76 in 1990, surpassing Korea's 1.69 percent. By 1995, China's OECD market share had increased to 3.57, compared to Korea's 1.8. The bank said that "competitive export items of the two countries are no longer limited to light industrial products. They now include heavy and chemical items such as machinery, electric and electronics goods." In past years, China mostly competed in light industrial goods. And Korean market share in the U.S. has continued to slip in the 1990s.[23] For 1999, however, Korea's share of the U.S. domestic market rose from 1.7 to 2.9, reversing the previous trend.

Aside from problems of competition and money, South Korea suffers from a built-in paradox. As it continues to step up a campaign to lure foreign capital, newspaper headlines from time to time remind everyone of the hazard to one's health represented by North Korea. One cannot completely ignore the possibility that the North may attack at any moment. The South uses this scent of danger to ensure American military support and the support of the U.S. Congress for the IMF funds. Money again takes on a security flavor. Korean defense spending has gradually fallen to 3 percent of the GNP, but unless North-South talks produce tangible results, the percentage will need to rise again. This is why Kim Dae-jung has launched his "sunshine policy" toward the North and has issued statements proposing the end of the Cold War in the Korea peninsula.[24] The hope to settle down the tension was at the root of the 1994 Geneva Accords to stop the North Korean nuclear program in exchange for presumably less hazardous light-water reactors.

The unresolved North Korean military problem aside, the conditions that allowed South Korea to make such a spectacular entrance into the international economic scene in the 1960s are no longer present, nor, in my opinion, are they likely to return. The IMF keeps up its self-congratulatory view that South Korea's economy will contract at six percent (in 1998), before turning around in 1999 and resuming "normal growth" by 2000. In an important way, the immediate futures of both the Republic of Korea (ROK) and the IMF are tied up in the apparent success of the efficacy of the IMF loan. The IMF program has drawn mixed reviews. The most criticized point was the excessively high interest rates, which were soon corrected. Some claimed this kind of intervention may have actually made matters worse.[25] Perhaps the IMF and Kim government have unrealistically insisted that the "recovery" happen too soon and without the excruciating pain that the readjustment of the chaebol system will require. Most of the pain to date has fallen on labor.

For example, a *Korea Herald* headline in late March 1999 said "Sluggish Exports Feared to Diffuse Momentum for Economic Recovery." The report was issued by the Korea International Trade Association (KITA). "The real-ity on the export front is in a stark contrast with the statistics the govern-ment recently released to support the optimism about an earlier than anticipated economic recovery, industry analysts say."[26] For the first two months of 1999, exports contracted 7.5 percent and in March, for the first 19 days, there was a further decline of 2.2 percent. Letters of credit (LC) ar-rivals declined 12.7 percent during the first ten days of March. This contin-ues a trend of decline for the past six months. The problem with exports is not Korean production but international demand, which the government and the chaebol regularly discount in their desire to find the silver lining sooner rather than later. From the chaebol perspective, an improvement in exports lessens the demand for "reforms," which they avoid; and from the government's view, if the recession is a self-correcting process through ever-expanding exports, then not to worry.

The need for systemic reform, however, in the view of the free econ-omy advocates, has not in the least slackened, and politics, as I have sug-gested, more and more is revolving around that issue, free economy of the future and the glories of the mercantilism of the past. This dilemma is nowhere more acutely felt than in the automobile industry.

Since the 1970s, Hyundai, the largest automobile producer, and Dae-woo have had a cartel. Then others entered: Kia, Ssangyong, and Samsung. Samsung started producing cars in March 1997, an exquisitely poor touch of market timing. Getting in the way of any rational solution to ease this vast over-capacity problem is the unrelenting intramural competition among the chaebol. Also at issue are the labor unions and a large helping of national pride.

National pride is perhaps the easiest to understand. In the 1960s and 1970s every country in the world wanted to have its own airline, a fad that has now run its course, largely because of the huge losses run up by inef-ficient carriers. Privatization and bankruptcy have taken care of the worse cases. Today, it is evidently considered a sign of economic maturity to have one's own auto factory. It is not enough simply to assemble the cars; one has to make them from scratch if possible. Hyundai has relied heavily on Mitsubishi; Daewoo has had an off-and-on relationship with General Mo-tors; and Ford Motor Company owned 11.9 percent of Kia, now consoli-dated in Hyundai after an auction in October 1998 among Korean firms and Ford. Auto manufacturing is considered to be a pillar of the South Ko-rean economy, earning $10 billion in exports in 1997, about 8 percent of Korea's export total. At 4.1 million capacity, Korea is either fifth or seventh in current rankings in auto production.

The leader of the Korean auto business is Chung Mong-gyu, chairman of Hyundai Motor Company and of the Korean Automobile Manufacturers

Association. In the Association's 1998 handbook, Mr. Chung says: "The growth of the auto industry in Korea also has a significant effect on secondary supporting industries including metals, plastics, machinery, rubber, textiles, electronics, petrochemicals, and many others. Thus, automobile production supports employment in a wide range of sectors throughout the economy, which is a benefit that is generally little noted." The aspirations of the association are worldwide. "We are becoming more active in mergers and acquisitions through which we support jobs and technology introduction all over the globe and we are helping developing countries establish and expand their own auto industry."

The Association was bullish for 1998. If we take the U.S. market as representing 100 percent in terms of cars per capita, then the Korean domestic market currently stands at a quarter of that. To promote further exports, Korean auto workers' wages are pegged at 40 percent of Japan's. (In 1999, Korean auto workers' wages fell from about $11 per hour to $7.) And with the dramatic 40 percent devaluation of the won, that advantage is even greater. The Association also felt it had a competitive advantage over China and Southeast Asia in terms of manufacturing facilities.

Yet the Kia bankruptcy in July 1997 exposed the more fundamental problem for Korea in the auto business. Korea had held onto fifth place worldwide for car production in the mid-90s. In 1998, car production was 2.1 million units, down 25.5 percent from 1997. In 1999, sales were projected at 2.25 million units, with exports at 1.4 million. (This compares to the U.S. as number one with about 11.1 million vehicles produced and Japan at around 10 million.)[27] Korean auto sales, despite the Daewoo Motor bankruptcy, or perhaps because of it, have improved in terms of price and reliability.

One of the obsessions of the Korean auto makers, leading to their colossal over-capacity, has been with the U.S. market. The first entrant was Hyundai in 1986, hoping at that late date to duplicate Japan's earlier success. The entry was ambitious—some said arrogant—and resulted in first-year sales of 168,882 units. In 1988 sales reached a high of 264,282 units, but they tumbled to 107,378 in 1995. The reasons for the decline were increased competition and "rock-bottom satisfaction ratings."[28]

Despite this Korean experience, Kia in February 1996 decided to have a gala launch. Both Daewoo and Samsung were also contemplating entering the U.S. market. This raised the question of why these Korean firms were so eager to sell in the U.S. The answer, the article suggested, had less to do with sales figures than with national pride. An American Hyundai executive commented: "It's the prestige of the American market. Everyone wants to be here. It's the toughest market in the world, and the perception is that if you're not here, you're not a player."

The article concluded that if the predictions of the Korea Development Bank were fulfilled by 2005 Korea would be the world's fourth-largest car-maker, behind the U.S., Japan, and Germany.[29] This will be delayed, as internal consolidation continues. To summarize, in 1998 Korea's new vehicle sales plunged to 570,000, then rose to 1.3 million in 1999, compared to 1.15 in 1997. Sales of foreign cars to this free-trading country follow their historic pattern, with WTO and OECD rules in place. A spokesman for the Korea Automobile Manufacturers said in regard to foreign car sales that for a company to break even, it would have to sell 1,000 units. BMW leads in sales with 885 units. But the good news is that foreign car sales in Korea jumped some 16 percent in 1999 since that down-time.[30]

Kia's bankruptcy in July of 1997 put a temporary kink in these ambitions. After Kim Dae-jung came to power in February 1998, the government decided to auction off the Kia company as the first step in rationalizing the Korean auto industry. So Kia was placed up for bids. In the first round, the bidders were Hyundai, Samsung, and Daewoo among the Koreans (Ssangyong having earlier been absorbed by Daewoo), plus GM and Ford. GM finally backed out, finding no fit, while the remaining bidders made their offers contingent on the forgiveness of as much debt as possible. Kia's debt was estimated at $11 to $12 billion (one notes that Japan's Nissan Motors had a debt of around $36 billion when Renault of France in March 1999 bought 35 percent). Also, in May 1998 the Daimler-Chrysler merger occurred, indicating the international consolidation of the car industry. Because of the demand for debt forgiveness, the first round was cancelled and then the second round in September also failed for the same reason. Ford threatened to back out altogether, saying that its pursuit of Kia made little sense in view of the unreasonable amount of debt. Ford may also have been adversely affected by a review in the *New York Times* Automobile section of September 6, 1998, where a new Kia model, the Sportage, was panned. The headline said "99 Kia Sportage Not Ready for Prime Time," and the conclusion was no better: "The primary appeal of the Sportage convertible is its devil-may-care looks, off-road capacity, and low price of $13,995. But the sacrifices in terms of ride, handling and fit and finish, are considerable." Since then, Kia's reputation in the U.S. has been on the rise.

A third round of bidding, including the three Korean companies and Ford, ended on October 19, 1998, with Hyundai the winner. This "purchase" produced no new external infusion of funds and no access to new technology that Ford would have provided. It was widely assumed that nationalism was the key ingredient in awarding Kia to Hyundai. Ironically, this maneuver assured Hyundai the top chaebol ranking in 1998 because of the unique calculation method of the government, adding both assets and debt as the measure of the chaebol rankings

The state of the Korean economy in 1999, after two years of Kim Dae-jung's administration, is in my view still improving, but vulnerable, like everyone else, to economic setbacks most anywhere. Unemployment is down to 5 percent from 10 percent. For the wealthy, this was the best of times, in terms of the recovery of the stock market from a low of about 285 points in December 1997 on the stock index to over 700 by mid-1999 and over 1,000 by the end of December. This may suggest a detachment of the market from the economy. Kim Dae-jung was given high marks for the stock market performance in terms of rallying investor confidence in Korea, as well as reviving international confidence in credit worthiness.[31] The Korean economic scene is filled with contradictions and those in the stock market who bet on an optimistic scenario in 1998 were among the international winners. Yet there is a lingering suspicion that all is not well and that the international investment confidence has been hyped by a combination of government statistics and the exuberance of the IMF. Clearly, the success of both entities is dependent in the short term on the sweet smell of success. By November 2000, the stock market had settled in the mid-500s.

Having come through the 1997 storm and the 1998 regrouping, the stage was set for gains in the economy for 1999, a year ahead of the anticipated recovery. How can this happen? Suspicions have been raised because such items as earning reports, dividend payments, and actual chaebol reform are lacking in the avalanche of government and IMF statistics. For example, at the end of March 1999, the KITA had some disturbing statistics going counter to the official line. Exports had contracted 7.5 percent in the first two months. Shipments abroad rose 3.1 percent in January, but then experienced a double-digit decline in February and dropped another 3 percent in March. For the first 19 days in February, exports were off 2.2 percent. And LC arrivals were down 12.7 percent in the first 10 days of March year-on-year. "The reality on the export front is in stark contrast with the statistics the government recently released to support its optimism about an earlier-than-anticipated economic recovery."[32] Business leaders were calling for a further devaluation of the Korean won, although such a measure might prick the stock market bubble.

There were additional ominous figures. Since June 1998, Korean exports to China were down 10 percent. Other exports to Asia were down 40 percent. Rising oil prices were also cited as deterrents to realizing a

$25 billion 1999 trade surplus. The decline in DRAM (dynamic random access memory) prices from $14 to $9 (which represent 60 percent of Korea's semiconductor exports) was also noted. The decline in steel shipments and stiffer enforcement by foreign countries of import regulations also was not helpful.

On April 4, 1999, a senior economist at the Daewoo Economic Research Institute warned that government statistics on an upturn could be misleading. The Korean Institute for International Economics and Trade said that the Korean economy would grow 3.6 percent in 1999 and 5.1 percent in 2000. Not to be outdone, the Bank of Korea governor is on record with a prediction of 3.8 percent growth in 1999.[33] By the end of 1999, these rosy export predictions had indeed come to pass.

Yet no sooner does one digest the idea that the auto industry is in serious trouble, with low domestic sales, huge over-capacity, and fierce international competition, than a glowing report arrives: "Industry sources" predict an export surge in Korean cars this year to two million. Further, this surge includes a change from small cars to larger cars, which are more profitable. There is the usual inflation of percentages because of low numbers: The Kia (now part of Hyundai) Credos enjoyed a 47 percent increase, shipping 3,286. More significant, however, is the growing acceptance of Hyundai's 1999 Sonata. Both the *New York Times* and *USA Today* praised this car. *USA Today* said it was a delightful surprise and "if you couldn't read the badges, you'd swear the Sonata was a premium Japanese car."[34] If this is the beginning of a real trend, this development is highly significant.

In the statistics cited from the official March 1999 data, one comes across mostly encouraging results. The real GDP growth through the third quarter of 1998 was down 6.8 percent, but as we have seen, the Bank of Korea is now optimistic. Industrial production is rising into the 70 percent area; the won-dollar exchange rate continues to weaken and remains around 1,290 to the dollar. The corporate bond yield is around 8 percent. Foreign debt stabilized for some months at around 120 billion. Foreign exchange reserves were around $50 billion. And so on. Public work projects may help to stabilize unemployment, but still raises the prospect of longer-term inflation.

To try to keep the domestic peace, the government has established a commission composed of the government, business, and labor. (If this resonates with the old fascist corporate state, the idea is correct. But the spirit of genuine cooperation is different.) The weak link here is the labor unions, both the Federation of Korean Trade Unions (FKTU) and the Korean Confederation of Trade Unions (KCTU), whose membership is largely concentrated in the heavy industries, plus financial services and teachers. This situation is typical of an IMF bail-out program, with the burden of financial pain largely borne by the working element of society.[35] The chaebol debts were paid off by the public, which has left the traditional industries in a stronger position than ever. There is considerable irony here, as President Kim Dae-jung has lectured from the day he took office on the need for chaebol reform, the "big deals" to rationalize (if not cartelize) all the industries, shed unprofitable businesses, sell marginal activities, and reduce the debt-to-equity ratio of the core business. This is truly a critical matter. Not only has almost none of these things happened, but the chaebol have basically continued on their own ways and have increased their strength in the economy under the blizzard of contrary exhortations.

Complaints about the chaebol and the family monopolization of the lucrative part of the Korean economy have been commonplace over the years, but never more strident than during the first year of the DJ administration. A good example of these complaints has been summarized in a newspaper editorial:

> More than a year has passed [since the demand for reforms began] and the outcome has been disappointing, to say the least. According to figures released by the Fair Trade Commission this week, the average debt ratio of Korea's top five conglomerates did fall considerably, from 472.9 percent in late 1997 to 335.0 percent late in 1998, but their total debt amount increased by as much as 5.9 percent from 221 trillion won to 234 trillion won. And all of the big five (Hyundai, Daewoo, Samsung, LG and SK) in the new order of scale had their total "assets," which includes debts under today's quaint bookkeeping, grow conspicuously. Most prominently, Hyundai's total assets jumped from 61.7 trillion won to 72.5 trillion won. The number of affiliates remains about the same.[36]

Upon receiving this report on April 6, President Kim "vented his displeasure" and repeated his call for restructuring to force the conglomerates to become "internationally competitive." Yet, according to the official figures, business is getting better again and the old system, long admired, is still functioning. The chaebol are being refinanced by the IMF loan at the expense of the Korean public and the treasuries of participating nations. What's to worry? The editorial also explains the chaebol view:

> They argue that their increased assets and debts resulted from their acquisition of debt-ridden firms as guided by the government under the big deals program. Hyundai took over Kia Motors and Daewoo, which absorbed Ssangyong Motors (no money changed hands; Daewoo assumed some debt). In April 1999 Daewoo was in the process of acquiring Samsung's auto

division, in exchange for an electronics unit, one of the few "big deals," but one that did nothing for either company. On the other hand, they say it is difficult to dispose of their oversized subsidiaries which have so far attracted little interest from potential buyers. They also cite labor resistance as the major hurdle to realizing comprehensive restructuring. Yet, their rationalizations can be countered with examples of some second-ranked conglomerates which substantially reduced their debts by selling their most lucrative subsidiaries and major assets.

The conclusion to the editorial is a familiar complaint:

> When will our chaebol learn that they can no longer dwell on the myth that mammoth vessels are unsinkable? Their mistaken investments with borrowed money precipitated the economic crisis, caused two million Koreans to lose their jobs, and contributed to a general sense of angst that continues to pervade society. The latest figures from the FTC compels us to doubt not only the sincerity of the conglomerates toward restructuring hut the resolve and competence of the present government in pushing through its reform tasks.

One scar left on the society by the economic crisis is the way that the population sees itself in terms of socio-economic status. In a poll of 993 married men and women conducted by the Hyundai Research Institute, about one third of the 61.1 percent who formerly called themselves "middle class" now identify themselves as lower class. Further, 79.2 percent of those who have fallen believe it will require three years to return to the middle class. Some believe it will be five years. The researcher concluded: "The rapid dismantling of the middle class will pose a serious threat to a sustained economic rebound."[37] And economic evidence favors the rich— 20 major luxury items were up 38.2 percent in January 1999 (month-to-month). "Sales of inexpensive consumer goods, meanwhile, remained sluggish," the Korean Customs Service said.[38]

This argument on politics and the economy has now run full circle. The economic restructuring debate is between the conservative mercantilists and the free traders. Our efforts to discuss politics separately from economics have been only partially successful; it will be necessary to place the two categories back together as we encounter again a classical Toynbeean dilemma. The miracle economy is undergoing a metamorphosis and the old question arises: How can an economy like this work?

By April 1999, the IMF had lost its upbeat mood. John Dodsworth, the IMF's senior Seoul representative, spoke before a meeting of foreign diplomats in Seoul. He said that the Korean economy would "have a difficult time next year." This was because of Seoul's anticipated deficit: "Korea's Fiscal deficit is expected to top 5.5 percent of gross domestic product

(GDP), which is very huge." Also, many structural reforms remain ahead: "It is naive to think that one can tackle these problems in two or three years."[39]

This issue will be considered in the concluding chapter, after dealing with the perennial problem of North Korea, which continues to permeate the South Korean political and economic scene, even more since active measures aimed at eventual reunification are now actually underway. In the meantime, the bumblebee is flying from flower to flower, dining on honey and pollinating for the future. Yet Korea is in a quandary: Its small economy is highly dependent on international trade, over which it has little control. In the meantime, George Soros, the world-class financier, said on April 14, 1999, as reported in the *New York Times,* that the currency crisis in Asia was over. That observation is correct. But what about the chaebol and the domestic restructuring problem?

On balance, after a hectic two years of pell-mell economic regrouping, the shimbaram approach—"let's get on with it"—once again saved the Koreas. The bumblebee went every which way, but in the end prevailed, taking the right course. One image particularly comes to mind. At the height of discouragement, a number of Southeast Asian countries saw long lines of people trying to get their money out of the banks. In South Korea, the contrary scene was long lines of women at the banks handing over gold jewelry, well over one billion dollars worth, to bolster the government's sagging reserves. This is a hidden Korean asset that does not show up on the balance sheet.

"Asian Markets ending 1999 on Steep Internet Ascent. Korea a Leader in Financial Crisis Recovery," said the *New York Times* on December 20, 1999. Economic forecasting of any validity is a notoriously scarce product. Coming to grips with the chaebol is certainly a flight in the right direction. The new emerging system will be judged by the crucible of history.

In the meantime, however, the old problem of excessive chaebol public and private debt continues. In 1999, in the biggest business story of the year, Daewoo went bankrupt (except for Daewoo Motors, which failed in November 2000). Under the leadership of the Kim family, Daewoo lost about $1.5 billion per year, going under at around the $60 billion level. Hyundai under the Chung family has done no better. The government, always the actor of last resort, desperately needs more money. It is a tough political issue, because the approval of a debt issue will require the approval of the National Assembly. But this must be done. According to the *Korea Herald* of August 23, 2000, about 100 billion won (or about 90 billion U.S. dollars) has been spent by the government to take over various financial institutions and businesses, making the free market government the largest owner in Korea. True, it will recoup some of this on future sales; but there is in fact no other way to deal with this endemic debt problem. Notably needed is a major foreign alliance for the car industry, but nationalism so far has stood in the way of such a solution. Solving the auto manufacturing problem is, in my view, the current critical issue. By mid-November 2000, the Korean stock market stood around 550, down about 50 percent on the year.

And Korea's export dependence on the American market will soon be tested, if the American economy actually heads for a recession in 2001. Korea is the third largest exporter to the U.S., accounting for almost one-third of its exports. A general slow down in Asian commerce also may occur, revealing the underside of globalization.

But despite all of this, the bumblebee flies on.

8

Democratic Politics and Korean Traditions

Looking at Korean politics in the context of the twentieth century, the first 50 years were dedicated to establishing Korean autonomy. This meant shaking off foreign rule. The 1945 success was soon eclipsed by the Cold War involvement of the superpowers. This froze the politics of the North into the old Stalinist mode; so only in the South was there the opportunity to experiment in traditional political development. In the struggle for political power, democracy was in a distant second place—for about four decades. A democratic historicism was not at work. As Victor D. Cha has put it, "In the past, the South Korean state generally has dictated to, not interacted with, civil society."[1] With the Korean election law revision, South Korean politics is truly opening up.

The tension between democratic politics and the politics of the past has created considerable misunderstanding of the nature and direction of Korean democracy by Americans and a conflict between well-established traditions and modern expectations on the part of South Koreans. (The totalitarian system established in the North in 1945 so far has had no challenges.) Since the conclusion of World War II, South Korea has gone through a series of political stages, all aimed at the dream of the (mainly American and Korean) political scientists for the "consolidation of democracy." This continuum divides into the nationalism of Syngman Rhee (1945–60); the ephemeral bubble of Chang Myon (1960–61); the garrison developmental state of Park Chung-hee (1961–79); the authoritarian regime of Chun Doo-hwan (1980–87); and then the transitional reign of Roh Tae-woo (1988–93); into the democratic term of Kim Young-sam (1993–98). South Korea has now reached the level of Kim Dae-jung's Korean democracy—"democracy" and "free markets"—which is to establish South Korea as a modern state. It is also the basis for the "new Korea," that is, the centerpiece of the drive for political reform. It is an effort to create a unique Korean society. In his new millennium speech, President Kim Dae-jung said that South Korea "without fail" will be among the top ten knowledge and information powers, and will be prepared to become an "electronic democracy."[2]

Some observers, both foreign and Korean, believe that to understand Korean politics, it is necessary to recall the imperial political past simply to draw the base line on where things were in 1910; and then, secondly, to see if any changes from that time indicate the introduction of new forces, or if today is simply a continuation of yesterday. The "consolidation of democracy," a political science catchphrase, is today's political prize, an indication of modernity.[3] Both the government and the opposition wish to capture this forward-looking slogan and then fill it with their own content. Here there may be evidence that the Korean politics of the next century will bring competing issues as well as competing personalities.

The legacy of the Yi Dynasty has placed a powerful imprint on the politics of this century, even though it publicly does not receive much attention.[4] No one wanted to try to revive the dynasty, yet the KPG during and after World War II claimed its legitimacy in part as the successor government of the Yi. The KPG's other claim was its resistance to the Japanese; generally, in the lull that followed the return of freedom on August 15, 1945, the population awaited expectantly the arrival of the KPG, led by Kim Ku, as their legitimate leaders.

But this was not to be. The 1945 Sian incident in August, related earlier, involving Major General William Donovan and Kim Ku and President Truman, got two birds with one stone—the OSS and the KPG. This provided an opportunity, as such turns of events always do, for someone else, in this case Syngman Rhee. At this moment in history, his lobbying work in Washington, D.C., and his Princeton Ph.D. paid off. He was a fervent anti-Communist at the right moment. After a staged interagency meeting in Washington arranged by the former OSS Deputy Chief, Colonel Preston Goodfellow, Rhee was sent off to Tokyo as the American favorite; General MacArthur provided his personal plane for the short flight to Seoul. Rhee's arrival on October 20, followed by a tumultuous reception by Seoul's citizens in front of the downtown Chosun Hotel (still flourishing), placed Rhee in the frontrunner's seat. He never relinquished this lead. Kim Ku and his group arrived from China the following month, but as individuals and not as the KPG. Rhee and Kim Ku began an uneasy alliance, with Kim Ku gradually sliding from power and toward his destiny of falling to an assassin in 1949. General Yi Pom-suk, although a long-time aide to Kim Ku, managed to find his way into Rhee's favor for several years (becoming the first Prime Minister).

After having had such a long period of denying recognition to the KPG on the grounds that it might not be representative of the people, the U.S. Department of State and the American military occupation both welcomed the old fiery anti-Japanese leader and embraced him. Considering how things appeared to the occupation commander, Lieutenant General John Hodge, the Rhee arrival was a blessing. As we have seen, the 45 years of Japanese colonialism were inimitable to the development of indigenous political organizations and any attempt by Koreans to exercise political power. The more ambitious, adapting to the situation that was not one of their choice, tried to get ahead in the Japanese system and became collaborators. These were the people who had some notion of how to exercise authority primarily through the economic system. The Japanese taint prevented this whole class of potential leaders from stepping forward as legitimate claimants to the very top positions. Some of the leading collaborators, like the Koch'ang Kims, were active in politics and succeeded in playing important second-tier roles.

With the announcement of Japan's surrender, the Japanese first looked around to see what they could do to guarantee the security of the Japanese occupation forces and the myriad of civilians in government and commerce. They had every reason to fear a bloody retaliation from the over 20 million Korean people they had dominated and humiliated. But the Koreans they approached to take over on an interim basis prior to the arrival of the Americans in mid-September demurred. This was not so much because of modesty but because of the opprobrium they knew they would receive from their fellow Koreans. The Japanese search was further confused by the initial information that the U.S. would only occupy areas around Pusan and that the Soviets would incorporate Seoul in their domain. Perhaps this rumor inspired the activities of Yo Un-hyong to rise to leadership and create the left-leaning Korean People's Republic, which was declared on September 6. The choice of name proved to be devastating. The Americans, after all, were to occupy the peninsula south of the 38th parallel. When Lieutenant General John Hodge received the first delegation of Koreans at Inchon on September 18 on his ship, he and his aides were taken aback. They did not wish to have anything to do with possible Communists. The People's Republic was short-lived in the South; and it fared little better in the North, against the real thing. Thus the indigenous political scene was essentially de novo.

Having eliminated what indigenous political resources were at hand, and seeing the Japanese dismantling their structure at the greatest possible speed, Hodge was left to make do with what was available to create a military government. Not surprisingly, the occupation turned to the police force and promoted the Koreans in the force to the senior positions.

This police apparatus soon became the only indigenous cohesive power the occupation could rely on, while it ineffectively looked around to find Korean groups and institutions that might be the beginning of the desired democratic society. Until the end of the year, the U.S. military occupation tried to create some semblance of order, but this was hard going. Food had to be brought into the truncated economy, the industrial North and the agricultural South. Both had difficulty standing alone. Only Soviet aid to the North and American aid to the South kept the economy above water.

Against this on-the-ground reality, the U.S. and its allies and the Soviet Union tried to decide the future of Korea. FDR had promoted the idea of a trusteeship of five years. This was in line with his views on the subject of how to bring colonial areas into the framework of independent states. This position was supported by the Soviet Union and North Korea, but with a different expectation: The trusteeship formula would allow the North to take over the South. In the South, the opponents of trusteeship were the conservatives, including Rhee and Kim Ku, who wanted to unify all of Korea under their terms. The Moscow conference in December 1945 showed the different expectations for trusteeship, and that approach was abandoned in favor of UN–supervised elections. By then it was clear that political events were taking different courses in the North and South. And finally the Department of State issued a policy statement for the U.S. military government to set up an interim government that would be prepared to bring stability and economic progress to the South. The prospect for the division of the country on a long-term basis was altogether too clear.

In the North, the Soviet Union decided to back a well-known guerrilla leader, Kim Il-sung, who had a record of fighting the Japanese, primarily in Manchuria from the Siberia sanctuary. The Korean Workers' Party was modeled on Lenin-Stalinist principles. Koreans of bourgeois background, Japanese collaboration, or religiously oriented were not wanted and had the choice of being purged or moving South.[5] Yoo Chang-soon (later the first prime minister under Chun Doo-hwan) decided in November 1945 that he should leave Pyongyang. He had been an official in the Chosen Bank (the Japanese bank of Korea). On his departure, his mother insisted that he take some money she had saved. "She gave me 3,000 yen. At that time you could buy a small house for about 300 yen. Finally, I accepted the money. I regret that I did that. I have often told that story to my children and still regret that I accepted that money."[6]

In preparation for the UN–supervised elections, the U.S. military government opened the way for the organization of political parties; over 100 were registered. And here the anomaly of the Cold War hit home. None of those parties in the South understandably represented a left-leaning view, and in the North, the Communists as the Korean Workers' Party mo-nopolized the political scene. So democracy as seen in the textbooks was denied in both parts of the divided land. Political competition in the South could not center on traditional left-right issues. Rather, personalities es-pousing anti-communism were de rigueur. This produced a truncated non-issue oriented politics.

Until the election of Kim Dae-jung in December 1997, there was a pe-culiar sterility in South Korean politics that was like a chess game in the Sunday paper, each side using the same designated moves. There were no surprises. There were two political parties (with some fragmentation based on individual feudal personalities). There was the ruling party, which was initially called the Liberal Party, and there was the opposing Democratic Party. (The "Liberal Party" was patterned on the Japanese Liberal Democ-ratic Party, with the hope that it could also monopolize power, which it did until December 1997. Like the Japanese, "liberal" indicates "conservative"; additional adjectives, such as "justice" or even "democratic" usually simply indicate a deeper hue of conservatism.) The objective was to obtain, exer-cise, and retain political power. Henderson described this as "the politics of the vortex." By this he meant that typical second-tier Korean politicians as-pired to the National Assembly, the putative legislative branch, not so much to exercise power there but to be in a position to influence the bureaucracy in such matters as obtaining funds and favors. They wanted access to the ex-ecutive power, which was the only power that mattered. The presidential competitors all focused on the main chance. Alternate sources of political power, in fact, still are scarce in South Korea, but that may be slowly chang-ing. In the 1960s, Henderson saw a mass society that was simply manipu-lated by the top leadership. Members of this society who wished to participate in power did so by entering the updraft of the vortex, seeking access. This was the only way to power, prior to the military dictatorships from 1961 through 1987.[7] Henderson states, "The chief base for party for-mation has been initiative from above. The result of the chief executive's or his associates' interest is the placing of some feasible limit on the unusually broad and intensive competition for position that besets Korean politics or in accomplishing some high policy objectives."

Part of this antidemocratic tradition stems from the Constitution, which requires any political aspiration to be exercised through political parties, not mass movements, interest groups, or other vehicles of political potential. In 1948, over 100 so-called political parties were formed, around personalities and a chiliastic motif. Beyond the dictator/authoritarian mil-itary commanders, the three main traditional politicians were the "Three Kims." These leaders depended on regional support—Kim Dae-jung from the southwestern provinces, Kim Young-sam from the Pusan area, and Kim

Jong-pil from south central provinces. Clearly, under this arrangement, no-body had a majority and the three Kims struggled to beat the dictators by clever manipulations and alliances. Two of the three Kims became presi-dent through such maneuvers; only Kim Jong-pil has not made it. He has been prime minister twice, once under Park Chung-hee and then under Kim Dae-jung for forging the alliance between his own party, the United Liberal Democratic Party (ULD) and the National Coalition of New Pol-itics, DJ's party (now the Millennium Democratic Party). Whether there is enough strength left in such mergers to allow him to seize the mantle in 2002 in face of changes in the election system in 2000, allowing the par-ticipation of groups other than political parties per se, remains an open question. The three Kims' historical importance through three decades is not, however, in question.

The vortex idea demonstrated the lack of grass-roots political institu-tions that, in the United States, for example, provide the road to special in-terest power in politics through the organization of like-minded individuals on particular matters. Alexis de Tocqueville made his trip through America in 1831–32 and produced his classic *Democracy in America* in 1835. He was much impressed by these civic voluntary associations at every social level that gave Americans access to participation in the society and by definition, a role in politics.[8] Stemming from these kinds of observations, a whole band of authors in the U.S. and the West in general have theorized on how democracy starts, how it is augmented, and how the "habits of the heart" in Tocqueville's phrase, become embedded in society. In this typology, the U.S. is, of course, the primeval democracy and others who wish to be democra-tic would do well to follow this model. Such is the folklore.

Samuel P. Huntington, in his book *The Third Wave: Democratization in the Late Twentieth Century,*[9] categorizes the conditions making for democracy and how various countries have progressed in the democratic direction. Some writers have seized on these trends to see democracy rising every-where, especially since the demise of the Soviet Union in 1989. Foremost among this literature is Francis Fukuyama's *The End of History and the Last Man.*[10] The South Koreans themselves seem to have an inexhaustible in-terest in the subject of democracy. It was the theme of the February 1999 celebration in Seoul of the President's first year in office, for example. "New Korea's" democracy is based on democracy itself and "free markets."

The problem in the first instance with the flowering of democracy in South Korea, however, is coming to grips with the Korean political past. There is no question that a South Korean living in Seoul toward the end of the twentieth century is a person not altogether comfortable with himself. Or such is the opinion of the well-known Korea scholar, Hahm Jai-bong, professor of political science and international relations at Yonsei University.

Hahm believes that Koreans, "despite expressing (and thinking) liberal democracy as their governing political ideology, are actually behaving under the Confucian influence of the past. In other words, they unconsciously choose to be Confucian, while consciously stating liberal democracy as their political ideology. Confucian in the private arena; while liberal democratic in the political."[11] One way to solve this problem of the psyche might be to restudy and reconstruct the experience and governing philosophy of the Yi Dynasty (1392–1910), somehow blending the Korean governance style into the modern age. Yet, to put it that way seems to spell out the overwhelming difficulty of such an application. There nonetheless remains much to review in that somewhat neglected experience from 1392 to 1910.[12]

The advance of democracy since 1948 has up to now been uneven at best. The lip service often given to the idea of democracy was to appear modern on the one hand and to honor the Confucian tradition on the other. This created a double crisis in legitimacy from 1961 through 1997. Military government was clearly an inferior model. Yet, with the overthrow of the old nationalist Syngman Rhee and the ascension of Chang Myon and the first attempt at real democracy in government, clearly the time was not ripe for textbook Western government. Chang Myon lasted just a year before Park's coup on May 16, 1961.[13] A weak indecisive leader was not the answer to the continuing military threat from the North and the endemic and permanent dangers to the South of poverty and indifferent economic growth. The dictatorial development state after the Japanese model that was beginning to astound the world was the obvious answer, and Park Chung-hee (nowadays hailed as the "economic president") was the personality to articulate it. One of Park's political advisors, the late Lew Hyuck-in, described the early '70s: "The slogan was annual personal income of $1,000. Considering that per capita income was less than $100 in 1961, this seemed impossible. There were banners on the buildings of Seoul setting that goal. And we actually achieved it in 1975."[14] Like Kim Jun-yop, average Koreans all understood the relationship between wealth and political progress.

Because of this, Park tried to monopolize political power through his *Yushin* (reform) movement. But the opposition to dictatorial rule continued. Kim Dae-jung, in his first presidential run in 1972, gathered over 40 percent of the vote. Park thereupon redoubled his efforts to hold power through a constitutional amendment to allow him to be president for life. The development state's ability not only to promote losers and winners in an investment sense, but to determine who those specific individuals would be, forged the steel bonds that united the ambitions of the governing bureaucrats with the chaebol leaders and the politicians. When a later president, Roh Tae-woo, was accused of having taken up to $700 million in favors and bribes during his five-year term (1987–92), some of his supporters considered it a sign of strength in the Korean economy.[15]

The economic growth, however, did begin to create the conditions that allowed for democracy, made it possible for democracy to work, if that was desired. When the choice for democracy was made in the Chang Myon moment, objective conditions in economics and security were not sufficiently strong to allow it to survive.[16] This factor, as well as the Yi Dynasty traditions, were the basis for Henderson's vortex thesis. His grasp of the particular character of Korean political power in the context he witnessed showed just how alien the idea of democracy was to the Korean man in the street.

The principle cause of this particular domestic power alignment, like moths fluttering around a single street light, was the absence of economic development. This was the feeling of President Park, seeing first-hand from the Japanese experience at home and in Manchuria (where he was an officer in the Kwangtung army) that heavy industry was the key to South Korea's future. He instituted five-year plan after five-year plan worthy of Stalin, contrary to the advice of many of his U.S. Agency for International Development advisers. At that time, in retrospect, the process for Korean success was a four-stage one, with stability as the necessary first building block. Then followed destabilizing economic development (but with the Schumpeterian risk—that is, the "creative destruction" of capitalism), then popular participation, concluding with aspirations for just goals for the society. This general model has been particularly successful in Asia, when we consider both South Korea and Taiwan, although there are many differences as well as similarities.[17] China, as well, has made great economic advances once it decided, as Teng Hsiao-ping suggested, that the color of the cat is not as important as whether it can catch mice. What is particularly important at this juncture is whether all of these economies in this interdependent trading system can succeed. And issues of fairness and distributive justice arise, as well. There is fierce competition, but all must succeed to a certain extent or the whole system will fail, as demonstrated by the Asian "economic crisis." While politics ideally should do well on its own merits (honest and inspiring), economic success, whether in the U.S. or South Korea, still looms large in politics.

Keeping in mind Schumpeter's "creative destruction" inherent in capitalism, encouraging economic development is a bold step for leaders with a totalitarian bent. Once those forces are unleashed, there are a series of consequences that are likely to occur that may not have been on the authoritarian agenda. As the decades passed in Seoul under Park, this became self-evident.

What are the uncontrollable results of economic development? By that I mean consequences that can only be modified or reversed by unacceptably high costs and problems, making the whole road to progress impassable. Change is the obvious first mover, and with change, the social order is shaken and the old ways of doing things must take on new ways.[18]

In fact, in regard to social change, one of the reasons for the slow development of China's economy over the centuries has been the unwillingness of Chinese leaders, either emperors or warlords or commissars, to risk "chaos" by risking change. The Chinese in the imperial days tended to prefer the status quo to innovation, thereby not making use of their own inventions. Examples are gunpowder and navigational instruments.[19] Park and his team took the other approach, the pell-mell shimbaram tactic. He was aided in this by a unique sense of circumstances. The war in Vietnam boosted the demand for many Korean goods (as the Korean war had for Japan) and the U.S. was also in a munificent mood in the peak Cold War years, ready to exchange U.S. markets for Korean goods for its worldwide security concerns.

After almost 20 years in power, President Park was assassinated by his intelligence chief, who was about to be dismissed, according to Park's former information minister, Kim Seong-jin.[20] The program stalled in 1979. Economic discontentment paved the way for another military coup by another general, Chun Doo-hwan, in a two-stage succession to full power. Some of the excessive investment in heavy industry was gradually but only partially corrected in the following years. The second stage of Chun's rise to power was in the spring through the ugly Kwangju incident, when paratroopers put down citizens protesting against the military rule. The current President, Kim Dae-jung, was blamed by General Chun for involvement in the incident and sentenced to death; Kim Dae-jung was finally released and pardoned and now holds supreme power, an incredible turn in Korean history. This bloody incident is memorialized now by Koreans, although final guilt and blame remain a matter of controversy.

Because of Kwangju, the crown of authority sat uneasily on Chun's brow as he struggled during his term to establish public legitimacy. He was somewhat immobilized by his early declaration that he would not seek another term, contrary to his predecessor. (In another twist in this saga, in 1996 under President Kim Young-sam, Chun was sentenced to death for sedition over the Kwangju incident; this was commuted in the final days of the Kim Young-sam regime in January 1998.)

By 1981, however, President Chun had things going his way in the economy. South Korea was able to move increasingly into niches left behind by Japan's increasing level of technology and before China became a serious and successful competitor. It is a conceit of classical economists that such obvious competition for South Korea as China is not important to the success or failure of Korean balance of payments every year. If China undercuts Korea, Korea can find other markets, say Luxembourg, to make up for this deficiency. The actual facts of such competition do not bear this out, but this in no way daunts the classical economists.

This raises questions about the role of the economy and the pace of democratization. For many Korean scholars there is a direct link.[21] In Professor Hyun Baeg-im's analysis, the economy is the single most important condition for the awaited "democratic consolidation."[22] Here he also cites the Seymour Martin Lipset thesis that the more wealthy a country, the more likely it is that it will remain a democracy. Yet, under Chun, while the economy flourished, so did authoritarianism. This tension resulted, however, in growing expectations for democratic input; one result of economic growth and the better education that accompanies it is first the expectation and then the demand for popular participation in government.

Here the dilemma was expressed in the anomalous position of the National Assembly. Half of the members are elected and the other half chosen by the parties on the proportional representation system. The institution itself has little power in the governmental process; legislation is handed down to it, rather than the other way around. Still, it can exercise a negative role, refusing to approve the budget or the appointment of the Prime Minister. But the ruling party usually can put together a majority by defections or coalition. The Henderson vortex principle prevails. Such tactics seem to be the current norm. This is the result of multiple candidates in presidential elections, denying the winner a majority. This has been true for the last three elections. The National Assembly reflects these divisions and has no opportunity to operate as a coequal member of the government any more than the judiciary. A more stable and useful system awaits a fuller development of the political parties.

Does this mean that politics may assume a more autonomous role than it has so far? Well into the Chun Fifth Republic, political legitimacy was equated with economic growth figures. An 8 or 9 percent growth rate was the equivalent of the Good Housekeeping Seal of Approval. (Paul Krugman was among the first to note that this "high growth" phenomenon was the result of huge inputs, greater than the comparative outputs, which helped set the scene for the 1997 financial crisis.)[23] On other grounds, another who noticed the changing character of Korean politics was Hyun Hong-choo, in 1987 Roh Tae-woo's campaign manager (later he was ambassador to the UN, Washington, D.C., and now he is a partner in the prestigious law firm of Kim and Chang). Our conversation occurred a day or two after the June 29 announcement of presidential candidate Roh Tae-woo that he favored the direct election of the president. Direct election of the president was one of the central issues leading to riots in the streets all over Korea. This Roh concession brought an end to these disturbances. A few days later the president, Chun Doo-hwan, endorsed Roh's position. In a three-way election, Kim Young-sam and Kim Dae-jung each collected about 26 percent. Roh won with 36 percent. This turned out to be a valuable lesson to both Kims, who later were elected president each in his own right. (There is still some argument over whether Roh or Chun was the originator of this popular concession. According to Don Oberdorfer's book, *The Two Koreas,* Lee Soon-ja, Chun's wife, credits this decision to Chun.)[24]

Hyun made the point that the time had come in Korea when there was finally the opportunity to make a clear separation between economics and politics. "No longer can we say that politics simply reflects economics. Our politics now have to stand on their own merits." In an elaboration on this, Hyun said, "What sets the leadership of the Fifth Republic (Chun's administration) apart from the earlier ones is its realization that economic progress is no longer a sufficient condition for legitimacy. Surely, it is a necessary condition, the absence of which will rock the very foundation of the country. The result of high economic development was the decoupling of politics from economics. Political legitimacy has to be established on its own merits."[25] In other words, political legitimacy would no longer flow from the hull of a container ship. This was all of a piece with the conference the Carnegie Council was having in Seoul during that momentous June of 1997. This was held with the Asiatic Research Center of Korea University, then headed by distinguished sociologist Hong Sung-chick. Among the foreign participants were Arthur Schlesinger, Jr., and Juan Linz of Yale University. The conference was focused on the progress of Korean democracy toward the end of the Chun regime. In an interview on TV, Schlesinger quoted Reinhold Niebuhr, the Lutheran theologian and philosopher: "Man's capacity for justice makes democracy possible, but man's inclination to injustice makes democracy necessary." That aphorism is still being played out in South Korean politics.

Can one be more specific about what kind of democracy South Korea and other Asian countries are striving toward? Too often the end game seems to be economic. I am not opposed to that as the first step, but one can see in South Korea and elsewhere the uneven distribution not only of income but of opportunity and expectation. Distributive justice needs to apply to the whole of society's expectations if all the sacrifice and hope for a democratic society can be achieved. In regard to Thailand, Barbara Crossette of the *New York Times* wrote: "So it is not just in Thailand that large groups of people are asking if economic progress will be accompanied by democratic reforms, as supporters of democracy in the area grow disdainful of the argument that Asians are somehow different, that they prefer the stability of even corrupt authority over the uncertainties that come with free expression and elections."[26] And elsewhere in that same article, Sidney Jones, executive director of the human rights group Asia Watch, said:

> The popular outrage against Suchinda (the unpopular appointed prime minister) and demand for democracy indicate that the notion, widely held in Administration circles, that Asians are somehow more comfortable with authoritarianism is utterly false. The Thai pro-democracy movement should also send a warning signal to Indonesia and Malaysia, who say that the developed countries focus too much on civil and political rights when the real priority of Asians is economic development.[27]

The Singapore Confucian scholar Wu Te Yao, in a statement later adumbrated by Confucian Lee Kuan Yu, the former long-time prime minister of Singapore, explained: "In all human societies, once the tummy is full, the mind begins to think. So whoever is going to rule, even in Japan or China, will have to pay attention to the people's heads and wishes."[28]

So again the Koreans have been in a leadership position in analyzing the components of democracy, the tensions created by the modernization process that point to a democratic outcome. There is no question that the roots of democracy were firmly established under the Roh regime. Right after Roh's June 29 declaration, at the same conference I mentioned before, Arthur Schlesinger, Jr., observed, "Democracy will be, I believe, more than a passing episode in human history. In the end it seems a natural aspiration because it responds in a deep sense not only to the needs of society but to the needs of human nature itself—because democracy expresses the complete amalgam in every breast of human courage with human frailty, of the desire to create with the impulse to do evil. Democracy rests on the mixed nature of man." Clearly the South Koreans have set out on this course.

This remains problematic in the advance of democracy in Korea in particular and in the world in general. In the triumphal spirit since 1989, there is a march to liberal democracy as a philosophy of government. This advance is allegedly irreversible and permanent, a form of Hegelian dialectic. This is well expressed in Francis Fukuyama's book, *The End of History and the Last Man*.[29] Liberal democracy will dialectically reach perfection in country after country. This argument from historicism is a thin reed, indeed. Diligence and dedication are stronger pillars to support democratic institutions and a democratic civic virtue. But herein lies the difficulty: Democracy is both progressing and at the same time under attack for its failure to meet often-idealized goals.

Nonetheless, there had been elements of significant "social and cultural transformation." From the Korean war to 1988, "the crucial transformations are clear enough: from poor to rich, unschooled to overschooled, rural to urban, and farmers to factory and office workers."[30] The gradual breakup of the chaebol system and the rise of young Korean entrepreneurs have been the keys to Korean economic recovery.

The problem in the democratic process in both South Korea and in the U.S. is that of incompleteness, that is, performance may not be what it should or could be. Democracy is not completed by simply 50 percent of the vote plus one. The expectation of democracy, in its insistence on the sovereignty of the people, is not simply to hold an election, but rather two more points that make the exercise worthwhile. First, the purpose of government (beyond security of the nation) is to develop the virtues and capabilities of the inhabitants to the fullest, in accordance to their own ability. (This was the expectation Kant had in promoting, in his book *Perpetual Peace,* the universal creation of republics, rather than kingdoms). And second, to allow power to devolve to the lowest common denominator, so that the habits of democratic processes are well exercised and strengthened through this process. In short, a citizenry of dedicated and practicing democrats is required. This means a high commitment and level of participation that cannot be taken for granted. A critical change in the March 2000 National Assembly election is that for the first time civic and other interest groups participated in the election as such. The Constitution gave a monopoly to political parties. But the modification of the election law allowed this popular change and further weakened the hand of the traditional political parties.

A good treatment of this disturbing democratic problem is in a book by David Norton on *Democracy and Moral Development.*[31] Norton argues that the way toward a better democratic society is the cultivation of virtues in the Greek way (and one may add, although he doesn't, the Confucian classical way). The prime virtues of Aristotle were wisdom, courage, temperance, and justice. Good citizens are necessary for good government. "The social utility of the virtues is apparent in their direct contribution to the well-being of others. The person of integrity can be relied upon to do what he or she accepts responsibility for; the courageous person better serves the collective interest too which she tends herself by her unwavering resolve when trouble arises."[32]

Suppose, then, that we have these virtuous citizens in the average democratic society. How do they lead the good life? This is at the core of "why democracy?" to begin with; yet it is often ignored in an ethical sense because of a preoccupation with GNP and per capita earnings as the hallmark of the essential performance of the state. Hyun Hong-choo, as mentioned earlier, raised the issue of a fuller definition of democracy by citing the autonomy of the political aspect of democracy, and implying that under Roh Tae-woo, there was the possibility that democracy might be defined in South Korea under increasingly pluralistic characteristics. Norton examines the possibilities for the citizen realizing himself through the eyes of Michael Oakeshott in *On Human Conduct*. According to Norton, Oakeshott holds two paradigms, "the collective enterprise association" and the "civil association." The former is the more common and powerful. "People often erroneously conclude that all durable human relationships must be enterprise relationships. They find it impossible to imagine association except in terms of a specific common purpose."[33] To the extent that Koreans have lost their jobs in 1998 and 1999 as a result of the Asian financial crisis, the Korean society today is under great stress. The change in the election law by popular demand is proof of that.

The "civil association," by contrast, composed of individuals voluntarily following certain "accepted" rules, allows freedom to its members to form groups to pursue mutually agreeable goals. The individual is supposed to realize himself, as opposed to the essentially involuntary nature of the "enterprise association," in which one's life is captured by the industrial (or whatever) job he is associated with. The company man, "the Man in the Gray Flannel," the salary man is not really free; if he thinks about it at all, he is a prisoner of the system. This does not mean that he is unconsciously in revolt against it; he may, in fact, prefer it. Nonetheless, if we are talking of Norton's standard of virtue and democracy, this is a serious handicap. This result can happen in democratic as well as authoritarian cultures. The "enterprise association," to the extent that it is involuntary, is dehumanizing, says Oakeshott. "It matters not one jot whether this undertaking is that of one powerful ruler (or coup d'etatiste), or a few, or a majority." The notion that the right of immigration, for example, "is a meaningful option to escape such an enterprise association is both naïve and impossible."[34] Korea is in the process of becoming a more sophisticated democracy, more so than many, and that should insure its political success.

This wider foray into the vision of an ideal democracy is not meant to downplay South Korea's substantial progress in this direction; but rather to demonstrate that these wider visions began to become relevant because of growing success. After five years of Roh Tae-woo in 1992, the *New York Times* (although still dissatisfied with the National Security Law) summarized his accomplishments: "In these his final months in office, President Roh Tae-woo has the opportunity to finish the job of democratizing South Korea. President Roh, who cannot run for re-election, has already earned a place in his country's history by leading the way to freely elected government and toward reunifying North and South Korea."[35] The *Financial Times* a bit later was also generous in its praise: "Democracy has taken root and is flourishing. . . . Labour and student unrest is subsiding as

Koreans exercise their democratic powers . . . [and] South Korea is winning its own Cold War with North Korea."[36] The trend was up. But the
problems anticipated with democracy by Norton grew more rather than
less intense because of the very success of more liberalization and expectations that outran reality and resulted in crisis in the Kim Young-sam and
Kim Dae-jung years. How to cope with distributive justice, broadly con-
ceived, in contemporary South Korea is the principal challenge of the Kim
Dae-jung administration.

The Roh Tae-woo presidency started the transition to democracy, especially in the sense of ending military rule. Kim Dae-jung was devastated
by Roh's victory: "I think my responsibility is overwhelming and I sincerely apologize."[37] The other defeated candidate, Kim Young-sam, shortly
afterward joined the ruling party, consolidated the rest of the opposition,
and five years later, in 1992, became the successful presidential candidate.
Whether during this period the autonomy of politics stood the test is an
open question. It did occupy a role in the sense of a "political economy,"
but the leading role of economics in Korean politics appears to have
strengthened over the last decade. Other desirable features of democracy in
the political and cultural spheres were blighted. The 1987 election marked
the beginning of the decline of the military in politics. Because Roh did
not have a majority in parliament, he could not prevent National Assembly investigations of corruption allegations against current and former defense ministers, for example, smearing their image. To control the fractured
National Assembly, Roh put together an alliance of the dissident Kim
Young-sam and former prime minister under Park, Kim Jong-pil, to establish a new party, the Democratic Justice Party. The price was a guarantee that Kim Young-sam would be the party's next candidate for president.
Herein was the germ of a later coalition, uniting two of the three Kims,
Dae-jung and Jong-pil, in a marriage of short-term convenience.

The Kim Young-sam presidency represented the first arguably democratic administration since independence. (Closely analyzed, however, the
New York Times' praise of Roh was mainly for having held free elections
rather than the content of his democracy.) Kim renamed the Democratic
Justice Party the New Korea Party, and his *Minju* (People's) faction was the
most powerful. Kim came in determined to reform the political system
and the key point of his program was instituting a "real name" system in
bank accounts.[38] Much of the business-political graft was possible because
one could open bank accounts under fictitious names, thereby making it
possible to conceal funds from the tax authorities (as well as political opponents), and prosecutors looking for political payoffs. This reform was
hugely popular with the public and Kim's own approval rating soared into
the 90-percent level, unprecedented in Korean politics. One of the victims

of this change was former president Roh Tae-woo. The reform exposed his corruption and played an important role in his 1994 trial (along with his predecessor, Chun Doo-hwan). Yet this reform obviously stirred up powerful opposition and soon was muted and slowed down. Kim's poll ratings went down, and by mid-1993, in an informal poll at Korea University, Kim Young-sam finished last among a list of world leaders, winding up just behind Hitler. Nonetheless, Kim ruled. For example, he transferred and retired many top military officers—often associated with corruption scandals—and so weakened the power of the military in domestic politics that a comeback to their glory years is highly problematic.

The ruling party under many names had remained continuously in office since 1961. Kim Young-sam was assumed to have the power to nominate his successor, but two things intervened. First of all, his son, Hyun-chul, took advantage of his blood relationship to behave in the eyes of his critics as "vice president," allegedly participating in influence payoffs. He finally was tried, jailed, and later released. Then, in 1997, there was more scandal among the chaebol. One such event, involving the Hanbo Steel group, involved bribing the government and bank officials to loan that company a staggering amount of cash (about $6 billion) to build a new steel mill. The economic need for such a steel mill was felt principally by the chairman.

The Hanbo scandal was the occasion for the reopening of old corruption wounds dating from the 1992 election. President Roh Tae-woo had generously given an undisclosed amount of funds to Kim Young-sam for his campaign and had even given a lesser sum (estimated at around U.S. $2 million) to the dissident candidate, Kim Dae-jung. When queried by reporters, Kim Dae-jung readily conceded that he had received those funds for that purpose. President Kim Young-sam, however, was not willing to disclose any details of his campaign financing. The President finally dealt gingerly with the subject in a nationwide television address on May 4, 1997. "In view of the [past] practices of the political parties and their election campaigns, it is true that every party needed huge amounts of money in the 1992 presidential elections." He said that such practices were wrong and reform was needed in this area. But he would not admit to any lapses and stepped aside from the demands of the opposition that he agree to any far-reaching probe into this matter. The election funds and now Hanbo were causing problems, but he stood firm.[39]

Still, both of these issues weighed heavily on the President. He kept more to himself; he quit jogging and avoided the public. He in effect withdrew from politics and announced a hands-off role in selecting the party candidate. So Kim Young-sam's party, which he had renamed the New Korea Party, was leaderless. The party convention then had its way. Emerg-

ing from this convention as winner was a virtual political unknown, Lee
Hoi-chang. For most of his public career Lee had been a judge and finally
a member of the Supreme Court. He was Kim Young-sam's first prime
minister, but resigned after six months because of the lack of real authority in that office. A squeaky-clean image seemed advantageous and he was
later appointed party president, as rumors of more corruption began to
swirl around the last months of the Kim presidency. The principal opposing candidate would be Kim Dae-jung, nominated by his own party, now
named the National Congress for New Politics (NCNP).

This would be Dae-jung's fourth try for the presidency, having run
against Park Chung-hee in the 1972 election; then in 1987 and 1992. He
had vowed he would retire from politics, but political ambition dies hard.
He attributed his failures in the past to government interference and their
description of him as a communist sympathizer. He asserted that if elected
he would seek a summit with the North. A study by the U.S. Embassy in
1987 gave him a clean bill of health.[40] DJ demanded that President Kim
disclose his 1992 campaign expenses, form a neutral cabinet, and even
leave the ruling party to demonstrate his even-handedness in the December election. "I am ready to help him if he meets these demands." DJ added
that he did not want to see President Kim go to jail. This would discon-
tinue the precedent of jailing former presidents, as had happened in the
cases of Chun and Roh.[41]

In this same interview, Kim Dae-jung discussed his putative alliance
with the United Liberal Democrats (ULD), which they had proposed. Kim
said he was willing to accept their idea of having a cabinet government
system (as opposed to the presidential system) "so that the long rule of the
ruling party will end."[42]

Lee Hoi-chang, the political newcomer to the New Korea Party (now
renamed Grand National Party), received the party's nomination; but
Rhee In-je, the governor of Kwanggi province (which contains Seoul),
split off from the New Korea Party to run on his own. Kim Jong-pil, the
leader of the United Liberal Democratic Party (ULD), joined in coalition
with Kim Dae-jung, and did not contest for the presidency. So it was a
three-man race. As the campaign entered December and there was a
media blackout on poll results, Kim Dae-jung was just leading Lee, and
the outcome was too close to call.

Then, right in the middle of this contest, on December 5, 1997 the financial crisis erupted like a volcano. Suddenly (or so it seemed), South
Korea was on the edge of bankruptcy. There had been no official warning.
The President's advisors told the President that the only way out was to
apply for a bailout loan from the U.S.–controlled IMF, which ultimately
reached $58 billion. The public in general was staggered by this event. Kim

Dae-jung at first opposed the idea of the loan as a surrender of sovereignty; but finally he, too, was convinced that there was no other way to deal with the staggering chaebol debt, now due, with foreign lenders in no mood simply to roll over the loans again as had been the practice. The unsteadiness of the Korean financial system and the recklessness of the chaebol had temporarily shaken the confidence of the international financial community. All of the candidates found themselves in the position of having to pledge their support of the IMF loan or risk losing the loan altogether with unfathomable consequences. During the final two weeks of the campaign, no one opposed the loan, but the Korean public placed the blame on the Kim Young-sam administration.

Still, the vote was tight: Kim Dae-jung 40.3; Lee Hoi-chang 38.7; and Rhee In-je 19.2 percent. The *Chosun Ilbo*/IMBC/Gallup Korea Poll of November 24, 1997 showed Kim Dae-jung with 31 percent, Lee Hoi-chang 28.4, and Rhee In-je at 20.5. In a two-way race, Lee received 44.6 percent and Kim Dae-jung 40.7 percent. The *New York Times* report was exuberant: "It is difficult to exaggerate the historical resonance of the scenes this morning, as Mr. Kim—the man who was nearly hanged as a traitor, the dissident whom American ambassadors used to shun for fear of annoying the dictators—stood before a forest of microphones and accepted the election to the presidency."[43] Kim himself was impressed with his accomplishment. "Since the founding of our nation, this is the most historic, most radical day. . . . The Korean people made their choice and broke all the barriers, transferring power for the first time in our history. Democracy will take root and prosper." The *Korea Herald* noted that the victory owed much to Kim's alliance with Kim Jong-pil and the United Liberal Democratic Party (ULD). The Alliance gave him a lift of 11–20 percent in provinces where he had never fared well.[44]

And so it had come about as the political scientists had all hoped: The opposition had been elected peacefully; power had been seamlessly transferred. The former ruling party could no longer simply pass the baton around among its members. Democracy had been consolidated. So far so good. But the new government was faced immediately with two urgent issues: How to stabilize and repair the economy; and how to deal with the new situation of making relations with North Korea a positive factor in domestic politics. Suspicion and animosity toward the North run deep in South Korea. The party that claims it can most consistently and competently deal with the reunification issue is likely to be the dominant force in South Korean politics.

Creating a new domestic politics—and political reform has been a DJ priority from the beginning—is a daunting task. The election reform measures are likely to have an uncertain outcome. His new party, the Millennium Democratic Party, with an ideology based on democracy, free markets, and protective welfare, is aimed at uniting the low-income class, an unprecedented approach in Korea. Also, President Kim's "electronic democracy" will allow citizens to reach him by e-mail, to be called the "internet shinmungo," after a drum used by citizens in former times to attract the attention of the king to citizens' complaints.[45] But in terms of contemporary politics, the three-Kim system is dying. Will a new popular leader rise from the ashes of DJ's old party and become the new presidential prospect for the MDP? There is no obvious heir apparent in the party. On the conservative side, Lee Hoi-chang, who leads the Grand National Party, stands out. But presidential elections will not occur until December 2002. The prognosticator must look through a glass darkly.

North Korea: Can the Cold War
Regime be Dismantled?

The ongoing division of the Korean peninsula, and the North's avowed objective of uniting the peninsula by force, is a powerful factor in South Korean politics. President Kim Dae-jung's focus on this issue since he assumed office in February 1998 has raised it to a new level of prominence, although it is still second to the ongoing concerns about the South Korean economy. There is no issue in South Korea that approaches that of North Korea. The ongoing division of this historically integrated land is a trauma in the South. For the North, the division provides its whole rationality and legitimacy: uniting the two halves by war. The South, by contrast, wants to bring about this mutually desired unification, but by peaceful reconciliation and cooperation. So, the North Korea problem represents the alpha and omega of both South Korean foreign policy and domestic politics. Everything, everywhere relates to relations with North Korea. The "sunshine policy" of the South, however, does not appear to the North as it does to the South, and there hangs the dilemma of peace on the Korean peninsula. The epiphenomenon represented by the June 2000 Pyongyang summit came out of a specific context. To understand this event it is necessary to review the past several decades in inter-Korean relations to see where things were, because they will still continue to shape the future.

By the beginning of 2000, both the tactics and politics of South Korea were rapidly changing in an all-out effort, as President Kim Dae-jung describes it, to "eradicate the vestiges of the cold war" and make 2000 "the first year of securing a stable peace on the Korean Peninsula."[1] At the same time, however, North Korea is showing signs of recovering from its economic slide, which had long been counted on (incorrectly)

to bring the North to the bargaining table on its way to becoming a normal state, i.e., in a manner acceptable to South Korean and U.S. interests.
An article by Richard Halloran in January 2000 in the *San Francisco
Chronicle* claimed that "North Korea's Recovery Dashes Hopes for Reunification."[2] Certainly the path to reunification will be a long one. Re-
viewing the history of this proposition is required before speculating on
prospects of a better, or even different, relationship between the North
and the South.

The South Korean and North Korean desire to create a united Korea
by force of arms did not end with the armistice at Panmunjom in July
1953. The "armistice" was signed by the UN participants on the one side
and China and North Korea on the other. Syngman Rhee refused to sign
for two reasons: (1) to register his fierce displeasure with the ending of the
fighting as a stalemate; and (2) as a heavy bargaining chip in negotiations
with the U.S. for a mutual bilateral defense treaty. He received the treaty
in October 1953, and the situation between the two Koreas—marked by
occasional moves toward better relations like the Mutual Accords of 1991,
never implemented—has a dreary familiarity. Threats by the North, sea in-
filtrations of heavily armed agents, espionage and dirty tricks by both sides,
most notably by the North in the case of the bombing of the South Korean cabinet in Burma in 1983 and the blowing up of a South Korean airliner over the Indian ocean in 1993—all these outrages are regular fare in
normal South-North relations.

While the North's position on unification by conquest has remained
constant, the South has developed more subtle and academic scenarios.
The unification problem in the South has attracted the attention of Korean political scientists, many trained abroad, and with this rich inventory
of scholastic talent, all kinds of ways have been found to move from humanitarian assistance to economic development, all foreseeing a future in
which the free market economy and democracy will prevail.[3] All of these
logical plans, varieties of rational choice, have all foundered on the same
rock—North Korea's rational position on regime survival.

There has been a significant change, however, in the attitude of South
Korea since the inauguration of Kim Dae-jung in February 1998.[4] Having witnessed these years of failure, Kim was willing to depart from the
"we're going to take them over" philosophy that had long prevailed. The
administration of each of the South Korean republics displayed a similarly
bellicose tone toward the North. The politics of this decade under presidents Roh Tae-woo and Kim Young-sam demonstrate the continuity of
the confrontation policy and now the transition to engagement under Kim
Dae-jung. There is, however, very strong opposition to DJ's "sunshine
policy" from the principal conservative opposition party. As the economy

has improved, there is once again time for politics, including schemes as to how to take over the North under the guise of humanitarianism.

While recommendations by South Korean scholars and politicians have dominated the debate, over the years on occasions foreigners have offered advice. For example, V. L. Ognev wrote in 1991 in a recommendation for peaceful resolution that "naturally, the Koreans themselves will gradually solve those issues within the framework of dialogue and according to the principle of self-determination, will choose the form of unification, acceptable to both."[5] The Korean tradition of being a united nation under a single kind of strong leadership is violated by the division.

Another article offering advice for President Kim Young-sam was by Kang In-duck. He felt that a more forward-looking policy, less dependent on threats of military measures, would be worthy of the support of the president and might lead to a gradual unification process.[6] These tentative approaches represented the growing dissatisfaction that, at the current rate, there would be no real progress on this issue since 1953. The ambitions of South Korea especially could not be met on the international scene, in terms of prestige and size, and were in jeopardy. It sounds so much better to talk about a united nation of over 70 million and a potential economy soon of say one trillion, rather than to be bound by lower numbers and the implication that Korea would always be among the middle-sized to marginal players in the world scene.

More proposals continued to come out of this milieu of dissatisfaction in the South. Nevertheless, however ingenious and sincere, these ideas did not reverberate north of the 38th parallel; and in the South, ideas of more immediacy prevailed. Professor Moon Chung-in proposed a variety of regional security cooperative efforts, but like all other imaginative initiations, they foundered on North Korea's refusal to take any move toward cooperation, as it instead stuck with threats of war. [7]

It was this unbending attitude of North Korea's, in fact, that created the myth of the irrationality of North Korean leadership. How could this cornered country, bereft of allies and living on hard-scrabble mountains, turn down every effort of important aid and assistance in favor of belligerence and rice bowl aid? I deal with this in more detail later in my interview with Hwang Jang-yop, the prominent defector. Others have pointed out that part of the problem makes North Korea quite rational, considering the hand it has been dealt and has to play. Denny Roy studied this issue at length and concluded that the North Korean posture arose out of placing a much higher priority on regime survival than on anything else, including national security as we understand that term.[8]

As the Kim Young-sam era wound down, there was a good deal of attention to new possibilities for the old, failed policies. Failure is an appropriate conclusion if the goal was to establish a relationship with the North that offered brighter possibilities for peace and prosperity on the peninsula. The failure was two-sided, if regime survival is not enough. Nicholas Eberstadt, a long-time American specialist on Korea, put this into perspective in his article titled "North Korea's Reunification Policy: A Long-Failed Gamble."[9] Eberstadt does not focus on the "irrationality" argument, but looks empirically on what North Korea has accomplished beyond regime survival and finds it lacking. His latest book, *The End of North Korea*,[10] carries his dim vision of North Korea to its ultimate conclusion.

The nuclear issue was raised in this context in an article by Jing Huang, "Why Is Pyongyang So Defiant on the Nuclear Issue?"[11] He relates this to regime survival, but is also critical in this article on the role of the U.S. in 1994 in the Geneva talks that led to the Geneva Accords and the controversial four-power agreement. The U.S. seized the negotiating lead because, on the U.S. side, it was considered an arms control matter and not simply a mutual security issue for South Korea and the U.S. against the North. South Korea, Huang believes, was basically shunted to one side, a view still dominant among South Korean conservatives and former president Kim himself. Had the U.S. offered South Korea more leeway, perhaps the agreement would have come out more favorable to South Korea's interests. As it is, South Korea is responsible for perhaps $4 billion of the total cost and has little to say on inspection issues and so on.

On the forward-looking side, in early 1994, studying the perennial North-South issue, Mark J. Valencia detected new signs of a spring thaw in the north Pacific and took a different tack: "Preparing for the Best: Involving North Korea in the New Pacific Community."[12]

This long series of failures on reunification, whatever one's political persuasion, was at the core of the dramatic shift in South Korean policy with the advent of Kim Dae-jung. He had long recommended a more conciliatory approach to the North; and this attitude had cost him the confidence of many of his fellow countrymen as "soft" on North Korea. In a society long accustomed to the Cold War and American military conservatism, Kim Dae-jung was a menace. The odd series of events in the South Korean elections of December 1997, which swept Kim to power, was viewed with apprehension by his opponents.

The root of the new policy was reconciliation and a willingness to "turn the other cheek" to start an "engagement" with the North, to use the jargon of the day. Kim was determined to extend his hand, even if it were rejected. Beginning with his inaugural address and repeated in May 1998, Kim spelled out his "sunshine policy." The five tasks for lasting peace on the Korean peninsula were these:

First, we must faithfully implement the agreed provisions of the 1991 Basic Agreement on Reconciliation, Non-aggression and Exchanges and Cooperation between the South and North; second, it would be desirable for the United States and Japan to begin the process of improving and normalizing relations with North Korea; third, all nations of the world, including the four countries whose interests intersect on the Korean Peninsula, should strengthen interaction with North Korea so that it can fulfill its role as a responsible member of the international community; fourth, we must eliminate from the Korean Peninsula weapons of mass destruction and realize arms control; and fifth, the current armistice regime between the South and the North must be changed into a peace regime.

In addition to these five tasks, President Kim restated the three basic principles of his North Korea policy: "First, no armed provocation by North Korea will be tolerated under any circumstances; second, we will not undermine North Korea or unify the country by absorbing it; and third, we will pursue across-the-board exchanges and cooperation with the North."

This policy has been in effect for only three years; as one would expect, the results have been mixed. A tourist program, now facing bankruptcy, from the South Korean port of Tung Hai to Diamond Mountain, North Korea, organized by the Hyundai chaebol, has attracted thousands of South Korean tourists (no reciprocity). Other cooperative schemes among the chaebols are underway, from enterprise zones to "excess" machinery sales, etc. Provocations continue, as demonstrated by the exchange of naval gunfire off the west coast and the sinking of a North Korean torpedo boat in June 1999. Provocations and cooperation advance hand-in-hand under this policy. To understand this better, it is now time to consider the overall view of North Korean policy that I gathered in a December 1998 interview in Seoul; the insights, I believe, remain fresh and significant.

The stereotype of North Korea as the consummate Stalinist state is unchallenged.[13] My efforts to visit the North have been unsuccessful. Beginning in the mid-1990s, the North Korean scene was dominated by descriptions of flood and famine, the terrible suffering of the average citizen (about 200,000 died), and the suspicion of the development of nuclear weapons. But even earlier North Korea's fate was dealt a hard blow by the collapse of the Soviet Union and its aid program, as well as the cutting back of aid by the Chinese. The famine convinced the Kim Young-Sam regime that the North was ready to implode and that the South would reluctantly have to go to the rescue, whatever the financial costs,[14] on the West-East German model. The South Koreans, however, would keep a stiff upper lip. There was nothing more that they wanted than to take over a self-destructed North Korea. General Gary Luck, the U.S. and UN commander, testified before Congress that it was not a question of whether North Korea would collapse, but when. So certain were the prophets of coming disaster that there was minimal disaster relief sent to avoid strengthening the North's outsized army, to which food would find its way rather than to the starving children, for example. While there was truth to the stereotype, and the powerful image of a stricken airliner coming down for a soft or hard landing persisted, the North held on. So it was for these reasons at the time that I determined whether I could arrange an interview with the famous defector, Hwang Jang-yop. What would the other side say about these things? He had arrived in Seoul via Beijing and Manila in April 1997. He had been debriefed by the Korean intelligence agencies and he had spoken to the press a number of times. He claimed he had arrived to head off another war on the Peninsula.

In November 1998 I sent in a request to interview Mr. Hwang through the consul general in San Francisco, which was approved by Seoul and the Hwang meeting was added to my schedule for December. When the news of Hwang's defection in December 1997 had arrived, I was in Seoul and discussed his possible motives with several friends, including Kim Jun-yop. I wrote a short piece for *Bridge News,* discussing the possibility of Hwang being a "Trojan horse." Hwang claimed that he was already a "dead man" and he lamented so much about leaving his family to its fate that curiosity was naturally aroused.

The National Security Planning Bureau picked me up at the Lotte Hotel promptly at 1:30 P.M. to attend the meeting. We were to go to a safehouse located in the *Itaewon* (foreigners') district, a popular shopping spot. There were four of us in the car; the driver, myself, the male escort officer, and a young woman interpreter who had been raised in California and later moved to Korea and then attended UCLA for a year on an exchange program. She and I and the male escort officer were dropped off near the safehouse. It was fairly unobtrusively guarded by young male civilians in inexpensive but natty Western suits. The safehouse was a two-storied wooden affair in Japanese style, with highly polished wooden floors and stairs. The North has shown the capability of striking down defectors and enemies in the South, so the precautions are necessary. The South cancelled a plan to send Hwang on an international tour because they were uncertain that they could assure his personal safety.

The second-story meeting room was furnished in the traditional manner—a low wooden table surrounded by three overstuffed chairs on each side and a single chair at the head of the table. This was for Hwang, who arrived promptly at 2 P.M. The interview would continue until 3:30 P.M.

I had given a good deal of consideration to what I might accomplish in talking with Hwang. I had submitted a general list of questions and thought the most useful to me was what he thought about the South Korean government's policy toward the North, the new "sunshine policy" of engagement, and whether he thought it would work. I had had a meeting with the South Korean Foreign Minister Hong Young-soon the previous day and an elaboration of the new policy had just appeared in the press. There were four points: (1) South Korea would help persuade the U.S. Congress that the U.S. should lift economic sanctions against the North. Since these sanctions had no real bite now—if they ever did—and could not be made effective through the UN because of China, this was not conceding much. This overt plan to influence Congress was a novel twist; the ROK for decades has had a close tie particularly with conservatives (the Tong Song Park "rice gate" of the mid-1970s) which was available for such occasions. (2) The North and the U.S. should exchange diplomatic relations. (3) The two Koreas should reach agreement on arms control. And then (4) the current "cease fire" which concluded the fighting in July 1953 at Panmunjom would be replaced by a peace treaty, finally ending the Korean war.

On this dark December day, Hwang wore a dark gray business suit, white shirt, and blue tie, and seemed weary. He had the nervous knee movement of many Asian overachievers. As for the "sunshine policy," he did not want to comment on that directly (being the line of the South Korean government). As for the North hoping for diplomatic relations with the U.S., Hwang was dubious.

> The North does not want to have diplomatic relations with the U.S., which would involve an exchange of missions to the capitols. Both Kim Il-sung and his successor, Jong-il, believe that the collapse of the Soviet Union came from two events: (a) the criticism of the state ideology by Khrushchev and the 1973 Helsinki pact that injected human rights into the Soviet Union; and (b) Gorbachev's weakening of the military.[15] The North would not allow such errors to occur.

As for the North's strategy, "it is still determined to take over the South by force. But it cannot do this as long as American troops are stationed in the South. So its main device is to threaten war on its neighbors in order to receive aid. This is the tactic toward South Korea, Japan, and the U.S. This is a cheaper method than to try to maintain a large number of bombs and missiles." So, with the bad economy, the blackmail continues.

If this were the actual situation, I wondered how a South Korean policy which had as its second point the normalization between the North and the U.S could succeed. "There may be other ways for the North to survive, but so far, the threat of war is the primary tool."

Hwang mentioned that for years the North had tried to normalize relations with Japan. They hoped that they would get the upper hand over Japan, but they finally realized that there was no way to do this without U.S. approval. Now, the North is again threatening Japan with new missiles. There would be no normalization there, not with the U.S. "Unfortunately," Hwang said, "my account of the North's position is not fully accepted by U.S. experts."

He went on to explain. "I have suggested a test, if they won't believe me. I say directly propose a liaison office in Pyongyang and see what they say." In the 1994 U.S.–North Korea–South Korea accord together with Japan, the "agreed framework" crafted at Geneva, there was a provision for an exchange of liaison offices, but that has not been realized. "I am convinced that the North's intentions remain quite contrary to any exchange of liaison offices."

From the point of view of the other signatories of the "agreed framework," there were what would appear to be advantages to the North in the exchange of diplomatic recognition and liaison offices. This would improve trade relations, promote foreign investment and more peaceful and secure relations with Japan, and so on. But Hwang believes this is outweighed by the dangerous prospect of having a U.S. Embassy in Pyongyang with its potential of creating tension and trouble for the regime through its exposure to North Korean citizens.

This circular argument goes back to how conditions on the peninsula might improve by direct North-South talks. In Oberdorfer's book, he recounts the exchange of emissaries in the 1970s between Kim Il-sung and President Park Chung-hee. Both Korean leaders wanted to talk about unification, but only in the context of an intra-Korean affair. This is why bilateral South-North relations are central. More countries may be helpful, said Hwang, but one should remember that "North Korea is never sincere in anything. It is absurd to expect anything from them. They are both feudalistic and fascist." Here Hwang cited his long personal relations with the two North Korean Kims, father and son, as an earnest proof of his analysis.

Hwang continued with his inside views of the North and I was intrigued to be sitting there with him. Ginseng tea was poured and was particularly satisfactory in the underheated safehouse. Hwang was 75 years old and had studied Marxist philosophy in Moscow. When he returned to Pyongyang, he had naturally been drawn in that direction, a solitary specialist in philosophy among the sea of economists and engineers. This proved to be a prescient choice, as he became an assistant to the "Great Leader" himself and helped to put the flesh on the bones of Kim's *juche,* (self-reliance), the official view of the North Korean regime. By 1983 he was secretary of the Korean Workers' Party. With the death of Kim Il-sung in July 1994 and the rise of his son Kim Jong-il to full power, Hwang believed that the party had lost its bearings, unable to see the evil of its ways, i.e., not dealing with the problem of famine, unable to see the misery of the common people, being so insane that they still believed they had created a workers' paradise.

There had been rumors about Hwang's disaffection for some years through academic conference circles, according to Kim Jun-yop. In Seoul, he continued to offer advice on how to prevent war. He believed the South should continue to provide some food and medicine to the North as a token of confidence-building. The support should be made in the name of humanitarianism, which was the only way to go about the opening to the North. This kind of aid from the South had to be handled carefully, restricting the quantity, so that the net effect was only to prop up the North. In regard to human rights in North Korea, the record is very bad; in fact, such an idea among the citizens of having any rights against the state did not exist. From Hwang's perspective, the people actually lived in a vast jail. He did not see how the people of the North could fight this system from the inside; he hoped that the South Koreans could take the initiative in exposing the evils of dictatorship. Hwang insisted that there would be change in the North, although the case he presented was weak. He was adamant that the North was under the absolute control of one man, Kim Jong-il. The feudal transfer of power from father to son had gone ahead smoothly. There had been no opposition.

The heart of the system, Hwang said, was power, an absolute totalitarianism. This was couched in terms of juche, which is based on the humanism of the people, and the class struggle between the proletariat in the form of the Korean Workers' Party and the rest. For me, it is difficult to see what elements in North Korea represent the counterweight to the "proletariat" to provide the basis for a "struggle." Hwang said the need for juche grew out of a requirement to establish North Korea's own identity. Before the Korean war, and just after liberation, North Korea was under the influence of the Soviet Union; during the war China was predominant. "Self-sufficiency" was the course Kim Il-sung chose through which to assert his independence. The Great Leader first articulated the juche policy on December 28, 1955; and when Hwang joined the secretariat in 1968, he worked with Kim Il-sung in developing the content. Juche was aimed at supporting the dictatorship of the Korean Workers' Party, modifying Marxism in a humanitarian direction. All of this separated North Korea from the domination of the "major powers." Nowadays, juche is used as an ideology to tighten the dictatorial hold of the regime.

I inquired whether a country whose national philosophy was "self-sufficiency" might have difficulty in international relations, perhaps being less concerned with developing relations with others. He said absolutely not. Juche first and foremost had to do with national sovereignty and humanitarianism. Juche has been subverted by the regime. What it says and what it does are two different things. Starvation, for example, is not connected with juche. Juche is now only a tactic. Juche does not approve of killing and starvation. North Korean human rights are 100 times worse than those of China and must be exposed for what they are. Also, Hwang said, it was not clear to him why the U.S. was bent on toppling Saddam Hussein but seemed content on leaving Kim Jong-il and the Democratic People's Republic of Korea (DPRK) alone.

It was closing time, 3:30 P.M. I said I had hoped that he had some practical ideas on unification. He smiled and said that he was beginning to write a piece on this subject for a Japanese magazine. I asked him to autograph the two small books he had given to me, which he did and off he went, down the slippery steps and out into the dark and dampness of a South Korean December day.[16]

Based on Hwang's analysis of the almost paralyzing pace of real success of Kim Dae-jung's "sunshine policy," despite the June 2000 Pyongyang summit, one is forced to recognize the reality of the status quo. For the past 47 years it has kept the peace, a powerful argument for its continuation. Eberstadt summarizes this point: One may indeed argue that fundamental conditions in Korea and throughout Northeast Asia over the past four decades demonstrate the soundness of the two-state formula for Korea. Commercially, the region has been transformed from an impoverished backwater into an engine of progress within the world economy; rapid growth, rising living standards, and burgeoning trade now typify the area. Although military forces in Korea remain poised for a resumption of hostilities at any moment, war has been avoided for nearly two generations. Not only Korea but all of Northeast Asia has enjoyed a long peace, albeit a tense one, and relations among the four great powers around Korea have gradually improved and are arguably better today than at any time in this century.

As the title of Eberstadt's book indicates, he does not think this happy situation can continue; change is inevitable because of the North's plight. Others claim, however, that North Korea is recovering and any reunification on the South's terms is out of the question. And so the stalemate continues.[17]

One can certainly argue that the opposing forces in the Korea peninsula must be in equilibrium to account for the peace and confrontation. In this situation, Kim Dae-jung continues to promote "sunshine," looking for supporters from both North and South. The North has never displayed any intention to alter its military solution; and the South has seemed to me quite content with the familiar stalemate. I decided in a small way to test the latter proposition. For my panel at a conference in Seoul in October 1999, I prepared a paper, "Crafting Peace in Northeast Asia: Opportunities and Challenges."[18] The idea was that since the U.S. is preoccupied with its own elections and the other powers in the region are preoccupied with other matters, might this be a good time for an intra-Korean initiative? Might the two Koreas consider a step toward concluding a real peace in the peninsula rather than the ongoing armistice? I asked a journalist friend of mine what he thought about this paper; he interviewed me on the subject and published the interview on October 27, in the *Joongan Ilbo*. This also led to a TV interview. At the conference itself, the discussants and participants were favorably disposed to the general line, but not the conservative analysts. The consensus conclusion was that any change in the status quo was a grave and risky matter. Henry Kissinger, who had been in Seoul the previous week, was asked whether he approved of the "sunshine policy." His response was that this was a matter exclusively for the Korean people to decide. Apparently he did not approve of it, but did not want to offend President Kim.

I was well aware that the conservatives, and specifically the Grand National Party and its leader, Lee Hoi-chang, had not strayed from the view of former President Kim Young-sam. In a speech in Washington, D.C. on September 15, 1999, sponsored by the American Enterprise Institute and the Heritage Foundation, Mr. Lee conducted a head-on attack on the "sunshine policy": "Let me submit to you that the sunshine policy is not working and must be revised. Not only has this policy had more negative results than positive but in a number of ways it has been counterproductive." Nonetheless, he conceded "nobody would quarrel with the goals of the sunshine policy." One can see that there is something out of sync here. The strategic failure, as Lee sees it, is giving up on taking over the North, in the previous tradition of Kim Young-sam. Lee longs for the Germany solution, playing the role of Kohl and at one stroke ending the matter.

Lee's litany of tactical negotiating measures with the North are the kind of things that have been done before on a "tit for tat" basis and have proven bankrupt. Concerns over nuclear weapons and missiles are expressed and their elimination has been at the heart of the Allies' negotiations with the North all this decade. Substantively, I see little difference between "sunshine" and Lee. Except for the German model outcome:

> In my view, German unification was in large part the product of West Germany's balanced, conditional, and consistent engagement policy toward East Germany. Even though the circumstances of German reunification cannot

be equated exactly with the situation on the Korean Peninsula, I believe the lessons of the German experience are very relevant. The fact that West Germany did not rush helped to lower East Germany's defensive guard which in fact hastened the reunification process. And although the Germans themselves may think the preparations were inadequate, the fact that such preparations were in the works enabled Germany to take advantage of the first opportunity that came for reunification.[19]

This speech shows the disagreement between the government and opposition, one that is not easy to bridge and that plays well in the North against the sincerity of Kim Dae-jung's policy. There is obvious difficulty in keeping a serious defense policy against North Korea in place in the South. Then, when one adds the different interests and perspectives of the more active players—the U.S., Japan, China, and Russia—the proper approach is not easy to sort out, especially, as we have seen, in the frame-work of Korean domestic politics and that of the U.S. as well.

Despite all of these up and down and sideways motions, it may come as some surprise that both Koreas make their way in the world, one as a U.S. ally and the other as a kind of rogue actor on the world stage, in a bittersweet romance, hated and yet wooed. North Korea is remembered in Washington only on rare occasions, such as the opening of the Korean War Memorial in Washington, D.C. in July 1997, as an international rogue terrorist in bombing civilian airliners, and so on. There is not much to like here. Yet, in the mix of international politics, where questions of interest and power intersect, North Korea occupies a troublesome place. The 1994 Geneva Accords, which have been mentioned previously, illustrate how a difficult process has become the cornerstone of a policy that has tamed down the rough edges of North-South and U.S. relations, that is, avoiding war on the peninsula.

Central to those year-long negotiations culminating in Geneva in October 1994 was the role of the South Korean foreign minister, Han Sung-joo. A well-known academic in Korea and the U.S., he had been a surprise choice as foreign minister by President Kim Young-sam. He had no experience in domestic politics and like all Korean ministers he was completely at the president's disposal. He accepted the post with enthusiasm. He soon became embroiled in a critical negotiation over the question of the inspection of nuclear reactors in North Korea, and his role eventually was pivotal.

Nuclear questions strike an awkward joint in South Korea–U.S. relations. The South looks upon the matter as part of the U.S.–Korea security treaty; up to a point, so does the U.S., but the U.S. very quickly puts its international apparatus into play. The issue of nonproliferation, for example, employs a different crew. This is what happened in the case of North Korea. As a signatory to the nonproliferation treaty, North Korea was subject to occasional checks by the International Atomic Energy Agency (IAEA) to determine whether nuclear materials designed for peaceful uses were being used to build bombs. North Korea felt the arms inspectors wanted to go too far, and were singling out North Korea—a fairly familiar story in regard to Iraq—for questionable treatment.

The U.S. supported the IAEA in 1994, even though it was also simultaneously negotiating a package with North and South Korea to settle the North's reactor question with a new exchange of light-water reactors for the old ones and also oil to carry the North over as the new reactors were built. Invective was exchanged, the North threatening to eliminate Seoul in a "sea of fire" and the U.S. threatening Pyongyang with referring the whole inspection matter to the UN Security Council. North Korea said such a move would be "an act of war." Aside from Defense Secretary William Perry, no one else used to dealing with the bluster of the North took this seriously. Perry brought back the generals and a military build-up was on the table in the White House to risk war over the inspection issue, as the preferable alternate to facing North Korean nukes later.

There was an Alice in Wonderland character to the situation, as the U.S. seemed paralyzed and mesmerized and languidly allowing itself to drift into war. Then the drama became richer. Jimmy Carter, until now not noticeably in the cast, telephoned President Clinton from Pyongyang, where Carter was visiting. Carter said that Kim Il-sung was agreeable to settling the matter and resuming North Korea–U.S. talks. Carter's call was resented by the Clinton officials as overstepping bounds. Here again, the attitude seemed to be to go to war to show their displeasure with Carter's miraculous intervention.[20] This incident is the theme of Leon V. Sigal's *Disarming Strangers: Nuclear Diplomacy with North Korea,* a cautionary tale of inept U.S. diplomacy.

By now it was July 1994. Saved from their own foolishness, Clinton's men followed on for the agreement: two light-water reactors (about $4 billion, to be paid for largely by the South Koreans and Japan), the oil, and no inspections for 10 years.

The inspection issue stood out like a boil, but this was the deal available. In Seoul, leaked information roused the easily rousable hard-liners, and President Kim himself began to oppose the agreement. Foreign Minister Han, realizing that this was the only deal available and critical to peace on the peninsula, was able to carry the day for South Korea and the agreement was signed in October 1994. As is well known, it does not pay to publicly oppose any South Korean president—including the current one—and Foreign Minister Han's tour was ended in December. Despite all the praises and misgivings about this accord, and the bureaucracy it established in the Korean Energy Development Organization (KEDO), the work has gone on and the two new light-water reactors are under construction. They will also produce nuclear materials, but perhaps less dangerous than the previous reactors.

That has not been the end of the matter, however. Political sniping from the U.S. right continued in Washington, prompting the Clinton administration to establish a commission under Secretary Perry, now at Stanford University, to come up with a new policy recommendation toward North Korea. Perry spent several months in 1999 consulting as many people as he could find with some knowledge of North Korean affairs; finally in November 1999, the Perry Report was revealed, recommending a carrot-stick approach, offering the reduction of trade embargoes against better behavior from the North.

This conciliatory kind of approach is not likely to sit well with the Republican congressmen. The Bush administration in the 1988–92 period has been described by Leon Sigal as "The Bush Deadlock Machine." This old mind-set is currently reflected by Congressman Benjamin A. Gilman, who wants to deal with the North Korean question by legislation. In May 1999 a draft version of this new legislation, "North Korea Threat Reduction Act of 1999," was introduced by Rep. Gilman, who argued that over five years after signing the Agreed Framework and undertaking a policy of engagement, the Korean peninsula remains poised on the brink of crisis. This legislation, however, was not passed.

The problem of dealing with North Korea remains, as it has been from the beginning, how to find a series of assurances that guarantees North Korea's existence as a state and at the same time receive security assurances of its good behavior. If threats of war remain its operative stance, the problem seems hopelessly compounded. During the division between East and West Germany (1945 to 1992) there was more open exchange of news, TV, and so on, leading to more common experiences. While North Korean TV can be shown in the South, there is no reciprocity, and of course no people exchange (until August 2000, when there were reciprocal visits by a few hundred families). The North remains almost airtight, except for intercourse with China. Even then, when North Korea was strong in the 1970s and 1980s, movement and travel to China was extremely limited. The unsettled war not only between the South and North but also the East and West in terms of the great Cold War struggle widened the gulf. Here we have the conventional Communist–Free World Cold War separation and antagonism, but also in North Korea an additional layer of state ideology. This element has remained constant over the past four decades. This is the North Korean doctrine of juche promoted by the Great Leader and now his son, perverted in the 1990s, Hwang said, into something other than he had in mind. This ideology stands in vivid contrast to the South Korean preference for democracy and free markets (including the globalization process).

As Hwang said, Kim Il-sung needed juche to establish North Korea's own identity to strengthen his internal hold and ward off his external enemies, particularly in South Korea. Kim's early ideas of juche meant the maximum contribution to rebuilding and rejuvenating North Korea outside the orbit of the two powerful communist allies. After World War II, first the Soviet Union and then China in effect exercised sovereignty over North Korea. Kim Il-sung's clever use of large amounts of Communist aid was so successful during the 1960s and early 1970s that the pace of economic growth in the North exceeded that in the South.

In a speech before the First Session of the Fourth Supreme People's Convention of the DPRK in Pyongyang on December 16, 1967, Kim Il-sung explained to the delegates his views on juche and its place in North Korea's political program.

> Only by firmly establishing Juche can each country repudiate flunkyism and dogmatism and creatively apply the universal truth of Marxism and the experience of other countries to suit its historical conditions and national peculiarities, and solve its own questions entirely for itself on its own responsibility by discarding the spirit of relying on others and displaying the spirit of self-reliance and accordingly, carrying on its revolutionary cause and construction.
>
> To establish juche is a question of special importance for us in the light of our historical development, and the complex and arduous nature of our revolution. Whether or not juche is established is a question of key importance on which depends the victory of our revolution, a vital question which decides the destinies of our nation.
>
> The Government of the Republic has been able to score great victories and success in the revolutionary struggle and construction work because it has endeavored consistently to solve problems in an independent manner, in conformity with the specific realities of our country and mainly by its own efforts, inevitably guided by the idea of Juche of the Workers' Party of Korea in its activities and adhering strictly to the Marxist-Leninist principles.
>
> As a result of our efforts to establish Juche in the ideological domain, the national pride of our workers and their consciousness of independence have grown to a great extent and they have come to acquire the traits of a revolutionary who does not follow others blindly but approaches things critically, instead of mechanically imitating or swallowing them whole; and strives to solve all matters with conformity with the actual conditions of his country and with his own wisdom and strength.

> Our Party's spirit of independence, self-sustenance, and self-defense finds its full embodiment in all fields of national construction, and the political independence and military power of the country have grown further still.
>
> As a full-fledged independent state, our country now determines its lines and politics independently and exercises complete equality and sovereignty in its foreign affairs (Juche!)[21]

Beyond the usual workings of international politics, interest, and power, the juche arguments give a particularly high moral tone to the operation of what appears by universal standards to be an inhuman society, as Hwang has described it. But juche does add another ingredient into the witches' brew that represents a problem of international politics that the world would prefer to ignore. One can argue whether too much or too little attention is paid to North Korea, but either measure will not make it go away. There is a book, for example, on North Korean negotiating strategy that would presumably prepare the negotiator with valuable tools of the trade. In the introduction to that book, former Ambassador to Seoul James R. Lilley writes:

> Dealing with North Korea is a tough proposition. There are no quick fixes. The North Koreans pursue every tactic in the book and they are especially adept as brinkmanship. By simply refusing to come to terms, they force tensions to the breaking point, leaving their cliff-hanging opponents biting their nails. They threaten war, engage in terrorism and infiltration, mobilize their public, call up their reserves, execute counter revolutionaries, put their oversized military on full alert, and appeal to humanitarianism. They make a show that convinces us that they mean business. Then they extract their price and celebrate. They take from the negotiating table what they are unable to do in any direct conflict. They survive not just to fight another day, but to create a new crisis when they are better equipped and stronger.[22]

What, at the moment, is U.S. foreign policy toward the North? The Perry Report is not so much a policy as an attitude. If North Korea cooperates on not developing and launching long-range missiles and continues the KEDO joint operation, then the U.S. will loosen trade restrictions, a version of the old "tit for tat" approach dear to the diplomatic mind. On January 24, 1999, U.S. Ambassador to Seoul Stephen Bosworth said in a speech before the National Assembly: "The U.S. policy toward the North remains intact. We may not be able to do anything in the short term. But we will continue to wait with patience. Using military force is never an option for resolving the Kumchang issue [the North Korean underground project then suspected of being a nuclear-related activity]. It will be done through dialogue."[23]

The setting in Seoul was probably the reason for such a soothing speech, calling for no use of military force. Yet, despite the verbal hawks in South Korea, détente is their thing: The breakout of war would destroy Seoul, only 30 miles from the underground entrenchment of North Korean artillery and missiles that would obliterate Seoul in hours. Seoul represents 25 percent of South Korea's population, an industrial base, and the very heart of the nation's culture. In 1993, then–Foreign Minister Han Sung-joo went to Washington out of Seoul's concern about U.S. belligerence. If there is war in Korea, it will not be initiated by either South Korea or the U.S.

Critics claim the U.S.–South Korea policy is little more than blackmail payments; but the money for arms control compliance is far cheaper than a war of any size and is in line with the relatively small American stake in North Korea. But regardless of the above objections, a "conventional" attack also might be considered, avoiding the fallout problem and the sensitivity of China to the use of nuclear weapons on the peninsula. Unless the current South Korean–U.S. engagement policy shows more immediate promise, a hard-line policy as the herald of a "strong and firm" U.S. policy cannot be ignored, however feckless such an approach might be.

A handmaiden of the hard-line policy would be Congressional legislation such as Rep. Gilman has crafted to take care of the North Korean problem. One can say at the offset that a legislative approach to a complex diplomatic problem is unsatisfactory. Whatever the weaknesses of diplomacy may be, skillful diplomacy, with its thrusts and parries, remains the best tool in dealing with the wily North. Legislation leaves no room for changes in circumstances, timing, and opportunities.

Another idea of resolving the North Korean issue is to involve more of the neighbors in Northeast Asia. This presupposes that the two Koreas and their neighbors have an agreed position on a new peace treaty, for example. There would seem to be advantages of converting the long-time armistice to a peace treaty. One downside is that the peace treaty would firm up the status of both countries, perpetuating the two-Korea, two-states system, and making political reconciliation more remote.

Former Foreign Minister Han Sung-joo, in his search for reconciliation in 1993 and 1994, concluded that the neighboring states would go along with a reunification program by the two Koreas; while China and Japan might not be enthused, they would not actively oppose it. It would not alter the balance of power. It is this assumption that led me to propose in a conference paper that the two Koreas take more initiative in unification now. It seems to me that the four- and six-power approaches to Korean unification presuppose that both Koreas are agreed, finally, and that China prefers some other arrangement than the current status quo.

As we learned from the earlier chapters of this book, China and Korea have a long relationship. China is pursuing its ties with the South as well as the North. The Chinese defense minister spent three days in Seoul in January 2000, for example. China's role on its borders in Northeast Asia will expand, and it may well develop a position based on continuing to opt for the status quo. During the height of the North Korean famine, China announced that it would not allow North Korea to fall. This was ignored by the "hard" or "soft" landing crowd in Seoul and Washington, who are still waiting for the "implosion" of North Korea long after the crisis has passed.

The U.S. has strong interests in this area, but over the long term it seems wise to support the Kim Dae-jung "sunshine policy" as the best vehicle available. North Korea's reciprocal diplomatic recognition of Rome met Mr. Hwang's criterion: no exchange of missions. The Italian ambassador remains safely posted to Beijing. But the European Union door is now open to the North. A new North Korean policy is evolving that will allow for new possibilities. As Sir James Fraser remarks in the Golden Bough, a study of taboos, even the mountains are slipping away.

The largest rock resisting change, however, may be the U.S. The foreign policy of the U.S. in East Asia is still embedded in the Cold War paradigm. North Korea has been so demonized that it serves as the Pentagon's rallying cry to justify both a theater missile defense and a national missile defense. Without North Korea as the ultimate "rogue state" led by a certifiable madman, credible attackers on the U.S. homeland are scarce. The Clinton administration's three-pronged policy toward the North seems to me to have been successful. The first defense is to try to dissuade the North from building either nuclear weapons or long-range missiles. If that fails, then there is the tried and true deterrence. This has shielded us from Russia during the darkest days of the Cold War, and now is in place for nuclear powers that contemplate trouble. The third circle is going to war, by whatever means are necessary. "Missile defense" brings up a whole range of issues beyond the scope of this book. So whether to maintain U.S. troops in South Korea to continue the current mutual security treaty is not moot. Whether cruise missiles targeted on the few North Korean missile sites would be a better alternate needs discussion. And finally, what the decision will be will revolve around U.S. relations with the powers of the area, China, Japan, and Russia.

A flurry of bilateral events between North Korea and the U.S. at the end of October 2000 briefly appeared to have set the stage for fundamentally new developments. This was against the background of President Kim Dae-jung being awarded the Nobel Peace Prize for his dramatic trip to Pyongyang and the beginning of a proposed unification process. North

Korean General Jo Myong-rok, second in command of the all-powerful Military Commission, visited Washington, D.C., meeting with President Clinton, Madeleine Albright, and Congressional leaders. This resulted in a trip to Pyongyang by Secretary of State Albright and a call by President Kim Dae-jung for President Clinton to follow up.

A note of reality entered the scene, however, when the South Korean Minister of Information disclosed that in September he had received a letter from the North saying that the pace of meetings on unification projects should slow down until spring; they were not prepared to move faster.[24]

President Clinton did not respond to the North Korea trip, and the actual situation was not much different than in the past. Attitudes may have changed, some minor economic projects are en train, but the real steps towards Kim Dae-jung's three-stage program will require dealing with the all-important security issues involving North Korean armed forces, nuclear weapons, and missiles. How quickly the interested parties wish to take on these issues has not yet been revealed.

Conclusion

Kim Dae-jung and the Future of Korea

This survey of the twentieth century on the Korean peninsula has revealed the challenges and responses so prominent in Toynbee's style of grand analysis. His method of describing the rise and decline of civilizations is entirely appropriate to Korea. Korea does represent a special civilization, and is not simply an amalgam of the cross-currents and debris of the cultural conflicts inherent in being close to both China and Japan. It is useful to think of Toynbee as a guide for the future. For one thing, this is because the current president, the person who is leading Korea into this new century, has said that Toynbee has been the primary intellectual influence on his life. Toynbee and Toffler and Confucius and the long row of legendary Korean kings, such as Sejong, and the Catholic religious experience make up the complex mind of one of modern Korea's most thoughtful and innovative leaders. True, he will compete with the vision of Kim Jong-il, his North Korean counterpart; but Kim Jong-il, as a Marxist, is a prisoner of the Marxian dialectic and is moving toward a destiny over which he has no control. Kim Dae-jung, on the other hand, has a future-oriented plan and a faith that man will determine, with God's help, his own destiny. These contrasting views make a profound difference in the probable outcome.

The South Koreans, who are clearly in the ascendancy, are determined to create a new society and a modern, leading state. There are obstacles in their path and success is not guaranteed under the system they have chosen, namely the democratic, market-oriented state. But this offers the best chance.

The important thing, if we wish to contemplate Toynbee, is that South Korea is a growing diverse state, and not a disintegrating monolithic one. Even North Korea is more likely to grow again rather than disintegrate, despite the disparate hopes of its friends and foes. How instructive some of these grand themes are in analyzing Korea's future is subject to debate; yet both Koreas are future-oriented, both carry on a variation of *shimbaram* (the agitation of the wind), and both are determined to succeed, alone or with each other. The lure of a "joint future" seems bright; yet the difficulties in the way of this outcome, as have been described, are enormous.

In the South, since early in the last decade, there has been a conviction on the part of the government that the time to create a "new Korea" is at hand. Why would this be a government program right at the time when the old mercantilist Japanese-model economy was pumping out its most attractive rewards, propelling the per capita income to over $10,000 per year by 1996, with promises of continuing successes?

This can be explained in part by the South Korean conviction and dedication to modernity in all of its aspects. One reason for the decline of the military government so quickly and completely was the perception on the part of the South Korean people that such a government was a symbol of the old and the backward; whereas the expectations and hopes of the Koreans were for the modern. In 1993 the new president, Kim Young-sam, moved quickly, and with high levels of popular support, to dismiss generals who were perceived as possible contenders for power and effectively defanged whatever opposition against his rule may have existed in the military. Over the decades many military officers have served in the government with distinction and are proud of the military tradition of service to the nation. But the number of former military cabinet ministers in the government has severely shrunk, aside from the minister of defense, and the idea of civilian rule has been completed during the Kim Dae-jung administration. It is fair to say that the demilitarization of the South Korean government is complete. But it turns out that this is not enough. In looking at the situation and to the future, there appears to be a ground swell for much more and successive presidents have tried to ride this wave. Because the reforms on paper were so comprehensive, Roh Tae-woo, Kim Young-sam, and Kim Dae-jung have all spoken of the imperative for South Korea to be a leading nation; but it was Kim Young-sam who first formalized these rather vague feelings into a program.

Kim Young-sam began his reform program in earnest in 1993, taking dead aim at the banking system that allowed accounts to be registered under aliases instead of "real name" accounts. This was a highly popular move, causing the President's approval rating to surge over 90 percent. These false accounts hid various illegal slush funds controlled by politicians (the previous president, Roh Tae-woo, was the biggest fish caught in this net). False name or alias accounts also hide all kinds of taxable wealth and the investigation of these accounts resulted in tax penalties and arrests. There was, in fact, fear generated that a strict enforcement of these accounts might cause an economic crisis. Gradually, this brave start weakened, as did the popularity of the president. His full reform package was published in 1997 by the Ministry of Information, Korean Overseas Information Service, with the title "Reform and Change, Four Years of the New Korea."[1]

This reform package, touching on all aspects of Korean life, aimed at ridding the new civilian democracy of its authoritarian past but preserving the strengths of the system that had seen South Korea ready to join the OECD, with Japan the only other Asian member. The first order of business was eliminating corruption and restoring public order; hence the drive for "true name" bank accounts. Because on paper the reform was so comprehensive, it is no surprise that DJ's program is so similar. The difference is that DJ is actually implementing it.

The second target was restoring the national spirit and righting past wrongs. The national spirit has been evoked on Independence Day, since August 15, 1945, and for the March 1, 1919, uprising against the Japanese, for example, as well as for the New Year's greetings on both the Western and lunar calendars. National pride and determination have long played a significant role in Korea's identity as a separate nation and culture and is part of the promise for the future. Past wrongs include the Japanese occupation and the long period of military authoritarianism, which is covered by the third category of reform. From that period, Park Chung-hee alone has retained his luster and remains an icon of economic progress.

Kim Young-sam's reforms were all exhortations for progress—strengthening national competitiveness and "restoring economic vitality"—which at that moment was very strong indeed; then Kim Young-sam would move on to creating an efficient government, a goal not only of his fellow Asian rulers but one of universal concern. Apparently recalling the sweatshop excesses of the 1960s and 1970s, Kim's reforms included a "quality of life" plank, paying attention to educational and political reform, new labor-management relations, and health and welfare reforms (beginning the weaving of a safety net). Items eight and nine were closely interrelated—building a foundation for unification as well as strengthening national defense. The ultimate purpose of these reform measures was the "preparation to become a first-rate nation in the 21st century."

With less than a year of the Kim Young-sam regime remaining when this was issued, it is no surprise that very little of this enterprise was realized. The most prominent reform, real name bank accounts, was beginning to falter; but it had accomplished a great deal of good and demonstrated that support could be found for worthwhile causes. The reform booklet is of value, however, in the context of the attitude of the South Korean leadership toward the close of the century, that for Korea to take its proper or desired place in the world, reform on a large and imaginative scale was a new imperative.

This background is necessary to explain the policies of Kim Dae-jung when he took over the helm of the Korean ship of state from Kim Young-sam after the December 1997 election. The economy, to be sure, was the immediate focus of Kim's energies; the IMF loan secured and the various ultimatums for chaebol reform issued, Kim Dae-jung was quick to move on to political reforms and to launch on August 15, 1998, a "second nation building program," which was to lead South Korea into the next century as the leader of the "information society."

The occasion for this pronouncement was the fifty-third anniversary of liberation and the fiftieth anniversary of the founding of the Republic of Korea. These occasions of celebration gave special impetus to DJ's dedication to the "second-nation building program." He stated that there were six major tasks:[2] "First, we must establish two-way political communication between the people and the government by achieving a great transformation from authoritarian rule to participatory democracy." This is part of his philosophy of making Korea a government of the people, including eliminating regional discrimination. Here he was referring to the bias against Cholla provinces, his native area, which have suffered from lack of government investment, government patronage, and so on. He included a point on German-style proportional representation, which presumably would help his own party, whose strength is still centered in Cholla provinces in the southwest and Seoul.

The second point is structural reform of the economy to assure better competitive position for Korean industries. This reform effort has met with stiff opposition from the chaebol and the GNP opposition party and results were slow but inexorable, as the slow demise of Daewoo, the second largest chaebol, demonstrates. Reform is coming from the growth of new, smaller industries. The Daewoo takeover of Samsung motors in exchange for an electronics business failed and Samsung motors took the path of bankruptcy. In a compiled book published by the Korea Development Institute (KDI) in 1999 called "Djnomics," DJ had this to say on economic reform: "Koreans should not worry about initial low growth after the reform, because it signals a fundamental and necessary change in the economy from previous years of extensive growth to an age of intensive development. Therefore, even though the economy will be expanding at a slower rate than in the past, the country will be growing qualitatively with transparent and efficient economic structures."[3] Attracting foreign investments in long-term projects was also to be encouraged.

For the third point, DJ also urged that Korea fulfill its obligations under the WTO system, welcoming competition and imports, but he was keen to reality: "It is regrettable, however, that many people in other countries still perceived Korea as less accessible." As this is overcome, it will help create a new value system based on "universalism and globalism, shedding self-righteous nationalism and other anachronistic ideas."

Earlier, I have mentioned the profound influence Kim Dae-jung has acknowledged to the "challenge and response" part of Toynbee on his own life, as well as the acknowledgement of the role of God in his life, which resulted in his conversion to Catholicism. Alvin Toffler has also influenced DJ. Toffler's *Future Shock* in 1970 brought him to the international scene. Writing from a Marxist perceptive, Toffler saw the world advancing through waves, from the agricultural to the industrial to the information society. Modern societies were those that mastered the science and technology of the new age. Toffler attended Kim Dae-jung's inauguration and his thinking has clearly affected Kim's future orientation in terms of the "second nation building" program Kim has laid out.[4] There is, however, more to the urgency DJ feels over the country's rise to the highest level than being on the edge of modernity. The "second nation building" program, organized in every province and denounced by the opposition political parties, has the possibility of shoring up DJ's party, the Millennium Democratic Party. Kim is furiously riding the reformist, modernizing bicycle and he dare not pause in his pedaling. Mergers of the old parties and creation (or renaming) of new political groupings are in the air.

If we can now switch analogies from the bicycle to the high wire, we are ready for the fourth reform: "We have to re-invent our economic system to build a knowledge and information based economy, shifting away from the current one based on industrial strength." This is the realm of Tofflerism, one that appears to be the professed goal of many societies of Asia. This is akin to Ahab's obsession with Moby Dick, the insistence in this case that the new Silicon Valley is just over the next ridge. Hong Kong, Singapore, Malaysia, and Taiwan are leading advocates as well as explorers in this quest.[5] This does not mean that they will not discover Alhambra some day, but this shift from the old to the new has more facets than are often considered.

In December 1998, in a talk to the Global Research Institute in Tokyo, I mentioned this Asian phenomenon and especially Korea's interest. In June 1998 Kim Dae-jung and his entourage visited Stanford University and Silicon Valley as part of DJ's official state visit to Washington, D.C., and the opening of the Metropolitan Museum of Art's permanent Korean art exhibit room in New York City. One of his party was Kim Ki-hwan, a durable member of several administrations because of his economic prowess. A Berkeley Ph.D. in economics and a former chief of the Economic Planning Board as well as ambassador-at-large on trade, Kim was promoting Media Valley, a government initiative to build a "Silicon Valley" near the west coast port city of Inchon (made famous by MacArthur), where a high-density concentration of technology firms is supposed to reach a fusion point. A software city is also in the works in the south part of Seoul. Media Valley will be competing with Singapore's Science Hub, Hong Kong's Cyberport, and so on, as Asia ratchets up to outrun the Western world.

In my Tokyo talk, I suggested that "when President Kim Dae-jung came to Stanford in June, he talked about having a South Korean Silicon Valley. But what he and his advisers perhaps have not completely understood is that you don't get a Silicon Valley artificially. For example, you have to start with great research universities." Here I was referring to Stanford, at root an engineering school, as well as the University of California system, which are responsible in the first instance for the rise of the technology phenomenon in the California peninsula south of San Francisco. I am not aware of any major universities in the Inchon area; it is, in fact, the lack of world-class universities in Korea that is a handicap to Korea's emergence as a leader in both theoretical and applied research.

How are these ideas understood by the public? One example is an article by Professor Yun Chong of Chungnam National University of Tae-jon. Professor Yun summarizes what these changes mean in terms of two factors: "One is the globalization and free trade and the other is the information revolution shifting the industrial society into an information-oriented one. Changes come rapidly, and against our will. Masayoshi Son, known as the Bill Gates of Japan, foresees the Information Age continuing for a minimum of 300 years. It is our task to overcome these tough waves in order to survive."[6]

Information provides access to power. There will be greater demand for creativity, and ideas will be more valued than "framed and systematic work abilities." Yun saw the change from a vertical to a horizontal structure of society.

The fifth point in DJ's reform program was to create a constructive labor-management relationship. The problem the government was anticipating was strong labor reaction to the rising level of unemployment caused by the Asian financial crisis. Unemployment in Korea had risen about threefold, to 9 percent, or almost two million of the over 20 million employed. In June 1998 in Seoul I had interviewed leaders of both of the major labor unions, beginning with the Federation of Korean Trade Unions (FKTU). This is the oldest trade union movement in South Korea, dating from 1945. It is considered the more moderate group. The leaders I spoke to expected to play a more open role in the DJ era, considering their long-time support as well as help in the December 1997 election. So the

FKTU anticipated good relations with DJ's government. The government's initiation of a three-legged stool composed of the government, business, and labor was supposed to address the economic crisis (this formula, identical with standard fascism, has encountered no criticism on that score, probably because the three interests refuse to cooperate). Both labor groups have been restive under this arrangement, threatening to withdraw if their demands for the right to strike and to organize and participate in politics (only partly protected) are not recognized.

One substantial reason labor expects DJ's support, they said, was that he will have to carry out many reforms and will need help beyond his party, then the NCNP, and coalition partner, the United Liberal Democratic Party (ULD), and the labor movement fills that need. (Labor is now a major beneficiary of the 2000 election reform laws.) The FKTU has a membership of over one million.[7] In 1997, membership was 1.2 million. Why lower now? Layoffs hurt, and also 40.7 percent of the total work force is "irregular," that is, not full-time, and not suitable for organizing.

In South Korea, the whole country employs about 20 million people and of those, only 13 million are possible prospects as union members. The FKTU's rival, the Korean Confederation of Trade Unions (KCTU), has about 500,000 members, mainly in autos and metals. The IMF program, as I mentioned, usually went forward at the immediate expense of unions. The leaders agreed, saying that the IMF program weakened the unions. Layoffs were taken in the name of efficiency; and that was all right if the chaebol reformed to actually improve efficiency, that is, by bringing in more capital investment. Labor unions, they said, have a fundamentally different approach than the chaebol: The unions love the company, are committed to it, are patriotic, and are forward-looking with a sense of belonging. But layoffs now occurring violate this unwritten compact. South Korea, they feared, is headed toward U.S.-style employment, with workers moving from place to place. There is no sense of belonging, no appreciation of skills and experience. This wipes out any reason for belonging to a particular company. (Since this interview, unemployment has dropped from about two million to one million.) One's future is not anchored to a particular company.

Labor unions, my respondents said, have a longer-term approach to workers and the companies. The current government program, supported by business, is short-term and destructive. Legislation allows people to be laid off. Labor is being singled out unfairly and other factors in the economic crisis must be handled. Only 10 percent of the cost of manufacturing is labor. High interest rates are a big factor (at the height of the crisis in the spring of 1998, interest rates were running in the high 30 percent range, before falling steadily to about 7 percent in 1999, which greatly contributed to the stock market boom—unconnected with the real economy). Low interest rates will help labor and the government must provide a social safety net for unemployed workers. A variety of tax measures were suggested—luxury taxes, transportation, bank interest. (In fact, the government has stepped into this problem by having a budget deficit of about 5 percent annually, which may create inflationary pressures down the road.)

In regard to the KCTU, its differences with the older FKTU largely had to do with the history of the labor movement from the early 1970s. At that time many people were leaving the rural areas for factory jobs. There were a great many young women who were exploited. In the textile industries, conditions were bad; there were fires and many deaths, for example. This dramatized their plight, but the government position was that they must control labor and wages. Cheap labor was considered to be one of Korea's main competitive advantages.

The danger from the North also handicapped labor. It was associated with Karl Marx and human rights and democracy. So under the conditions of the time, it was difficult for labor to establish its legitimacy. The unions began as little more than tools of the government.

The Kwangju uprising in June 1980 against the Chun Doo-hwan military dictatorship was put down brutally by Chun's paratroops and several hundred were killed. From this a pro-labor democratic movement began and it obtained the support of Kim Young-sam and Kim Dae-jung. Community organizations were formed after the pattern of Saul Aulinsky, the American labor organizer. Learning about labor rights was a good thing in itself, but this was not sufficient to launch the movement. Organizers concentrated on small companies with 200 or less workers.

In 1985, the KCTU spokesman said, there were two important events for labor: (1) there was a strike at Daewoo motors, (2) there was a successful textile strike. The government considered both strikes illegal, but they went forward anyway; the issue was wages, not—as the government contended—pro–North Korean sentiment.

But the event that really prepared the way for the KCTU, spokesman Yoon said, was June 1987, when protests began over the subject of direct elections of the President. Students initially led the way, but labor union members and young adults also joined in the vast nationwide demonstrations, which were dispelled when the ruling-party candidate, Roh Tae-woo, agreed to the direct election demand. Over a million people participated in this event, although workers did not demonstrate as such. Yoon described this outcome as a dramatic step forward for the democracy movement. This was a favorable moment to organize unions. In three months, there were 4,000 individual labor disputes, including 2,000 in newly organized places. New leadership arose. The slogans of the day now seem laughable: hair styles, better lunch, etc., leading to union recognition. This was the first time that workers in big companies started to organize.

The KCTU began a training program and provided some assistance to workers. The initial focus was in the Masan area (autos, metal works) and then it spread to other regions. Most unions were small—from 100 to 1,000. There was a need for a central organization to tie these groups together. Hence the shabby, non-air conditioned office in downtown Seoul. But the KCTU was not officially established until 1995. They concentrated on industrial workers, large chaebol, and white-collar workers. One other thing they worked on was new efforts to change strict labor laws. One law they wanted to remove was the one allowing only one union per plant, which gave the company control. Also, unions were realigned into federations by industries to give labor more influence. By November 1995, they had 428,000 members and by March 1998, 520,000 members. But by June 1998 (the time of the interview), people were losing jobs and the unions were passing out leaflets opposing this. The unions were also reluctant to participate in the tripartite groups of government, business, and labor, because they do not have equal influence.

I asked Mr. Yoon to talk more about himself, beyond college at the University of Melbourne and so on. Since 1985 Yoon was a student of politics and literature and joined the KCTU in 1996. He wanted to devise new rules for labor in the companies, so that labor's position would be better. There had to be an acceptable balance. One issue, Yoon said, is participation. Power must be shared. There must be an understanding of the social significance of chaebol restructuring, considering both economic norms and social norms:

> There is a tradition in Korea of social engineering, "untouchable kings," which means there is no sense of pluralism. Now there is a delayed catch up of 30 years of single-minded economic growth. Korea claimed to be the 11th largest economy. Now most want to see themselves as victims. The chaebol are worried about what to do with their wealth. There is no sound moral and political substantive program to handle economic growth. There is no consensus on what to do. The civil society is growing, but without consensus. No one is suggesting alternate ways. But the future of Korea will be decided within the next two or three years. One thing that is required is a more accessible government.

The DJ government is in no way indifferent to the concerns of labor or about the future direction of the country. DJ's fifth point addresses directly the labor issue: "We are now at a historic crossroads when we have to create a constructive labor-management relationship conducive to the new age of harmony and cooperation. It is imperative that we put an end to the confrontation and animosity between the two major sectors in society."

Labor seems more ready to do this than the chaebol, which has steadfastly refused to "restructure." The "big deals" have not amounted to much. The original auto consolidation between Daewoo and Samsung failed in June 1998, with Samsung opting for bankruptcy. (In 2000, Renault of France formed an alliance.) The chaebol position was well-stated in June 1998 by Kim Seong-jin, chairman of the Daewoo Research Institute: "DJ's restructuring plan is all right, except that he must keep in mind the private sector. There are three factors: (1) private ownership must be protected; (2) free competition must be maintained; and (3) there must be a fair system of justice. None of these exists in Korea today."[8] The resolution of the twin and related issues of social justice and fairness remains open. For its part, labor has been quiet and circumspect, facing the then reality of 8–10 percent unemployment. They have supported the national interest in economic recovery over their workers' issues of higher pay and benefits. So far, there have only been a few strikes in banks and hospitals.

And the sixth point is the perennial national security issue, better relations with the North: "I intend to promote a new relationship of exchanges and cooperation between the South and the North based on a firm national security posture, overcoming the 50-year confrontation on the Korean peninsula." This subject was analyzed in the preceding chapter on North Korea, with the conclusion that South-North relations are likely to improve, but progress toward reunification is not likely to advance quickly.

What about the prospects for the other big reforms of the "second nation building"? The whole program has been denounced by the opposition parties as brazen efforts to strengthen DJ's party to improve his position in the National Assembly as the government moves toward a parliamentary system. It has become more of an unofficial movement rather than a government program. In April 1999, Kim Jun-yop, the last Confucian scholar-figure, now 80, was approached by a representative from the Blue House and asked if he would serve as chairman of the "Second Nation Building" Committee. Kim Jun-yop, well known for turning down the offer to be prime minister under both Roh Tae-woo and Kim Young-sam, found this offer easy to refuse. "Just repair the economy," he advised, "the remainder of Korea is all right." DJ's nation building program is now going forward under the banner of the Millennium Democratic Party.

There are some signs of change in the basic society through the development of grass-roots organizations that in the long term will transform Korean society. Park Won-son, a lawyer, and his wife, visited the Stanford campus in the spring of 1999. He is the Secretary General of People's Solidarity for Participatory Democracy. He is a long-time DJ supporter and came to the U.S. as a 1999 Eisenhower exchange fellow. Issues that his organization follows are minority shareholder's rights; Korean unification; sexual harassment law; and election campaigns. This kind of effort is representative of a growing interest by Korean citizens in nongovernmental organizations. In time, these changes will open up Korean society to help create the "participatory democracy" that Mr. Park and his associates are seeking. But this represents only a brick or two on the way to rebuilding the nation.

Still, repairs are in order for Kim Dae-jung's other five points, which collectively are political party reform, economic reform, and transition to the information age. These things will finally come about, but the pace is undetermined and whether it will add up to a "second nation building" is problematic. The big political reform will be the switch to the parliamentary system, so that the cabinet will be controlled by the legislative branch. The power of the president will be restricted, unless his party is the main force in the legislature. Whether such a reform will give South Korea a better or worse government is chancy. The Korean style, both North and South, is that the leader is all-powerful. While Koreans often spoke of wanting a democratic government, they nonetheless seemed to have a preference for a leader in a military uniform. Politics has certainly advanced by now well beyond this point, but weak governments, particularly based on parties, have an uncertain future. Given Koreans' notorious inability to compromise, the possibility of stalemate and quagmire cannot be overlooked. But by the summer of 1999, it appeared that Kim Dae-jung's coalition with Kim Jong-pil and the UDP was frayed and that more parties would be created by opposition figures, including Kim Young-sam, so that DJ would by the end of this century already occupy a lame duck role and his bright hopes for a "second nation building" and the brave new information society would be on hold. Eager academics who rushed into the meetings to start the rebuilding by the summer of 1999 were no longer attending and were labeling the effort a "farce."

Nonetheless, the DJ-KJP alliance held together to maintain a ruling majority. In December 1999 Kim Jong-pil resigned as Prime Minister and the president of the UDP smoothly replaced him in January 2000. The new prime minister, Park Tae-jong, is the former chairman of Pohong steel. Park soon left in a cloud of scandal, and lesser personalities have since occupied the Prime Minister post.

Chaebol reform did not seem to be a serious project. The list of announcements soon dried up and the results were scarce, encouraging me to write a piece on "South Korea's Lagging Economic Reforms."[9] As the South Korean economy improved, led by a roaring stock market (up over

three times from the low, to over 1,000 by July 1999), the chaebol continued to lag on restructuring performance. The *Far Eastern Economic Review*
noted in a piece called "Test of Wills," that it was unclear who was winning. Both Hyundai and Daewoo claimed they would do their own internal restructuring to streamline their activities and reduce debt:

> Such sharp restructuring by the nation's two largest chaebol would prove a
> turning point for Korea Inc. If the companies follow through, it would sig-
> nal that the chaebols finally recognize the need to discard their long-held
> strategy of debt-financed expansion and focus on a few profitable ventures
> to survive global competition. But that's a big if. Many analysts say Hyundai
> and Daewoo can't possibly accomplish everything they have announced by
> the end of the year. "It's a total hoax," says Stephen Marvin, head of research
> at Jardine Fleming in Seoul. "They're buying time."[10]

One of the prominent big deals that went wrong was the government-
ordered swap by Samsung of its auto factory near Pusan to Daewoo for an
electronics business. Not only was there no agreement on equitable prices,
but by June Samsung decided to simply go bankrupt. The factory was already closed, and now the citizens of Pusan as well as opposition politicians publicly blamed DJ for depriving Pusan, the second largest city, of a
premier business that had employed at peak 6,000 workers. As such issues
smolder, the appetite of the government to come forward with restructuring ideas becomes severely impaired. (In 2000, however, Renault formed
an alliance with Samsung that seems promising.)

On May 23, 1998, chaebol mistrust of the DJ government flared over
an article in the *Chosun Ilbo*. The article pointed out that the credit status
of many smaller groups and banks was rising, while those of Daewoo and
Hyundai (the two largest chaebol) were falling. To Seoul's leading newspaper, this showed that the government needed to restructure those weak
chaebol. "Now is the time for the government and creditors to face the
huge insolvency in a brave way, according to public opinion." The article
continued that, "after the IMF crisis, several companies are making every
effort in their restructuring; however, parts of them continue to resist
change. Again, some chaebol are trying to recklessly expand their business
in the financial world and maintain its management style, that is, the company owner decides all matters."

Even more, the article said, "owner's wives of the chaebol continue to
manage golf clubs and art galleries as their hobbies. We don't want to live
any more under the circumstances that the chaebol control the Korean
economy."[11]

Kim Woo-chung, the chairman of Daewoo, was in Tokyo that Sunday
and telephoned to Kim Seong-jin, his longtime president of Daewoo Eco-

nomic Research. He asked Kim if he had read the article; when Kim said no, he gave him five minutes and called again. Kim Woo-chung was furious at the newspaper's attitude toward the chaebol and told Kim to go and register a complaint. So Kim went to the editorial offices to learn on Monday that the publisher and editor were already at the Blue House receiving decorations for their contribution to Korean democracy.

The pent-up ire of the conservatives toward the DJ regime was kept under control for over a year as the economic situation improved. It would have been both unseemly and unprofitable to strongly criticize the government in the midst of economic crisis. But once that was on the mend, the complaints were unleashed, particularly over the "sunshine policy" toward the North. The weakness of that position, however, is that no one has an effective substitute. The proposed "proactive" policy simply leads to reciprocity and diplomatic reprisals, which are the hallmarks of the past 50 years.

The evolution of South Korean politics and economics will continue under the pressure of the international globalization process, which South Korea simultaneously plays and also avoids to the fullest extent possible. The downside of globalization, insofar as it makes mid-sized countries like South Korea vulnerable to financial flows, commodity prices, and market fluctuations, places new risks on the economy and hence politics. But efforts to protect domestic markets can only be partially successful, say in agriculture, as the forces of globalization relentlessly move ahead.[12] Nonetheless, South Korea will make its own way and its own national policies will continue to make a difference. Its entry into OECD in 1996 was criticized in some quarters (notably by former Prime Minister, Kim Jong-pil), but is proving to be a successful move. OECD countries represent about 80 percent of international trade and South Korea, as the newest member, will benefit both in results and in mindset.[13] As part of the commemorative celebration for Kim Dae-jung's first year in office in February 1999, the Korean Ministry of Information commissioned a book of congratulations to the President from foreigners, who in some cases were friends of the President and in others long-time observers of the Korea scene. These contributions, including mine, are in general praise-worthy but subdued. John Dunn, a professor of political science at Cambridge who knew DJ when he was in England in the 1980s in semi-exile, wrote a sympathetic and insightful general analysis. He began by focusing on the power and wealth of the chaebol:

> The existing and drastically inefficient concentrations of ownership are to be altered, and the overmanning of many segments of Korean industry are to end, many powerful individuals and groups must change their minds or

be made to do so. If the president falters or stumbles at this formidable historical task, Korea may well find itself slipping into a far more violent vortex of economic failure or into much bitterer social or political conflict. But on the evidence of the last year and a half it is far likelier to do so as a result of all too effective resistance from many different quarters to the pressure which he has steadily exerted throughout his presidency to build a society which is politically far more democratic, socially more inclusive and less unjust, and economically more efficient than any previous stage of Korea's long history.[14]

Each nation creates its own system of government and style of governance. Democracy is now the mode and South Korea is democratic. North Korea sticks to its version of Stalinism with North Korean characteristics. There are discussions about "democratic consolidation" in South Korea, after the Huntington-Diamond model, particularly among political scientists in Seoul.[15] On the Freedom House scale, South Korea rates a 2 as a liberal democracy (1 through 2.5 qualify for that rating); while North Korea and China, for example, weigh in at 7 (the most authoritarian).[16] This is a real achievement in meeting the democratic goals first expounded in 1987. Elections are now being held from the local to the national level; and just as important, the government tries to act in a democratic manner; and when it fails, it can expect criticism. And the president accepts the responsibility and apologizes, as DJ did, when in May and June some minor scandals, involving the receipt of expensive clothing by cabinet members' wives, caused a minor furor in the public and gave the opposition several more seats in the national assembly. Another larger scandal occurred in July, involving the governor of Kyonggi province (which contains Seoul), a close supporter of DJ. Corruption, in my view, is a facet of universal human nature, not restricted or special to Korean politics. Considering the real national security threat posed on Korean democracy by the North, freedom in the South is remarkable, although security laws against subversion are still in place, and in my view, necessary.

South Korea and the future, rebuilt or not, will be on the edge of Asian technology, competing against its neighbors. Exactly what the future holds for South Korean technology is difficult to ascertain. What difference will size make? Japanese GNP is 15 times that of South Korea, for example, and South Korea still needs Japanese technology, which Japan is increasingly unwilling to either sell or transfer. Since 1997, the chaebol have invested very little in either research or new plants under the government stricture to reduce their debts and liabilities. This move may have longer-term bad consequences. On the other hand, the quality of South Korean manufactures is improving, especially in autos, and South Korea, mainly through

Samsung, is internationally competitive in chips and semiconductors. As an outside observer, an area where South Korea might improve dramatically is in graduate-level education, although in the global economy perhaps that problem is already being taken care of through the outpouring of South Koreans to the world's best graduate schools.

South Korea will make its own way in the Toynbeean recovery phase of its present cycle, perhaps not as quickly as in the past because of intense international competition, but nonetheless moving forward. The North Korean albatross is still there, defying gravity in its single-minded pursuit of sustaining the regime's power. But even that will not stop the South, although unification has the potential for releasing latent energies, enormous defense savings for both North and South, and opening significant possibilities of reorientation of the whole peninsula. It is to that future that the Toynbeean philosophy leads, as well as Toffler's information society, and the always-powerful idea of progress—properly tended—speaks well for a strong Korea in the twenty-first century.

By mid-July 1999 the South Korean labor ministry released new figures, showing that the economy had recovered to precrisis levels, and that the profits for the top 100 companies were up from 1998 as much as 100 percent. The stock market surpassed 1,000, the highest level in four years. And all of this with very little chaebol reform, raising the question of whether the rise in unemployment solved part of the problem and/or that the crisis was really a narrowly based banking and speculation problem. In June 1998, I interviewed Park Ung-suh, a senior Samsung executive. (He is a onetime CEO of Samsung Petrochemical and then was head of Samsung's economic research. In June 1999, he became president and CEO of KOHAP, an ailing petrochemical chaebol that he hopes to turn around.) He unambiguously blamed Korea's financial troubles on the financial system, but there has been no alternative way for South Korea to industrialize: "One reason for the chaebol's drive for bigness and success was to overcome the traditional bad image of business in a Confucian-oriented hierarchical society. Under the Confucian ethic, business was at the bottom. Casting the chaebol's efforts as nation building, contributing to the rise of Korea, was only in part successful."

Park said that the whole nation embraced shimbaram, determined to succeed by overcoming all obstacles. It was an obsession with growth. The entire emphasis was on volume, not quality:

> At the Blue House luncheons for business leaders, the seating arrangement was determined by which chaebol had the largest business volume, not profit or loss. The banks were caught up in the volume approach. To earn money they kept the loans coming and the government in effect guaranteed

them. But there was no alternate source of capital. If loans could not exceed equity many times, there would have been no growth. There is no source of capital in Korea other than loans. The equity market is underdeveloped.

Japan was the Korean model for globalization, still playing the mercantilism game. "The world was like Mother Nature. Go out and harvest it. It is there to be exploited. Now in Korea, with some fairly minor changes, Korea will be all right. The standard of living is still high. Our industries are strong. Samsung is still the leading semi-conductor company in the world with 17% of the market. This position will not be given up."

What the world is facing now, Park said, was a new phase of capitalism. Here, the financial people are playing the key role. Manufacturers take the long view of investment, while financial people take the short. This creates the nontransparent hidden hands of funds that create havoc: "The financial people have no stake in any community and have no moral purpose."

During the same June 1998 trip, I visited with Kim Ki-hwan, a Berkeley-trained economist. Where Korea was headed was the topic. As Kim saw it, there have been three separate Republics of Korea. The first was the long period of industrialization, under Park Chung-hee; then there was the period of corruption generated by the new wealth; now third, Korea will become a regional operational center, based on a new service economy, perhaps based on a Hong Kong or Singapore model. Basically, the last ten years have been a period of economic stagnation. Kim Young-sam early in his term decided to get interested in globalization, but then he became involved in investigating former presidents Chun Doo-hwan and Roh Tae-woo. He wanted to punish them to "correct history." Then the Hanbo scandal came in 1997, completing the period of stagnation. Now, Kim Ki-hwan was enthusiastic; one of his duties was the Media Valley project, to replicate Silicon Valley and the ancillary expectations that go with that. (In 1999 he accepted a position with Goldman-Sachs.)

President Kim Dae-jung is the only philosopher, or man of ideas, who has been president of South Korea. In his book, *Letters from Prison,* he wrote:

> In this difficult time I have learned much and have discovered a conviction for Toynbee's philosophy of history. I have read most of his works, as you know. Their principal analytical perspective on historical understanding rests on the view that the colossal drama called the birth, growth and collapse of civilizations is determined by the relationship between challenge and response. Although he never taught me directly, I have always recognized him as my intellectual mentor.[17]

And in a later collection of essays, he writes on the Toynbee theme, "A man is challenged by his fate to move up one step higher. When he does that he is again challenged constantly until his time expires. A man successfully responding to the challenge naturally succeeds in life, while a man failing to meet the challenges will have far less to show for his time on earth."[18] To his credit, Kim Dae-jung has moved boldly in all areas of Korean national life. In October 2000 President Kim was awarded the Nobel Peace Prize for his efforts to bring peace to the Korean peninsula. But success will mean the accomplishment of these long-term goals, which will not be settled during his lifetime. Unification will be the work of the twenty-first century to determine Korea's ultimate possibilities.

Notes

Chapter 1

1. *Korea Herald*, December 14, 1996.
2. Michael Lewis, "The World's Biggest Going Out of Business Sale," *The New York Times Magazine* (May 31, 1998), p. 34.
3. "The Faltering Economic Reforms of South Korea," Robert J. Myers, (JPRI Working Paper No. 51, November 1998, San Diego: Japan Policy Research Institute, 1998).
4. Ithaca: Cornell University Press, 1993.
5. *San Jose Mercury News,* November 28, 1999.
6. For example, at the Miller Center, the University of Virginia. See Kenneth W. Thompson, ed., *Korea: A World in Change* (Lanham, MD: University Press of America, chaps. 1 and 3, 1996).
7. Lee Jay Cho and Yoon Hyung Kim, eds., *Korea's Political Economy, The International Perspective* (Boulder, CO: Westview Press, 1994).
8. Miller Center News Letter, Spring 1998, vol. 14, no. 1, p. l.
9. *The Passing of Korea* (New York: Doubleday, Page & Company, 1906).
10. *Korea Focus,* (July-August, vol. 3, no. 4), "Modernizations vs. Risk in Korean Society," by Han Bang-jin, Professor of Sociology, Seoul National University, 1995, pp. 55–69.
11. Ibid., p. 68.
12. Kim Se-jin, *The Korean Military Government* (Chapel Hill, NC: University of North Carolina Press, 1971).
13. *Korea Update,* March 2, 1998, vol. 9, no. 2, p. 5.

Chapter 2

1. See John K. Fairbank, Edwin O. Reischaurer, and Albert M. Craig, *East Asia: Tradition and Transformation* (Boston: Houghton Mifflin, 1973), chaps. 11 and 12.
2. See Martine Deuchler, *The Confucian Transformation of Korea: A Study of Society and Ideology* (Cambridge MA: Harvard University, 1992), pp. 14–27.

3. Kenneth Scott Latourette, *The Chinese: Their History and Culture,* 3rd revised edition (New York: Macmillan Co., 1946), p. 518.

4. James Legge, *The Chinese Classics,* vol. 1, *Confucian Analaects, The Great Learning and Doctrine of the Mean* (Hong Kong: at the authors; London: Trubner & Co., 1861), 13–27, p. 274.

5. I am indebted to the late Professor Herlee Creel of the University of Chicago for his courses in Literary Chinese by the Inductive Method, for my life-long interest in literary Chinese and Confucian philosophy.

6. See Fung Yu-lan, *A History of Chinese Philosophy,* translated by Derk Bodde (Beijing Henri Vetch, 1937), pp. 73–75.

7. *Analaects,* 13–27.

8. Ibid., 12–2, p. 251.

9. Ibid., 13–25, p. 273.

10. *Hsiao Ching* (Filial Piety), chap. 14.

11. Wu Hung-chu, "China's Attitude Towards Foreign Nations and Nationals Historically Considered," *Chinese Social and Political Science Review 10* (January 1926), 23.

12. M. Frederick Nelson, *Korea and the Old Order in Eastern Asia* (Baton Rouge: Louisiana State University Press, 1945), p. 89, passim.

13. T.C. Lin, "Manchuria in the Ming Empire," *Nankei Social and Economic Quarterly,* viii, April 1935, pp. 1–43.

14. Ibid., pp. 17–18.

15. Lin Mou-sheng, *Men and Ideas* (New York: The John Day Company, 1942), p. 120.

16. J. K. Fairbank and S. Y. Teng, "On the Ch'ing Tributary System," *Harvard Journal of Asiatic Studies* (1941), p. 141.

17. Ibid., p. 160.

18. See H. F. MacNair, ed., *Modern Chinese History: Selected Readings* (Shanghai: Commercial Press, 1927), p. 17.

19. Chinese Repository, 20 vols. (Canton, printed for the proprietors, 1835), 3: 417.

20. Ibid.

21. Ibid., p. 419.

22. E. R. Hughes, *The Invasion of China by the Western World* (London: A. and C. Black, 1937), p. 102.

23. Frederick Wells Williams, *Anson Burlingame and the First Chinese Mission to Foreign Powers* (New York: Charles Scribners' Sons), p. 97.

24. Latourette, *The Chinese . . . ,* pp. 525–26.

25. Nelson, *Korea and the Old Order in Eastern Asia,* xiv.

26. See Statistical Department of the Inspector General of Customs, Treaties, Regulations etc. between Corea and Other Powers (Shanghai, 1891), pp. 41–50.

27. Harold M. Vinacke, *A History of the Far East in Modern Times,* 2nd revised ed. (New York: F. S. Crofts, 1937), p. 115.

28. See Nelson, *Korea and the Old Order in Eastern Asia,* p. 152.

29. Alastair Ian Johnston, *Cultural Realism: Strategic Culture and Grand Strategy in Chinese History* (Princeton: Princeton University Press, 1997).

30. Arthur Waldron, review of *Cultural Realism: Strategic Culture and Grand Strategy in Chinese History,* by Alastair Ian Johnston, *New Republic,* June 22, 1997, 36–41, quote on p. 39.

31. Ibid., p. 38.

Chapter 3

1. Rikitaro Fujisawa, *The Recent Aims and Political Development of Japan* (New Haven, CT: Yale University Press, 1923), p. 174.

2. See Richard Connaughton, *The War of the Rising Sun and Tumbling Bear* (London: Routledge, 1988), pp. 22–27.

3. See a discussion of the findings of a Korean scholar, Kim Ki-sok, of a memoir of Homer B. Hulbert in Columbia University Archives *Korea Newsreview* (April 30, 1994), p. 26.

4. New York: Doubleday, Page & Company, 1906.

5. In May 1997 I went by the temple to confirm that this gruesome monument still existed and took a few photos.

6. See Dennis L. McNamara, *Trade and Transformation in Korea, 1876–1945* (Denver, CO: Westview Press, 1996), p. 165.

7. See Carter J. Eckert, *Offspring of Empire, The Koch'ang Kims and the Colonial Origins of Korean Capitalism 1876–1945* (Seattle: University of Washington Press, 1991).

8. Max Weber, *The Religions of China. Confucianism and Taoism* (Glencoe, IL: The Free Press, 1951).

9. Ibid., p. 85.

10. Eckert, ibid., p. 6.

11. Eckert, ibid., pp. 224–225.

12. Ibid., p. 225.

13. See Tetsuo Najita, *Visions of Virtue of Tokugawa Japan. The Kaitokudo Merchant Academy of Osaka* (Chicago: The University of Chicago Press, 1987).

14. Ibid., p. 15.

15. New York: Basic Books, 1986.

16. See Peter Duus, *The Abacus and the Sword. The Japanese Penetration of Korea, 1895–1910* (Berkeley: University of California Press, 1995). First paperback printing, 1998. Part 1, chap. 6, "The Politics of the Protectorate, 1905–1910," 201–241.

17. *Korea Since 1850,* New York: St. Martin's Press, 1993.

18. Interview in Seoul, June 1998.

19. Lone and McCormack, ibid., p. 58.

20. Hulbert, ibid., p. 208.

21. Lone and McCormack, ibid., pp. 59–64.

22. Interview with Hong Sung-chick in Seoul, June 1998.

23. See Philippe Burrin, *France Under the Germans* (New York: The New Press, 1997); and Richard H. Weisberg, *Vichy Law and the Holocaust in France* (New York: New York University Press, 1997).

24. "The Special Committee for Anti-Nation Investigation," in Karum Planning 1995, translated by Professor David Chun for this book.

25. Ramon Myers and Mark Peattie, *The Japanese Colonial Empire,* (Princeton, NJ: Princeton University Press, 1984), pp. 494–495.

26. *Korean Herald,* March 29, 1997.

27. Hulbert, ibid., p. 465.

28. Hulbert, ibid., pp. 465–466.

29. See Lone and McCormack, ibid., pp. 68–69.

30. Ibid., p. 87.

31. See unpublished Ph.D. dissertation by Dennis L. McNamara, *Imperial Expansion and Nationalist Resistance: Japan in Korea, 1876 to 1910,* (Harvard University, 1983). Published by University Microfilms International, Ann Arbor, Michigan, U.S.A.

Chapter 4

1. See Lee Hyun-hee, "A Study of the History of the Provisional Government of the Republic of Korea," (Seoul: Jipmundong, 1983), translated by David (Hwang-soo) Chun.

2. Ibid.

3. See Cumings, *Korea's Place in the Sun* (New York : W. W. Norton, 1997) p. 157.

4. Lee Hyun-hee, ibid., p. 29.

5. See Mon Il-soek, "If Kim Ku Were Alive," (Seoul: Deoksu Publishing Co., 1994), translated by David Chun.

6. See Yu Mahchun, *OSS in China: Prelude to the Cold War* (New Haven, CT: Yale University Press, 1996).

7. The Korean government has compiled all the relevant Department of State documents of this period in a bound publication called "Documents Related to the Recognition of the Korean Provisional Government: Documents Related to the Independence Movement, (in Korean, *Haehan min'guk imsichongbusungin kwannyon munso haewaeui han'guk tongnip undong charyo mijupyon kukka bohunch'o*). This volume was presented to me in June 1998 in Seoul by Mr. Lee of the Ministry of Patriots and Veterans. This source volume will be referred to as "Independence Documents."

8. Independence Documents, p. 243.

9. Ibid., p. 245.

10. Ibid., pp. 245–246.

11. Ibid., pp. 246–247.

12. Ibid., p. 247.

13. Ibid., p. 252.

14. Ibid., p. 255.

15. Ibid., pp. 255–256.
16. Ibid., pp. 256–57.
17. Ibid., p. 375.
18. Ibid. pp. 375–76
19. Ibid., pp. 349–50.
20. Ibid., p. 360.
21. Ibid., p. 364.
22. Ibid., p. 404.
23. Ibid., p 402.
24. Ibid., p. 430.
25. Ibid., pp. 382–399.
26. Ibid., p. 425.
27. Ibid., p. 462.
28. Ibid., pp. 465–66.
29. Ibid., p. 467.
30. Ibid., p. 487.
31. Ibid., pp. 495–96.
32. Ibid., p. 539.
33. Ibid., p. 545.

Chapter 5

1. The Monthly Report of the Intelligence Officer, China Theater, from the Strategic Services Officer, China Theater, APO, John T. Whitaker, Col. Infantry, Intelligence Officer, July 1945.
2. See Han See-joon, *A Study on the Korean Kuang-bok Kun (liberation) Army* (Seoul: Iichogak, 1996), also translated by David Chun.
3. OSS Documents, "Operational Report from 1200 Thursday 10 August to 1200 Thursday 16 August 1945," pp. 63–64.
4. P. 28 of the OSS documents.
5. Yu, op. cit., p. 230.
6. Op. cit., p. 230.

Chapter 6

1. Chicago: The University of Chicago Press, 1943.
2. See Mark Paul, "Diplomacy Delayed: The Atomic Bomb and the Division of Korea, 1945," in Bruce Cumings, ed., *Child of Conflict: The Korean-American Relationship 1943–1953* (Seattle: University of Washington Press, 1983).
3. See Robert R. Simmons, *The Strained Alliance: Peking, Pyongyang, Moscow and the Politics of the Korean Civil War* (New York: The Free Press, 1975), chap. 1, "A Partial Korean Genealogy of the Korean Civil War." While domestic factors did indeed play a role, the war in Korea and its consequences clearly places it within the Cold War Great Power context. For

more discussion of this point, particularly as raised by Professor Bruce Cumings, see below in this chapter. Also see William Struck, *The Korean War: An International History* (Princeton, NJ: Princeton University Press, 1995).

4. Ibid., p.71.
5. See *United States Relations with China, with Special Reference to the Period 1933–1948* (Washington, D.C.: The United States Department of State, 1949).
6. See Michael H. Hunt, *Crises in U.S. Foreign Policy: An International History Reader* (New Haven, CT: Yale University Press, 1996), p. 199, citing *Washington: Department of State Bulletin,* 22 923, (January 1950), 114–116.
7. See Hunt, ibid., p. 188.
8. Ibid.
9. Ibid., p.189.
10. Ibid.
11. Ibid.
12. See Chen Jian, *China's Road to the Korean War: The Making of the Sino-American Confrontation* (New York: Columbia University Press, 1994); and also Sergei H. Ginchabov, John W. Lewis, and Xue Litai, *Uncertain Partners: Stalin Mao and the Korean War* (Stanford, CA.: Stanford University Press, 1995).
13. New York: Monthly Review Press, 1952.
14. Princeton, NJ: Princeton University Press, 1980 and 1990.
15. New York: W. W. Norton, 1997.
16. Vol. 2 (of *The Origins,* chap. 18). He returns to this theme twice more toward the end of that chapter.
17. Cumings, vol. 2, p. 568.
18. Ibid., p. 500.
19. Frank Holober, *Raiders of the China Coast* (Annapolis, MD: Naval Institute Press, 1999).
20. Ibid., preface, xvii.
21. The Gaston Sigur Center, George Washington University, Washington, D.C.
22. *Korea's Place in the Sun,* pp. 263–64.
23. See Sung Chul Yang, "A Convoluted Approach to the Study of the Korean War," *Korea and World Affairs,* vol. 17, no. 2, Summer 1993, p. 323.
24. See Chen Jian, Working Paper No. 1, "The Sino-Soviet Alliance and China's Entry into the Korean War," Woodrow Wilson Center for Scholars, Cold War International History Project, June 1992.
25. Ibid., p. 3.
26. Lee, op. cit., p. 10.
27. Ibid., pp. 9–10.
28. Ibid., p. 13.
29. See Anthony Farrar-Hockley, *The British Part of the Korean War, Volume I, A Distant Obligation* (London: HMSO, 1990), p. 204.
30. Chen Jian, ibid., p. 25.
31. Hunt, ibid., p. 206.

32. Ibid., p. 207.
33. Ibid., pp. 211–12.
34. Chen Jian, Working Paper, ibid., p. 28.
35. Ibid., p. 28.
36. See Dr. Chang-il On, professor of military history and strategy, Korean Military Academy, Seoul, Korea, "Military Operations and Strategies of Two Koreas in the Korean War." A paper prepared for "The Korean War: An Assessment of the Historical Record" July 24–25, 1996. International Center Auditorium, Georgetown University, Washington, D. C.
37. See Max Hastings, *The Korean War* (New York: Simon & Schuster, 1987), chap. 27, pp. 305–329.
38. See Kathryn Weatherbee, assistant professor of history, Florida State University, "The Soviet Role in Prolonging the Korean War, 1951–53." Prepared for "The Korean War: An Assessment of the Historical Record," July 24–25, 1996. International Center Auditorium, Georgetown University, Washington, D.C.
39. See Lee, ibid., p. 32.
40. Ibid., p. 51.
41. Hastings, ibid., pp. 318–319.
42. Ibid., p. 305.
43. Ibid., p. 329.
44. See Han Sung-joo, *The Failure of Democracy in Korea* (Berkeley: The University of California Press, 1974), chap. 2, pp. 7–32.

Chapter 7

1. See the Korean Annual, now in its 39th year (Seoul: Yunhap News Agency); and for a analysis for 1998, see Joint U.S.–Korean Academic Studies, vol. 9, 1999. "Korea and the Asian Economic Crisis: One Year Later." Symposium Sponsored by Georgetown University, The Korean Economic Institute of America, and the Korea Institute for International Economics Policy. Washington, D.C., November 13–14, 1998.
2. See Paul Krugman in *Foreign Affairs,* "The Myth of Asia's Miracle," vol. 73, no. 6, pp. 62–78, for example.
3. Ibid., pp. 29–54.
4. Ibid., pp. 9–27.
5. See Selig S. Harrison and Clyde Prestowitz, Jr., *Asia after the "Miracle:" Redefining U.S. Economic and Security Priorities* (Washington, D.C.: Economic Strategy Institute, 1998). These factors are true and were necessary, but hardly sufficient to account for the Korean success, measured in large part by hard work, diligence, and bold leadership.
6. See Louis Uchitelle, "Ounces of Prevention for the Next Crisis," *New York Times,* February 1, 1998.

7. See "A Korean Company Town Suffers as Steel Mill Fails," *New York Times*, December 30, 1997; and defense-related, "South Korea's Financial Crisis Hinders Atom Deal with the North," *New York Times*, February 5, 1998.

8. Also immediately affected were the traditional costly Korea weddings. "Seen Atop Wedding Cake, A Shaky Future for Korea," *New York Times*, December 28, 1997.

9. Ibid., p. 4.

10. See my article, JPRI Working Paper No. 51, "The Faltering Economic Reforms of South Korea," November 1998.

11. Amsden is the author of *Asia's Next Giant: South Korea and Late Industrialization* (New York: Oxford University Press, 1989).

12. *Korea Herald,* April 4, 1999.

13. See Leo Gough, *Asia Meltdown: The End of the Miracle* (Oxford Capstone Publishing, 1998), pp. 112–13.

14. Ibid., p. 112.

15. *Cambridge Journal of Economics* 1998, p. 22.

16. In July 1993 the Kim Young-sam administration issued a report, "Shifting Towards the New Economy, Korea's Five Year Economic Plan 1993–97." This was prepared by the Korea Institute for International Economic Policy. The plan called for a "new strategy" and key reforms: fiscal, financial sector, deregulation, and new patterns of economic behavior, or chaebol reform. None of these proposals, however, was carried out.

17. In Kenneth W. Thompson, ed., *China, Taiwan, Japan, the United States and the World* (Lanham, MD: University Press of America, 1998), p. 100.

18. See the *Wall Street Journal,* October 26, 1998.

19. *Dow Jones Newswires,* October 14, 1998.

20. *Korea Herald,* November 19, 1998.

21. *Korea Herald,* September 29, 1998.

22. See Han Sung-joo, ed., *The New International System: Regional and Global Dimensions* (Seoul: Ilmin International Relations Institute, 1996).

23. *Korea Herald,* March 31, 1999, by Kang Seok-jae, staff reporter.

24. "Kim Urges Major Powers to Help Bring Peace: Calls for an End to the Cold War on Peninsula," by Chon Shi-yong, staff reporter, *Korea Herald,* February 3, 1999.

25. See David Sanger, "U.S. and IMF Make Korea crisis worse," *New York Times,* December 3, 1998.

26. *Korea Herald,* March 31, 1999, by Kang Seok-jae, staff reporter.

27. See *Korea Herald,* November 4, 1998.

28. See *New York Times,* "The Koreans Are Coming! But Where Are they Going?" February 25, 1996.

29. Ibid.

30. *Korea Herald,* January 7, 2000.

31. See John Dunn, "Record and Future of Kim Government," *Korea Herald,* April 6, 1999.

32. Ibid.

33. *Korea Herald,* April 9, 1999.
34. *Korea Herald,* April 9, 1999.
35. Robert J. Myers, *The Political Morality of the IMF* (New Brunswick, NJ: Transaction Press, 1987).
36. *Korea Herald,* April 8, 1999.
37. *Korea Herald,* April 14, 1999.
38. *Korea Herald,* February 18, 1999.
39. *Korea Herald,* April 30, 1999.

Chapter 8

1. Victor D. Cha, "Politics and Democracy under the Kim Young Sam Government; Something Old, Something New," *Asian Survey,* vol. 33, no. 9, September 1993.
2. *Korea Herald,* January 5, 2000.
3. See, for example, "Where does South Korean Political Development Stand Now? From Legitimacy Crisis to Democratization Trial," Sung Chul Yang, *Korea and World Affairs,* vol. 18, no. 1, Spring 1988, pp. 5–22, and Myuongsoon Shin, "Democratic Transition and Consolidation in Korean Politics," *Korea Observer,* vol. 27, no. 2, Summer, 1986, pp.165–183.
4. See James B. Palais, *Politics and Policy in Traditional Korea* (Cambridge, MA: Harvard University Press, 1975).
5. Ibid., pp. 332–334.
6. Interview in Seoul, April 1997.
7. See Henderson, ibid., chap. 10, "Political Parties."
8. *Democracy in America,* edited by J. P. Mayer and translated by George Lawrence (New York: Harper & Row, 1969), pp. 189–195.
9. Norman, OK: University of Oklahoma Press, 1991.
10. New York: The Free Press, 1992.
11. *Korea Herald,* November 18, 1998.
12. See Martina Deuchley, *The Confucian Transformation of Korea* (Cambridge, MA: Council on East Asian Studies, Harvard University, and distributed by Harvard University Press, 1992).
13. See Han Sung-joo, *The Failure of Democracy in South Korea* (Berkeley: University of California Press, 1974).
14. Interview in Seoul, June 1998.
15. See John C. H. Oh and Bruce Wiegard, "Democracy, Development, and Corruption: The Case of Korea," *Korea Observer,* vol. 27, no. 4, Winter, 1996, pp. 492–495.
16. See Han Sung-joo, ibid., pp. 207–215.
17. See Linda Chao and Ramon H. Myers, *The First Chinese Democracy: Political life in the Republic of China on Taiwan* (Baltimore, MD: The Johns Hopkins University Press, 1998).
18. Professor Hong Sung-chick, former head of the Asiatic Research Center at Korea University and now chairman of the Asian Social Science

Research Institute. On behalf of the National Academy of Sciences, Republic of Korea, Professor Hong initiated a study in 1997 "On A Study On Historical Review of Social Change in Korea." In brief, in 1997, there were 215 books, 55 dissertations published within Korea, and 105 dissertations from foreign countries. All of these were written by Koreans. So the materials for a detailed study of this subject are at hand.

19. See Lester C. Thurow, *The Future of Capitalism* (New York: William Morrow & Co., 1996).

20. Interview in Seoul in January 1998.

21. Hyun Baeg Im, "Korean Democratic Consolidation in Comparative Perspective," at a conference on Consolidating Democracy in South Korea, June 19–20, 1996, pp. 5–6.

22. Ibid., p. 7.

23. See his "The Myth of Asia's Miracle," *Foreign Affairs,* November/December 1994, vol. 73, no. 6, pp. 62–78.

24. See p. 172.

25. See *Progress in Democracy: The Pacific Basin Experience* (Seoul: The Ilhae Institute, 1987), p. 69. Also see Robert J. Myers, "The End of the Hermit Kingdom," *Ethics and International Affairs,* vol. 2, 1988, pp. 99–114.

26. *New York Times,* May 23, 1992.

27. Ibid.

28. Ibid.

29. Francis Fukuyama, *The End of History and the Last Man* (New York: The Free Press, 1992)

30. John Lie, *Han Unbound, The Political Economy of South Korea* (Stanford, CA: Stanford University Press, 1998), pp. 158–59.

31. Berkeley: University of California Press, 1992.

32. Ibid., p. 197.

33. Norton, ibid., p. 172.

34. Norton, ibid., p. 173.

35. April 18, 1992.

36. May 19, 1992.

37. *Korea Herald,* December 26, 1992.

38. See Cha, ibid., pp. 153–58.

39. *Korea Herald,* May 5, 1997.

40. See Oberdorfer, ibid., p. 134.

41. See *Korea Herald,* May 24, 1997, citing an Asahi Shimbun interview.

42. *Korea Herald,* May 24, 1997.

43. December 19, 1997.

44. December 20, 1997.

45. *Korea Herald,* January 6, 2000.

Chapter 9

1. *Korea Herald,* January 6, 2000.

2. *San Francisco Chronicle*, January 6, 2000.

3. See, for example, a booklet published by the National Unification Board of the ROK, November 30, 1994. This study collects four articles published elsewhere by four Korean scholars—"The Economies of South and North and the Problem of Unification: How to Overcome Gaps and Variances," by Yoo Young-ock; "Inter-Korean Economic Cooperation, Current Status and Future Prospects," by Kim Kwang-yong; "The Method of Monetary Integration and the Decision of Exchange Rate in the Unification Process of North and South Korea," by Kim Young-yoon and Lee Young-hoon ; and "Supply and Demand for Grains in North Korea: A Historical Movement Model for 1966–1993," by Lee Hy-sang.

4. DJ published a book on this subject, *Three Stage Approach to Korean Unification* (Los Angeles: The Center for Multiethnic and Transnation Studies, University of California, 1997). This book, too, places much weight on economic and cultural exchanges but has a kinder tone.

5. "Prospects for a Peaceful Settlement in Korea: A Soviet Perspective," *The Journal of East and West Studies* (Yonsei University, vol. 20, October 1991, no. 2), pp. 13–2.

6. "Unification Policy of Kim Young-sam's Government—The Pending Requirement." *East Asian Review* (vol. 6, No. 4, Winter 1994, Published by the Institute for East Asian Studies, Seoul), pp. 38–50.

7. Moon Chung-in, "Peace and Arms Control on the Korean Peninsula: A Search for Alternatives, " *Korea Focus* (September-October 1996), pp. 5–19.

8. "The Myth of North Korea's Irrationality," *The Korean Journal of International Studies* (vol. 25, no. 2, Summer 1991), pp. 129–145.

9. *Korea and World Affairs* (Fall 1996), pp. 406–430.

10. Washington: American Enterprise Institute, 1999.

11. Jing Huang, "Why is Pyongyang So Defiant on the Nuclear Issue?," Korea and World Affairs, vol. 20, No. 3 (Fall 1996), pp. 380–405.

12. *Journal of Northeast Asian Studies* (Spring 1994, vol. 10, no. l), pp. 64–73.

13. See, for example, Chung-in Moon, *Understanding Regime Dynamics in North Korea* (Seoul: Yonsei University, 1998); and Thomas H. Henriksen and Jong-ryn Mo, *North Korea after Kim Il-sung* (Stanford, CA: Hoover Institution Press, Stanford University, 1997). For a more favorable view of the North Korean scene, see Han S. Park, ed., *North Korea Ideology, Politics, Economy* (Englewood Cliffs, NJ: Prentice Hall, 1995); Martin H. Landsberg, *Korea . . . Division, Reunification, & U.S. Foreign Policy* (New York: Monthly Review Press, 1998); and Bruce Cumings, ibid., pp. 304–433.

14. See Elizabeth Rosenthal, "In North Korean Hunger, Legacy is Stunted Children," *New York Times,* December 10, 1998.

15. Some would say there was no alternative; see the author's *U.S. Foreign Policy in the Twenty-first Century: The Relevance of Realism* (Baton Rouge, LA: Louisiana State University Press, 1999), reflections of Gorbachev, pp. 145–46.

16. The two booklets were "Reform for North Korea's Politics, Economics, Culture and International Relations and Creating Opens," and "The True and False of North Korea," (both published in Seoul: Institute of Unification, 1998).

17. Nicholas Eberstadt, *The End of North Korea* (Washington D.C.: American Enterprise Institute, 1999).

18. Published in the FDL/ap, "Peace and Democracy for the New Millenium," October 25–26, 1999, Seoul, Korea.

19. Speech by Lee Hoi-chang at the Heritage Foundation, Washington, D.C., September 15, 1999.

20. See Leon V. Sigal, *Disarming Strangers: Nuclear Diplomacy with North Korea* (Princeton, NJ: Princeton University Press), 1997. Also, see Don Oberforter, ibid., chaps. 13 and 14.

21. *Juche! The Speeches and Writings of Kim Il-sung*. Forward by Eldridge Cleaver. Edited and introduced by Li Yik Sa (New York; Grossman Publishers, 1972), p. 157. When I checked this book out from the Green Library at Stanford University in September 1997, a library assistant remarked that this was the first time anyone had checked it out.

22. Chuck Downs, *Over the Line: North Korean Negotiating Strategy* (Washington, D.C., The AEI Press), 1999.

23. *Korea Times,* January 14, 1999.

24. *Korea Herald,* October 27, 2000.

Conclusion

1. Seoul, Korea: The Ministry of Information Korean Overseas Information Service, 1997.

2. See *Newsreview,* vol. 27, no. 34, August 22, 1998, pp. 6–7.

3. P. 52.

4. See also, Alvin and Heidi Toffler, *Creating a New Civilization: The Politics of the Third Wave* (Atlanta, GA: Turner Publishing, 1995).

5. See Edward Neilan, "Silicon Valley clones lack the right stuff," *Japan Times,* April 18, 1999.

6. *Korea Herald,* September 29, 1998.

7. See also "Handbook of the Social Agreement and New Labour Laws of Korea," (Seoul: KILF [Korea International Labour Foundation], 1998).

8. Interview, Seoul, June 25, 1998.

9. JPRI Working Papers No. 51, November 1998.

10. May 6, 1999, p. 52.

11. Chosen Ilbo, May 23, 1988

12. See especially the preface to *Challenges of Globalization and Korea's Response* (in Korean), by Kim Yong-won and Im Hyun-jin (Seoul: Nanam Publishing Corp. September, 1995).

13. See Paul Hirst & Graham Thompson, *Globalization in Question* (Cambridge, MA: Polity Press, 1996), pp. 195–196.

14. Reprinted as a guest column in the *Korea Herald,* April 6, 1999.
15. See Larry Diamond, *Developing Democracy, Toward Consolidation* (Baltimore, MD: The Johns Hopkins University Press, 1999).
16. Ibid., pp. 279–80.
17. *Letters from Prison,* translated by Choi Ra-jung and David R. McCain, (Berkeley: University of California Press, 1987), p. 62.
18. *New Beginning: A Collection of Essays,* edited by George Oakley Totten III, Ph.D., translated by Young Jaik Lee, Ph.D. and Young Mok Kim, Ph.D. (The Center for Multiethnic and Transnational Studies, Los Angeles: University of Southern California, 1996), p. 15.

Annotated Bibliography

Allen, Richard C. *Korea's Syngman Rhee. An Unauthorized Biography.* Tokyo, Japan: Charles Tuttle Co., 1960. This is a portrait of South Korea's first president, warts and all. Rhee's determination to obtain a bilateral security treaty with the U.S. succeeded. Whether both countries are now equally served is an open question.

Amsden, Alice. *Asia's Next Giant: Korea and Late Industrialization.* New York: Oxford University Press, 1989. Since 1997, there has been empirical evidence to cast doubt on the validity of Korea's real economic growth and prospects for the future. It may be that consistent "overachieving" is beyond South Korea's reach.

Carter, Ashton B., and William J. Perry. *Preventive Defense.* Washington, D.C.: Brookings Institution Press, 1999. A controversial notion that curbing the means of war-making—nuclear and biological weapons—somehow deals with the politics and passions of international rivalry.

Cha, Victor D. *Alignment Despite Antagonism.* Stanford, CA: Stanford University Press, 1999. This detailed account of how the U.S. and Japan and the U.S. and South Korea harmoniously handle their conflicting affairs is masterfully done, while explaining through many examples the still rocky relations between Japan and the ROK because of Japan's late colonization of Korea. This sour note is expected to continue to sound, despite the best efforts of their respective leaders.

Chen Jiang. *China's Road to the Korean War. The Making of the Sino-American Confrontation.* New York: Columbia University Press, 1994. This insightful book shows the wider results of the Korean war, especially its long-term damage to U.S.–China relations, which persists.

Cumings, Bruce. *Korea's Place in the Sun.* New York: W. W. Norton, 1997. This is an exceptional book, encapsulating in a readable way the entire sweep of Korean history and culture up through the twentieth century.

Deuchler, Martina. *The Confucian Transformation of Korea. A Study of Society and Ideology.* Cambridge, MA: Harvard University Press, 1991. This study examines traditional

Korean society and how the arrival of Confucianism changed Korean values and worldview in line with China's, but with a strong Korean residue.

Diamond, Larry. *Developing Democracy: Toward Consolidation*. Baltimore, MD: The Johns Hopkins University Press, 1999. The author is one of the most thoughtful of the Third Wave school of political science, which sees the whole world becoming democratic. Through a process of "consolidation," democratic prospects appear good, despite the many obstacles.

Duus, Peter. *The Abacus and the Sword. The Japanese Penetration of Korea, 1896–1910*. Berkeley: University of California Press, 1998. This is the basic account of Japanese preparation for annexing Korea as a colony in 1910.

Eberstadt, Nicholas. *The End of North Korea*. Washington, D.C.: American Enterprise Institute, 1999. The systemic failure of North Korea's dictatorship by any measure of performance is well argued and documented. While there may be an end of North Korea as it was, it is likely to remain with us as an exasperating problem that leads to flights of military fancy on how to rid the world of this pestilence. But it is here to stay.

Eckert, Carter. *Offspring of Empire. The Koch'ang Kims and the Colonial Origins of Korean Capitalism, 1876–1945*. Seattle: University of Washington Press, 1991. This is an important study of how a certain class of Koreans managed not only to survive Japanese colonialism but also to continue in their privileged role in post–1945 South Korea.

Fairbank, John, Edwin O. Reischauer, and Albert M. Craig. *East Asian Tradition and Transformation*. Boston: Houghton Mifflin, 1973. In studying Korea, it is appropriate to understand the larger Asian landscape. This gives a context to observing Korea as a "shrimp between two whales," and the adversities that a small place in a strategic location must endure.

Gough, Leo. *Asia Meltdown. The End of the Miracle*. London: Oxford Capstone Publishing, 1998. This was one of the genre of quickie publications that rejoiced in the embarrassment of many Asian countries caused by the collapse of their oversold economic competence. Shrill and over-stated.

Han Sung-joo. *The Failure of Democracy in Korea*. Berkeley: The University of California Press, 1974. This is an authoritative account of the brief interregnum by a participant between the overthrow of Syngman Rhee in April 1960 and the coup of Park Chung-hee in June 1961. The regime of Chang Myon, while democratic, was too weak to deal with the politics and demands of the day.

Harrison, Selig, and Clyde Prestowitz. *After the Miracle. Redefining American Economic and Security Interests*. Washington, D.C.: The Economic Strategy Institute, 1998. This is a revisionist history of how South Korea achieved such a high growth rate and apparent success, attributing this achievement more to the Vietnam war and American security trade-offs for aid to South Korea than to miracle workers. It calls for a reappraisal of what the U.S. is doing in Northeast Asia, but nothing of that sort has been undertaken by the Clinton administration and seems unlikely in the short term by its successor.

Hastings, Max. *The Korean War.* New York: Simon & Schuster, 1987. Of the many books on the Korean war, this one strikes me as the most complete and satisfying. Hastings, a British historian, covers all aspects of the war: the Soviet pilots in the North, whose activities both sides minimized to avoid escalating the war; the "intelligence war"; the POW issue, which prolonged the war for John Foster Dulles' high principle of voluntary choice by each prisoner on whether to return home or opt for resettlement; and the armistice negotiations and the activities of Syngman Rhee to determine the outcome.

Henderson, Gregory. *Korea: Politics of the Vortex.* Cambridge: Harvard University Press, 1968. Henderson caught the essence of Korean politics and social structure, which makes the book valuable reading to this day. Like moths to the light, Korean politics revolve around a few powerful figures and larger political institutions, like the ministry of finance. The lesser members follow the leaders for their share of the political pie. Politics of party and principle have yet to develop in Korea, and perhaps nowhere else either. Henderson may well be describing a growing universal phenomenon.

Hickey, Michael. *The Korean War. The West Confronts Communism.* Woodstock, NY: The Overlook Press, 2000. As part of the commemoration of the 50th anniversary of the Korean war, Hickey has cast the Korean war scenario as the opening round of the defense of the West against Communism, the beginning of the Cold War strategy against the Soviet empire. He also raises up the real contributions of the other U.N. members who sent contingents to assist the U.S. and South Korea turn back the invasion by North Korea and China.

Hughes, E. R. *The Invasion of China by the Western World.* London: A. and C. Black, 1937. This is a good single-volume account of how the entire Chinese worldview was changed by the West with short-term disastrous results for China.

Hulbert, H. B. *The Passing of Korea.* New York: Doubleday, Page and Company, 1906. This is a nostalgic and classic account of how old Korea fell into the hands of the Japanese by a perceptive and compassionate American missionary. All the lamentations and predictions of the missionary group went for naught. Full of photos, folktales, and foreboding incidents.

Hunt, Michael H. *Crises in U.S. Foreign Policy. An International History Reader.* New Haven, CT: Yale University Press, 1996. Among the documents selected, some highlight the confrontation between MacArthur and Truman, and show the intelligence failure of MacArthur's staff, which totally miscalculated Chinese intentions and capabilities.

Johnson, Alastair. *Cultural Realism. Strategic Culture and Grand Strategy in Chinese History.* Princeton, NJ: Princeton University Press, 1997. This study places Chinese military strategy firmly within the Western realist tradition. It is an important contribution toward understanding Chinese military power.

Johnson, Chalmers. *Blowback. The Costs and Consequences of American Empire.* New York: Metropolitan Books, Henry Holt Company, 2000. The chapter on South Korea is an iconoclastic and chilling account of American connivance with the South Korean dictator Chun Doo-hwan in the bloody suppression of the Kwangju Uprising in Cholla province in May 1980. In this account, Johnson draws an analogy between this and the Hungarian Uprising of 1956 that is not flattering to either the American or Korean image.

Kim Chong-soon. *The Culture of Korean Industry.* Tucson: The University of Arizona Press, 1992. An idealized view of the development of Korean industry and labor relations under the chaebol system, which rings hollow in light of the present state of the South Korean economy.

Kim Dae-jung. *Conscience in Action.* Seoul: Chung-do Publishing Co., 1987. A favorable interpretation of Kim's earlier political career leading up to his unsuccessful presidential run in 1987.

Kim Dae-jung. *Three Stage Approach to Korean Unification.* Los Angeles: University of California. The Center for Multiethnic and Transitional Studies, 1997. Because of the June 2000 summit meeting in Pyongyang, this three stage plan—confederation, federation, complete unification—acquires more salience.

Kim, Richard. *The Martyred.* New York: Braziller Publishing, 1964. This novel shows the Korean war from a Korean perspective as a particular test and sacrifice. It also demonstrates the intensity of Christian religious belief among the faithful (about one third of South Koreans are Christian; the rest Buddhists).

Kim Se-jin. *Korean Military Government.* Chapel Hill: University of North Carolina Press, 1975. This was an early effort by a Korean graduate student to explain what was happening under the Park Chung-hee dictatorship. After Park, Kim then served his country in the diplomatic corps.

Koo, Hagen. *State and Society in Contemporary Korea.* Ithaca, NY: Cornell University Press, 1993. This is an excellent introduction to life in Korea in a broader sense. One sees Korea through the eyes of a highly professional group of Korean and American specialists and these essays remain valid and informative.

Korea Development Institute. *DJnomics: A New Foundation for the Korean Economy. Part One: Philosophy and Vision of the Government of the People; Part Two: Complete Reform of Economic Structure, A Vision for the Future.* Seoul: 1999. This was compiled in haste by a combination of Korean ministries, institutes, and agencies, and it shows. This is not a typical product of the KDI. Its significance is that it shows President Kim's determination to try to change fundamentally the Korean economy.

Korea Economic Institute of America. This group, sponsored by the Korean government, turns out a large quantity of excellent material. Its annual review of the Korean economy is reliable and outstanding.

Korean Annual. Seoul: Yonhap Press. Now in its fortieth year. This is an annual production by Yonhap News Service that provides a plethora of statistics on the Korean economy, and politics and a brief biographic section. A basic source.

Ladd, George Trumball. *In Korea with Marquis Ito. Part I. A Narrative of Personal Experience. Part II. A Critical and Historical Inquiry.* New York: Charles Scribner's Sons, 1908. The first part is a bucolic account of a young American travelling with a Japanese noble around the Japanese protectorate of Korea. The second part is the justification for the "yellow man's burden."

Lewis, John, and Litai Xue. *Uncertain Partners.* Stanford, CA: Stanford University Press, 1995. The Korean war presented through a different lens. Stalin reneged on his pledge to Mao to provide air cover for Chinese troops when they entered Korea. Such incidents probably served to create the Sino-Soviet split in the 1960s. Having the Chinese and Americans fight each other was highly agreeable to Stalin and he promoted the war until his death, after which the armistice soon came.

Lie, John. *Han Unbound. The Political Economy of South Korea.* Stanford, CA: Stanford University Press, 1998. The title is a play on words, with the Korean word *Han* meaning both Korea and suffering. Professor Lie himself is a Korean who has lived in Korea, Japan, and the United States and brings a wide range of personal experience and insight into this subject.

Lone, Stewart and Gavan McCormack. *Korea since 1950.* New York: St. Martin's Press, 1993. This is a concise treatment of the development of modern South and North Korea, from an Australian perspective.

McNamara, Dennis. *Trade and Transformation in Korea, 1876–1945.* Boulder, CO: Westview Press, 1996. This is a study of the gradual progress in economic development in Korea beginning from early encounters with the West, leading to an increasing all-embracing Japanese economic and military supremacy over Korea.

Mittleman, James, Ed. *Globalization: Critical Reflections.* Boulder, CO: Lynne Rienner, 1996. This is a genre of revisionist books that attack the easy suppositions that globalism is good for every country on an equal basis.

Mo, Jongryn and Chung-in Moon. *Democracy and the Korean Economy.* Stanford, CA: Hoover Institution Press, 1999. The authors raise the question whether the Korean financial crisis of 1997 was in part because the Korean democratic process had eroded the ability of the government to control the economy.

Myers, Ramon, and Mark Peattie. *The Japanese Colonial Empire.* Princeton, NJ: Princeton University Press, 1984. This is a professional and reflective account of this contentious subject.

Myers, Robert J. *U.S. Foreign Policy in the Twenty First Century. The Relevance of Realism.* Baton Rouge: Louisiana State University Press, 1999. My book on international relations stays close to the classic "realist" theory of politics, where the struggle for power and the flawed nature of man are important principles.

Najita, Tetsu. *Visions of Virtue of Tokugawa Japan.* Chicago: University of Chicago Press, 1987. This is a Japanese account of efforts of Japanese merchants to obtain status and respectability in a Confucian society that cast a cold eye on those who spent their time making money.

Nelson, M. Frederick. *Korea and the Old Order in Eastern Asia.* Baton Rouge: Louisiana State University Press, 1945. This was an early effort to explain how Korea functioned within the ancient Chinese tributary system. The destruction of that arrangement left Korea an easy prey to the Japanese.

Oberdorfer, Don. *The Two Koreas. A Contemporary History.* Reading, MA: Addison-Wesley, 1997. Oberdorfer delivers a well-told tale of U.S. relations with both Koreas, as well as the competition between the two Koreas. Closely researched and very well written, this is an excellent resource for the modern period.

Park, Han S., Ed. *North Korea: Ideology, Politics, and Economy.* Englewood Cliffs, NJ: Prentice-Hall, 1996. This is a collection of pieces on the North by a group of scholars generally sympathetic to their subject.

Sigal, Leon V. *Disarming Strangers. Nuclear Diplomacy with North Korea.* Princeton, NJ: Princeton University Press, 1997. This is the story of the incredible mishandling of U.S. interests in the North Korean nuclear program by both the Bush and Clinton administrations. The blundering almost caused a mindless nuclear exchange, or, in any case, a conventional war with the North with disastrous consequences for all parties.

Toffler, Alvin. *The Third Wave.* New York: Bantam Books, Inc., 1980. This is the original Toffler discussion of the development of society, depending on Marxist philosophy, to see the world going through first the agricultural stage, second the industrial, and then the information phase (Marx' progression was feudalism, capitalism, socialism/communism). This simplistic way of looking at the world had a powerful effect in the U.S. and elsewhere. It seems to have caught the attention and imagination of President Kim Dae-jung as he contemplates rebuilding South Korean society. *The Third Wave* theme is reinforced by a later book by the Tofflers, *Creating a New Civilization. The Politics of the Third Wave*. Atlanta, GA: Turner Publishing, 1995.

Toynbee, Arnold J. *A Study of History. (First American Edition)*. New York: Oxford University Press, 1947. A classic study of the movement of world history, now out of favor in some quarters. The shape of world history, according to Toynbee, depends on each civilization's response to the challenges that come its way. This idea played a powerful role in the intellectual life of President Kim Dae-jung during his years in jail and under house arrest. In his writings, he mentions Toynbee as his "mentor."

Wang, Gungju. *The Chinese Way. China's Position in International Relations*. Oslo, Norway: Scandinavian University Press, 1995. Professor Wang emphasizes China's unique position in the world, as both a nation-state and a great civilization.

Weber, Max. *The Religions of China. Confucianism and Taoism*. Glencoe, IL: The Free Press, 1951. This is a book that raises the hackles of China-area specialists. How dare Weber point out a significant fact, that China did not develop a capitalist society, without being a member of their club?

Weintraub, Stanley. *MacArthur's War. Korea and the Undoing of an American War Hero*. New York: The Free Press, 2000. MacArthur's brilliant surprise landing at Inchon to drive the North Koreans back over the 38th parallel was overshadowed (in the author's view) by his desire to carry the war farther including China, with atomic weapons, if necessary. His policy was at odds with Truman's determination to limit the scope of the war in Korea as part of a larger strategy on how to deal with the Soviet Union.

Yu, Mahchun. *OSS in China: Prelude to the Cold War*. New Haven, CT: Yale University Press, 1996. This is the best account of a minor subject, but the OSS' organizational and political problems in China profoundly shaped the successor organization, the CIA.

Index